THE HIVERNANTE

To David & Kria and Dicevy

THE HIVERNANTE

Marie Anne Lajimoniere,
the White Mother of the West

with best wishes

MARY WILLAN MASON

iUniverse

THE HIVERNANTE
MARIE ANNE LAJIMONIERE,
THE WHITE MOTHER OF THE WEST

iUniverse books may be ordered through booksellers or by contacting:

iUniverse
1663 Liberty Drive
Bloomington, IN 47403
www.iuniverse.com
1-800-Authors (1-800-288-4677)

Because of the dynamic nature of the Internet, any web addresses or links contained in this book may have changed since publication and may no longer be valid. The views expressed in this work are solely those of the author and do not necessarily reflect the views of the publisher, and the publisher hereby disclaims any responsibility for them.

Any people depicted in stock imagery provided by Thinkstock are models, and such images are being used for illustrative purposes only. Certain stock imagery © Thinkstock.

ISBN: 978-1-4917-5258-6 (sc)
ISBN: 978-1-4917-5257-9 (e)

Library of Congress Control Number: 2014921956

Print information available on the last page.

iUniverse rev. date: 02/26/2015

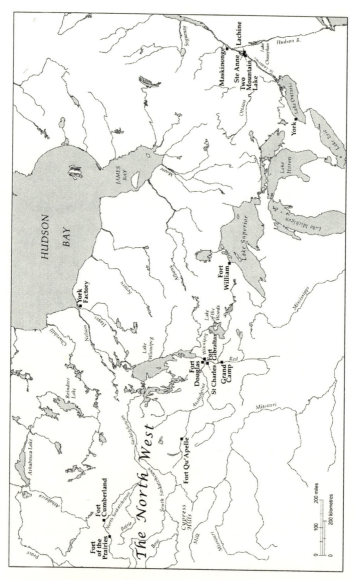

Map by the GIS and Cartography Office of the
Department of Geography, University of Toronto

CHAPTER 1

Marie Anne trudged along the hot dusty road dragging one wooden shoe after the other. The farther she got from home, the more she dragged her feet. A sympathetic passer-by might have noticed that the slender young girl was sobbing in desperation, with her head held high but her teeth biting her upper lip.

As she trudged, it crossed her mind to take herself and her pathetic little bundle containing all her possessions and just walk straight into the Mastigouche River. Then perhaps her mother would be sorry for sending her off to earn a living as assistant to the priest's housekeeper until she died a dried-up old spinster. She would show them all – her mother, her nine brothers and sisters, Father Vinet, and everybody in the world.

"I'm still thirteen, but I'll be fourteen in November. Lots of girls are married at fourteen. My sister was fifteen when she married." Marie Anne sobbed her complaints out loud, but there was no one to hear, and besides, no one could have done anything about it.

"Why did God have to take Papa? We were so happy together before he died and everything changed." Staring down at the slow-moving current, Marie Anne caught a reflection of her dusty and tear-stained face. She was suddenly horrified at what had just passed through her mind. Without even thinking about it, she had followed the path to the river, and now she stopped short, aghast at what she might have done.

Hearty yells and the sound of splashing upstream caught her attention. Two of the Lajimoniere boys chased each other in the water like a pair of young seals. Marie Anne turned away quickly in embarrassment, but the boys had already seen her, and with whoops of laughter they sent a cascade of water, covering her from head to toe.

"That's for you, skinny Marie Anne," called out Jean Baptiste, a strapping sixteen-year-old, as he sent another wave of water her way.

Marie Anne ran as best she could in her heavy wooden shoes, her clothes clinging to her and her bundle now heavy and soaking wet. Knocking on the priest's door a few moments later wet, dirty, and bedraggled, she felt like a prisoner begging to be locked up.

The housekeeper noted the appearance of her young helper with disgust, scolded her, and sent her off to the pump for a cold-water scrub.

Marie Anne felt more anger at Jean Baptiste than dread at the housekeeper's disapproval. That taunt from Jean Baptiste was the last straw. She hated him, just as she hated having no dowry and no prospects, only these everlasting tasks of learning the housekeeper's rules. "Who does he think he is anyway, splashing me like that?" she muttered.

Jean Baptiste, eldest son of the richest man in the Maskinongé area, was a full-of-fun, devil-may-care fellow if ever there was one. There were rumours about the village that he was off to fight the Iroquois, who were still making the occasional raids on the village. Some folk had it that he would try to join other French lads to tussle with British soldiers after the Battle of the Plains of Abraham, now thirty-seven years past.

Marie Anne tried her best to clean herself up to Madame the housekeeper's standards, thinking how unfair it was that those boys should be off on their adventures and she would have to live like a hermit in the priest's home. At last she doused her head in the freezing cold water and plaited her hair into its accustomed pigtail.

Madame sniffed her acceptance and noted that the dry garments she had produced would last a long time before the child grew into them. She set about at once giving Marie Anne her first job: scouring the iron pots. By the time the evening meal had been served and cleaned up, the new assistant was exhausted.

Marie Anne climbed the steps to the upper floor of the presbytery and her little bedroom with its narrow cot. She tried to peer out of the small window, but all she could see was a bit of cloud in the sky. She sighed, knelt at her cot to say her prayers, rolled into bed, and sniffled into her pillow. It seemed to her that her whole life had changed that freezing cold day, just four and a half years ago, when they had buried Papa.

It was in 1792 at the gravesite of Charles Gaboury, a hard-working and prosperous farmer, that the entire family's fortunes had taken a turn. Although his farm was well situated on the outskirts of Maskinongé on the Mastigouche River – only a half-day's journey on horseback or by fishing dory from the St Lawrence River – it was simply too large to manage for his widow and the children still at home.

Not that the first ten years of Marie Anne's life had been all play. She had been taught to help out with a great number of tasks both inside and outside the Gaboury homestead.

Her mother, another Marie Anne – Marie Anne Tessier Gaboury – made sure that her daughter was capable in all the household chores, including helping to card the fleece a little at a time and then spinning the wool into yarn until her fingertips ached. The girl had even progressed to knitting that yarn into socks for the menfolk and toques for the whole family. Marie Anne especially loved to help her mother with the baking. The scent of fresh bread coming into the house from the outdoor bake oven gave her immense pleasure, a feeling of satisfaction in providing for those she loved.

Before the death of Charles Gaboury, the home had been a happy place indeed, despite the hard work. As Marie Anne thought back, it was after his death that her mother had found such difficulty in caring for and feeding her children. With the eldest off and away farming his own portion of his inheritance and the eldest daughter married to a farmer nearby, it was left to the children still at home to somehow do a man's work on the farm as well as their own assigned chores. A young woman needed a strong back and robust health to become a successful farmer's wife.

Marie Anne sighed as she remembered the way Grandmaman Tessier never tired of telling the story to anyone who had the time to listen to the old lady about how delicate a little body she, Marie Anne, had been as a baby, and how it was thought necessary to bundle her up only a few hours old and take her straight to Father Rinfret at the Church of St Sulpice to be christened.

"Who knew," her grandmother always said while telling the story of Marie Anne's early days, "whether she would live to see another day after that terrible storm on the night of November fifth back in 1782?" She added, "It was always the great hope of the family that my uncle, my father's brother, should be sent to the parish as our priest and christen his great-niece, but that had not come to pass, and so it was Father Rinfret who baptized her after all. I still had hopes that my uncle might come to St Sulpice in God's good time and then she would be housekeeper for her great-uncle. What a fine thing that would have been." She would cross herself as she concluded the story.

During the four years since her father's death, Marie Anne had felt her mother's increasing anxiety about managing the farm and ensuring that there was enough food on the table and thatch on the roof. Marie Anne had happily taken on more and more of the tasks of caring for her younger siblings – tasks she loved – but that meant seeing less and less of her friends in the village and being unable to take part in their games.

Angrily tossing her pigtail over her shoulder, Marie Anne looked around now at her tiny room and fumed, "I really am in a prison. This is the closest to becoming a nun without taking on the vows, and I don't feel any calling to take on a religious vocation at all. If only I had a little more time, perhaps somebody, approved of course by Maman and Grandmaman, would have asked for my hand, but now I suppose it's too late." A few tears trickled down her cheeks.

"Was it just this afternoon that I bade goodbye to Maman and hugged my brothers and sisters?" she asked in despair. Sunk in her gloom and with no mirror in her room, she had no way of realizing that she had grown into a strikingly handsome young girl with a long braid the colour of buttercups and eyes as blue as the cornflowers in her mother's garden, a true descendant of her Norman ancestors. She had also become a little woman as determined as water running downhill, a fierce little ramrod with an iron will despite her sweetness and grace.

Both Madame Tessier and Madame Gaboury felt satisfied that Marie Anne would become a source of needed help to the aging housekeeper. The child was proficient in her weaving and spinning, handy with a needle and thread, could knit socks and other simple requirements of a household, could bake bread and make a good soup out of dried peas that was everyone's favourite, could make a tasty dinner of fish when times were good and out of fish heads when times were not good, and could preserve greens in a salt mix to be used all winter long to flavour soups, rabbit stews, or deer meat. There were many skills to be learned, and both Madame Tessier and Madame Gaboury were satisfied with the girl's progress. They also convinced themselves that since Marie Anne was not considered robust, a necessity for the hard life of a homemaker, placing her in the priest's home would be to her best advantage.

Marie Anne had not voiced her disappointment to her mother in the matter of dedicating her life to the presbytery. She knew better than to try to thwart what had been pointed out as God's mission for her in this life, but she did resent being sent away into a very straight-laced and strictly controlled way of living for the rest of her life. She was both a resourceful and a quick-witted young person, but it had simply never occurred to anyone to ask her opinion about something that would affect her so deeply. Madame Gaboury had no doubts that Father Vinet's housekeeper needed an assistant, and having come to that decision, it was a small matter to convince the priest and his housekeeper that her daughter was the ideal choice.

And so it was that Marie Anne had packed up her few belongings, patted her pillow in the big bed in the sleeping loft she shared with her sisters, and noted with a tug at her heart with what alacrity the next oldest sister appropriated her place in the comfy old bed. At the gate, Madame Gaboury had given her a blessing. With a flick of her skirt, Marie Anne persuaded one of the hens to stay where she belonged and not dash for freedom right out on the road. "Even a hen wants freedom too like me," crossed her mind as she latched the gate.

"We never thought we would be able to raise you," her mother sighed, "and now see the wonder of it. The Good Lord has preserved you, and you are off to make your way in the world."

Now she wriggled down in her lonely cot, missing her family and the give and take of family life. Too tired to think anymore, she drifted into sleep until the housekeeper roused her to the morning tasks.

The presbytery was a solemn place. So solemn and quiet was it that the high-spirited laughing little girl began speaking in a hushed voice like the housekeeper. The fun-loving Marie Anne tiptoed about in a very subdued manner like a little mouse so as not to disturb the priest. For the first few weeks, she was kept too busy to be lonesome for the rough and tumble of home. She remembered her sisters and brothers faithfully in her prayers each night, but it was in the mornings that she first began to realize that she missed them deeply. There were no small people to dress and fuss with, to laugh with or sometimes to scold if they were tardy or wilful. Having a narrow cot all her own was no gain, for she missed the joking and giggling that had gone on in the big bed for the girls.

Marie Anne loved to help with the baking. She was used to that. She helped with the washing, a back-breaking job that involved stirring the dirty clothes with a stick in a big tub filled with hot water and harsh homemade soap, and then wringing them out by hand and hanging them out on the clothesline. She was used to that too – although it did strike her that it took a lot of linen to keep up the standards of the priest's house, even though only three people lived in it.

"All these surplices and altar cloths and everything, it does make a deal of extra washing," she thought.

Marie Anne learned to starch the priest's vestments. They had to be stiffened just so, not so much that they'd crackle when he genuflected during the masses but enough so that they hung straight and smooth and kept their shape. The housekeeper was extremely fussy about the starch, which they made themselves from the finest of ground wheat, sieved until not a trace of bran was left.

"Wheat that could have been made into bread and fed to people," thought Marie Anne, remembering the times in her home in the last four years when flour was a scarce commodity and she had gone to bed wishing there had been larger servings of food at the supper table.

Year followed quiet year in the presbytery. There were times when Marie Anne was present at the wedding of a sister or one of her playmates in the village. She had even stood in the chapel of St Sulpice at a niece's or a nephew's christening, holding a new life in her arms and aching to be holding a baby of her own. She was happy for each bride in turn, of course, and wished her well, but for a few weeks after each of the weddings, Marie Anne was unusually subdued and restless. The housekeeper noted the young woman's sadness and the expression of resignation on the usually bright little face and recalled her own youthful longings. Marie Anne saw her family in church each week, but the breaking up of the tight family circle and her own removal from it was beginning to bring a tightness around her mouth and her eyes.

"Life seems to be passing me by," thought Marie Anne. "There's excitement outside in the world, but nothing stirs in here ... except those starched frills on the curtains in Father Vinet's reception room when we've opened the windows to let some warm breezes freshen things up."

By the time eleven years had passed, Marie Anne had become the trusted and efficient helper of the household, and it was obvious to everyone in Maskinongé that the young woman would be taking over the entire responsibility of housekeeper when the time came. Even her own family had started to think of her as the unwed, middle-aged housekeeper of the priest's house. Except for Josette, her closest sister in age and her fondest, no one gave a thought to Marie Anne's feelings. Lively young Josette had hatched one or two schemes of rescue, but they had come to naught. Well and happily married, Josette now wanted happiness for her big sister.

In those eleven long years, Marie Anne had become an accomplished chatelaine, learning to keep all the details of the presbytery in order, bake the small wafers of bread used in the Mass, even crochet lace for Father Vinet's vestments and the altar cloths. These required fancier patterns and a much smaller hook, but basically it was the same craft of hooking thread that the men of Maskinongé used to fashion their fishing nets. Marie Anne had watched her father mend his nets in days gone by, as he and all the farmers whose lands abutted the river had fishing rights on it. Sometimes when she was working on something to beautify the church, she was reminded of her father – his joking with his children and the happy laughter in the Gaboury household in the past.

Now it was November again, a chilly dark November afternoon. Marie Anne looked at herself in the pewter salver she was polishing to a bright sheen.

"I'm twenty-five years old this month," she said to her reflected image. She peered as closely as she could to get a look at herself in the bottom of the salver. "I guess I'm getting to be old. Too old ever to be asked to be anybody's wife. I'll never have any babies of my own. Oh! How I wish things had turned out differently. If only Papa were still with us, everything would have been different for me, I know. Is this all there is for me in this life? Polishing salvers? I should be grateful. I know that. But starching Father Vinet's vestments and mending the lace on the altar cloths and …." She sat down at the kitchen table feeling utterly forlorn.

Marie Anne had every good reason to think of herself as an old spinster. Most girls married before they were sixteen, and Marie Anne's chances of finding a husband in her present circumstances were slim indeed. Much of her golden hair was hidden in a white cap she wore day in, day out, winter and summer. Marie Anne dabbed at her tears with a corner of her apron. With an effort of will, she straightened her back and took up the polishing cloth again.

"Maybe this is my darkest hour, and a whole new and beautiful dawn waits for me. They do say that the darkest hour is just before the dawn, and everything is so dark right now." She wiped away the last of her tears and sniffled a little.

"Maybe by next spring, when the days get longer and the world warms up ... maybe something nice will happen. I must try to pray each night that it will. Sometimes," she went on mournfully, "I wish I had been born a boy. I could have gone hunting in the forest with the other boys and the men, or maybe even have gone away to the western deserts for adventure and excitement. Or at least I could have stayed at home and helped Maman with the farm, doing the hard chores in the fields for her. It must be so hard for Maman to keep our farm going with only the young ones to help."

Marie Anne shook her head. "I'm just making pictures in the clouds," she said quietly as she put down her polishing cloth and got up to set the pewter dish back in its rack. She called to mind the radiance in her sisters' faces and the way the young bridegrooms looked at each of them, ready to gobble them up right then and there in the middle of the wedding Mass with everybody looking on. "It must be so wonderful to be special like that to the man who makes you his wife."

Marie Anne sighed again and looked around for another task. A smart tapping on the door jogged her out of her miseries. She swept the polishing cloth out of sight and went quickly across the room to open the door.

The housekeeper came in quite out of breath and all aflutter. She took a deep breath and thumped the willow shopping basket down on the table. The fish heads she had bargained for bounced up and down as though they had something to add to the excitement.

"Such talk in the village!" she managed to splutter when she had caught her breath. "What a surprise!"

"What on earth is the commotion about?" asked Marie Anne. "Dear Lord, preserve us. You don't mean to say there's been an Indian attack? It's been a few years since we had that to worry about. Is it a war? God help us! Have soldiers from France come to help us so we fight the English all over again? Have the English from south of the river attacked us again?"

"Heavens no, child." The housekeeper fanned herself. "Nothing like that at all. It's really some good news, and, oh my goodness, what excitement there is for everyone."

Marie Anne winced at being called a child. Here she was twenty-five almost and an aunt several times over. Being called a child only worsened her despondent mood and made her voice a little petulant as she demanded of the housekeeper, "Well then, what is it that's made you so breathless? Tell me the news of the village."

The housekeeper took off her shawl and hung it on its peg. Coming over to the table, she sat down and began.

"It's the Lajimoniere's son. You know, the family of the seigneur who is descended from a count, so they say. Do you recall the son who went off to make his fortune in the western deserts? Jean Baptiste is the one. Well, Jean Baptiste has come home to us. He must have had enough of that terrifying life, living with savages, trapping beasts in winter, and always moving about. He was always such a restless little fellow, I recall, but now they say he wants to take up his portion and farm. Everyone is saying he has such tales to tell. Imagine! Jean Baptiste a *coureur de bois*, living out in the western deserts without a hearth to call home for all those years, and then coming back to us. I cannot bring to mind any other lad from around here who returned to his village from the west. It's like the story of the prodigal son." Madame sank back in her chair, exhausted.

The life of a *coureur de bois* life was never an easy one. To live by trapping furs all winter, which were then taken to the forts of either the Hudson's Bay Company or the North West Company and traded for ammunition, tobacco, tea, and a couple of other treats, and then by hunting down the buffalo in summer to provide food, tenting material, footgear, and blanketing, was indeed a hard life. It did, however, offer challenge and the excitement of risk to health and life that many a young man found irresistible. Adventuring into unmapped and unknown lands and overcoming danger was the life they craved. Many a young man throughout Lower Canada would have given a great deal to be part of the heroic band of risk-takers. Those who returned were the most envied of heroes, but very few did.

The ermine, fox, and beaver pelts the hunters gained were sent off either to the Hudson's Bay post on Hudson Bay or to Montreal and then shipped to the European markets, eventually making enormous profits but not for the hunters. A *coureur de bois* who returned home did not do so as a rich man, although he did have hair-raising accounts of his experiences and enough tales to be told and retold to last for the rest of his life. Few of the *coureurs de bois* who stayed in the west to hunt and trap lived to be old men. It was a perilous life.

Jean Baptiste, however, arrived home a hero.

Marie Anne was astounded at the housekeeper's news. Here she had been thinking that her life was doomed to routine and frustration, and now the entire village would have stories of adventure, excitement, and high jinks enough to last the entire winter. She sat down opposite the housekeeper, and the two women grinned at each other, some real entertainment in store for them both.

"It will be almost as good as being there myself," Marie Anne thought to herself. "I can hardly wait to hear what Jean Baptiste has to tell us. I wonder what he looks like now and if he remembers the day he splashed me and called me skinny?"

CHAPTER 2

Marie Anne looked with concern at the elderly housekeeper, who was still trying to catch her breath and compose herself. "I wonder whether I should pour a little of that restorative strawberry cordial for her or put the kettle on the hearth to boil?" she thought. "Something is certainly needed for Madame to settle her nerves."

Just as Marie Anne had decided on the kettle, there was a knock on the door.

"What a busy time we are having this afternoon," she said to herself. "Who on earth can be knocking so hard this time?"

"Answer the door! Answer the door!" The housekeeper was still not quite calm, and in her excitement – just in case it was an important visitor – she was busily tying on a fresh apron and thinking ahead to heating the griddle for Marie Anne to make scones.

Marie Anne ran to the door. Flinging it wide, whom should she see but her favourite younger sister, holding a baby in one arm and guiding a sturdy little two-year-old with the other.

"Josette!" Marie Anne exclaimed, and her voice rang with pleasure. "Dear Josette and the little ones. What a surprise! Do come in."

After the two sisters had embraced and the babies had been kissed, the housekeeper made Josette welcome and helped Marie Anne take off little Pierre's outer clothing.

"What a fine young son you have, Madame," she murmured.

"Oh! Madame. Thank you." Josette bobbed a little curtsey. "And now, oh ladies, such excitement! You have heard the news surely. The Lajimoniere's son, Jean Baptiste, has returned to us. He must have had enough of the western deserts. Oh! Marie Anne, you must see him. He looks so handsome, so manly and so strong." She flexed her arms, made fists of her hands, and pirouetted about.

All three ladies laughed uncontrollably.

"Josette, you never change. You always make so much merriment wherever you are." Marie Anne reached into her pocket for her handkerchief to wipe an entirely different trickle of tears from the ones she had shed earlier that afternoon.

Josette looked around at her audience with her eyes sparkling with mischief. Even wee Pierre and the baby were captivated by her animation.

"Monsieur and Madame Lajimoniere are having a gathering," she went on, "a reception to welcome back the mighty hunter. Everyone says he has quite changed, and that now he wants nothing more than to settle down here with us and farm like his brothers. All that wilderness and yearning for adventure is behind him now. His father is so pleased."

Josette paused for breath and sat down.

"He told his sister who told my mother-in-law that he has determined to take up his patrimony. My father-in-law says it is a fine parcel of land with frontage on the Mastigouche and good bush in the back."

Then she whispered, "Marie Anne, they say he is alone and seeking a wife. You know he is three years older than you. You would be a perfect match. You must come with us to the reception. How long is it since you were present at a party? And this will be the most brilliant gathering anyone has ever seen in Maskinongé. You must come, Marie Anne. You haven't taken the vows of a religious, you know."

Marie Anne kept smiling at her lively sister, hoping that Madame had not overheard her remarks.

"It does sound wonderful, very wonderful, Josette, but I have nothing to wear to such an occasion. You would be ashamed of me. No, no. Just come by and tell us all about it."

Josette turned to the housekeeper. "Please persuade my sister that she should come with my husband and me to the reception. Besides, the Lajimonieres are inviting everybody, and that surely means that you and Father Vinet will be honoured guests." Josette smiled prettily.

Marie Anne noted that her sister could still charm the birds out of the trees. "No wonder she was such a favourite of Papa's and could get her own way with both Maman and Papa."

The housekeeper smiled back at Josette. "It will be an evening to savour indeed. Of course Marie Anne must go, and I shall be delighted to chaperone her."

"Thank you, Madame. Then it is all settled," said Josette with a *don't cross me I've made up my mind* look that reminded Marie Anne sharply of the old days when she was little mother to the strong-willed Josette.

"Now for your gown, my slender elegant sister. You must wear my blue linsey – my wedding dress. It's been wrapped away in lavender and cedar ever since I got too large to wear it again after carrying Pierre. It's just the right blue for your eyes, and it may even be a little too big for you in the waist, but I can take it in and then it will be perfect. You must wear it. I insist."

Out of Madame's earshot, she whispered, "It would be a beautiful gown for you to wear at *your* wedding. Just think of us both, the happiest brides, wearing the same gown."

Marie Anne blushed. "Jean Baptiste has only just arrived in town. I haven't even seen him yet, and you have my wedding dress all arranged. Really, Josette, you haven't changed one tiny bit." She shook her head in wonderment. "But I do love you, and I have missed you so much and in so many ways since we have all grown up, dear Josette." Marie Anne grinned.

"Now, child," the housekeeper said as the sisters exchanged glances.

"I'm no longer a child" was Marie Anne's first thought, but Josette's whisper was more to the point: "It's high time you were rescued from this penance with all its incense and sanctity."

"This very evening then," said Josette, bowing to the housekeeper, "my good man and I will come to escort you, Madame, and Father Vinet, and you, my dear sister, and we shall all arrive in style together. Now I am going home at once to air that blue gown. Expect me back soon so we can have a try on to see how it fits you."

Later the same afternoon, Josette was making little tucks in the waist and talking non-stop with a pin or two between her lips. "And remember, if Jean Baptiste should ask you to dance with him, don't hang back. Just watch me. Don't forget, he has been in the western deserts and must be out of practice after five years away – unless of course he can teach us some quaint native steps. Oh! This will be so enjoyable."

She stuck in a final pin. "There. I think I can claim to be the swiftest seamstress in New France – oh, I mean Lower Canada – and now you look so much younger and absolutely adorable. If Jean Baptiste doesn't fall helplessly in love with you, he isn't the man we have all been led to believe he is."

Josette hopped back on her feet and turned around to hug little Pierre and the baby in turn. "Thank you, Madame, for amusing them while I was dressmaker deluxe to my beautiful sister."

"A pleasure, Madame, a pleasure I assure you," beamed the housekeeper, and it struck Marie Anne for the first time that perhaps she too had known frustration and that at one time, years ago, she too had wondered and wished that someday, somehow, she might have babies of her own to cuddle and love.

Josette lost no time in bundling Pierre into his warm outdoor clothing. Marie Anne noted with pleasure that the toque Pierre was busily trying to pull down over his eyes was one she had knitted for him. Josette wrapped the baby swiftly and expertly in her shawl, and taking Pierre by the hand made her hasty exit. Marie Anne stood stock still in the middle of the kitchen, feeling a little awkward in such finery, the first time she had ever worn anything so well fitted and elegant.

The Lajimoniere's house was the largest in the entire district, even larger than the priest's presbytery. Candlelight gleamed from every window. Three fiddlers were engaged in playing lively airs, and the music mingled with sounds of chatter and laughter. As the conversation got louder, the fiddlers bowed harder. Marie Anne, watching from the sidelines, thought with amusement, "Finally no one will hear anything until at last all the chickens in the village will wake up and join in."

Even over the din, however, she was able to hear a deep ringing voice behind her.

"The Gaboury girls, how are they all? They must be grown and married off by now, I suppose. Five years have brought a lot of changes, and I've a lot to catch up on."

Marie Anne turned quickly but was only in time to get a fleeting glimpse of a head of dark brown hair and a pair of broad shoulders belonging to an unusually tall man, quick-moving and very much assured of himself. The room seemed too small for him, large and high-ceilinged though it was. To Marie Anne, he seemed to bring an air of excitement of far-off lands, something exotic, right into quiet little Maskinongé.

By this time, he and his companion had moved away, and Marie Anne was only able to hear the companion say something about a young Gaboury still at home.

"He couldn't possibly mean me," she thought sadly, suddenly wondering if at nearly twenty-five years of age, she really was too old to think of attracting so handsome a man. "I must really seem like a regular maiden lady of advanced years. How has it all happened? I wonder if he remembers splashing me on that miserable day?"

It was Josette who caught his eye.

"Now here, I am sure, is one of the beautiful Gaboury girls" said Jean Baptiste, bowing as gracefully as if he hadn't spent the past five years out of touch with polite society.

Josette sparkled at being thus singled out and, during the course of a few moments' conversation, managed to press upon him an invitation to come to her home and regale them with his stirring tales. Jean Baptiste promised that he would be delighted to visit the charming Madame Josette and her husband and to entertain them with a few of his recollections. The day was decided at once.

"Before you are filled with boredom with the telling and retelling of your adventures to the entire diocese," she said archly.

On the way back to the presbytery, Josette kept asking Marie Anne, "Did you see him? Did you speak to him? Everyone wants to entertain him and hear his remarkable stories about the fur country. He has promised to come to us first, that is, early next week, isn't that a coup? Think of it. His great-great-grandfather was a surgeon before he came out to New France, so that means he is fifth generation in the New World. His father dropped the title of Comte de la Jimoniere too. Just think, Marie Anne, if you marry him and he is persuaded to revive his grandfather's title, you will be Countess de la Jimoniere. That's a different life for you, my dear sister, than being called 'child' by Madame in the presbytery. Isn't it all going to be splendid? Oh! I am so happy for you."

"You seem to know a great deal about Jean Baptiste and his forebears," grumped Josette's husband as he gave a sharp flick of the reins to let his horse know at any rate that Josette was off on one of her wild schemes again and talking nonsense.

Josette laughed and snuggled affectionately closer to him. "I just want to see my sister as happy as I am," she said with a grin. She buried her nose in the sleeve of his warm coat.

After that outburst of chatter, Marie Anne was relieved that Madame had left earlier at the kind invitation of a parishioner who had offered to take Father Vinet home and could see that the housekeeper was showing weariness.

"Josette has me married to a man already when the only glimpse I had of him was the back of his head," she thought, but the manliness of his voice was like a bell ringing in her head. "I mustn't let Josette carry me away with her in her imaginary travels."

So thinking, she hopped down from the wagon, waved goodnight, and made her way up the path to the presbytery door in a confusion of emotions. Her cheeks felt hot, and she took off her mittens to cool them.

"I'm behaving like a silly little girl," she said softly to herself as she lifted the latch to let herself into the warm kitchen. Madame had thoughtfully left one of the precious candles burning for her to light her way up to her room.

The following week, permission was granted by Madame for Marie Anne to go to another social gathering. The blue gown was pressed into service again, and this time Marie Anne felt more comfortable and self assured in her finery at her second appearance in Maskinongé society. With her heart beating rather more quickly than was its usual habit in the presbytery's understated atmosphere, Marie Anne set off on foot to Josette's house in high anticipation of some wonderful entertainment, tall tales but true, delivered by the village's returning hero.

Throughout Lower Canada, the tall tales (some of them too tall to be creditable) from the returning *hivernants* – those trappers and wanderers who had elected to brave the intense cold and the rages of the howling winter storms and then had decided to come home and settle down – were a favourite source of entertainment for the villagers and townsfolk. To hear of wintering in a buffalo-hide shelter and then to snuggle down in a real house with a stone fireplace and a cosy bed seemed the height of luxury. The stories were apt to take on a life of their own and grow in the recounting. And as it was extremely unlikely that another *hivernant* would arrive to dispute the veracity of the yarns, the storyteller had the floor to himself.

On the other hand, the *mangeurs de porc* – "porkeaters," the hands taken on by the trading companies to travel to the west in springtime with supplies and return with the fur pelts long before freeze-up in Montreal, were not nearly as much in demand for their yarns around a neighbour's fireplace.

Jean Baptiste was in good form. He'd had a few days of practice in recounting his adventures to his family and had found to his amusement that his old friends in Maskinongé and its surroundings were enthralled and enchanted by his accounts of life in the wild. He had always been known as a restless sort of fellow, always dreaming of taking to the woods as a voyageur, a traveller, a *coureur de bois*, a runner through the forest, dealing with wild animals, Indians, anything that was challenging and dangerous. But in the last five years, he had come to decide that he'd had a bellyful of harrowing escapes and back-breaking portages, to say nothing of encounters with murderous beasts and humans. And by no means, he had told himself ruefully, had all the humans been Indians – far from it. He'd had close calls and lucky escapes from fellow Canadians as well as Metis, the people who claimed an Indian mother and a Canadian or British father.

When the British employees of the Hudson's Bay Company were recalled home, they frequently left without their Indian wives and half-breed children, sometimes promising to send to send for them or to return themselves. Many a deserted wife found it hard to readjust to the tribal life of her people after having a position of great respect as the wife of a post manager, or "factor" as they were known. The Metis who survived to adulthood were frequently at loggerheads with both white and red-skinned men.

Listening to Jean Baptiste's accounts of bravery and endurance, the villagers all declared that his five years of wandering had made a man of him, and they welcomed him back to the quiet ways of the village, hard as they were. Farming, raising crops, and keeping the cradles filled under the approving eye of the priest – that was the way of the village, and most considered it a good life. A few were thinking ahead to the time when more settlers arriving would want to purchase lumber already dressed and make a regular town of what had been a clearing beside a river not too many years before. Some were going into business in a small way, setting up a sawmill or a gristmill or selling fish, all at a tidy profit of course. It was not every farmer whose holdings were so large that after dividing up his farm among his many sons, a large enough tract would be left to sustain yet another generation. Everyone wanted frontage on the river, and already many of the farms had begun to take on a narrow and lengthy ribbon aspect.

Everyone hoped to be one of Josette's guests at her modest reception, but she had to be selective. Her home was not nearly half the size of the Lajimonieres' – and besides, she had no intention of inviting pretty younger women to outshine her Marie Anne.

Josette need not have been so careful. Jean Baptiste was no sooner launched into a harrowing tale of rescuing his partner on the winter traplines from a pack of wolves circling round the fellow, whose attention was fixed on capturing a fine white fox, than he found himself bedazzled by a pair of very bright, very blue eyes hanging on every word he said.

Jean Baptiste glowed. The blue eyes belonged to a strikingly handsome young woman. Not only did she seem enthralled, but she had an air of quick comprehension that intrigued him. The wolf story completed, he settled back and started on the tale of the Hudson's Bay factor, Mr Kite.

"This was far up the North Saskatchewan River," he began, "a couple of weeks' paddle upriver from Fort of the Prairies. One day this fellow, Kite, remained alone in his fort. He sent all his employees, his clerks, upriver to an even smaller fort to bring them fresh provisions and trade goods. He figured the smaller fort would be receiving traders any day by then, and the fort would be needing fresh supplies of ammunition and spirits. His four clerks were called Montour, Milet, Morin, and St Germain, all Canadians. A Metis named Tourangeau followed the Canadians in a small canoe.

"The first day that Kite was alone, Indians camped across the river from his fort, and they sent a young boy across to trade for powder. After the trade was concluded and everyone was satisfied, the factor ruffled the young boy's hair in a playful way. He certainly only meant it to be a gesture of friendship. He never dreamed that the Indian lad would resent being touched and think it an insult. Hardly had the boy reached the encampment across the river again than he complained of feeling sick. Before the day was out, he was dead."

Jean Baptiste paused and glanced around at Josette's guests. No one made a sound. No one moved. A log in the fireplace crackled and shed sparks. Everyone was startled.

Marie Anne found herself murmuring, "What happened then?"

Jean Baptiste returned to his story, finding it a little difficult to focus his thoughts under the penetrating gaze of those bright blue eyes.

"Well," he went on, "before he died, the boy told his people about the factor touching him on the head and giving him an evil spirit. The boy insisted that the factor was the cause of his illness. Sad to say, the Indians believed the boy. To their way of thinking, the factor had done something evil, and so he must possess an evil spirit to be able to own such power. If the factor could do this powerful thing, he was not to be trusted, and they reasoned it was necessary to get rid of him and his strange powers as quickly as possible."

He paused for a breath. "As dawn broke the next morning, the entire band of Indians crossed the river with but one intention and one thought in their minds: to kill the white man in the fort as quickly as possible. They stabbed him with knives, and from what was found later, each brave must have stabbed him at least once. Then they tore the fort apart. They dumped powder, skins, kettles, sugar, anything and everything all in a heap and leaped on it, stabbing with their knives, and I suppose shrieking at the top of their lungs to rid the area of poor Mr Kite's 'evil power.'

"In the meantime, the four Canadians, the clerks, who had gone up the river a couple of days before, were coming back to the fort singing light-heartedly the way the Canadians always do and never suspecting that anything could be wrong. An elderly Metis woman had seen what had happened, and very bravely she decided to risk her life by warning the Canadians. She knew they would be massacred as soon as they returned to the fort. Her idea was to signal to them as they passed her. Of course, if the Indians at their camp knew what she was up to, they would have killed her too. The sad thing is that she waited all day long for them, and when they finally paddled into sight, it had grown dark and they could not see her waving to them, even though she was frantic. As she had feared, when the four reached the fort the next morning at first light, the Indians were waiting for them and butchered them too, all four of them."

There was complete silence in the room. Even the logs in the fireplace were silent. Memories of Indian ambushes in the area around Maskinongé were recent enough in the memory of those listening to Jean Baptiste that fear and horror were registered on every face. Marie Anne's expression reflected her complete absorption in the tale as she took in every detail and made vivid pictures in her mind's eye.

Jean Baptiste cleared his throat and continued. "Tourangeau, the Metis who had paddled along behind them, was still behind on the way back, and he only reached the fort the next day. By this time, the Indians had moved on, except for the Metis woman who told him what had happened. Tourangeau paddled up to the dock at the fort, and as he told us afterwards, everything seemed so very still, a quite unnatural stillness."

Once again, Jean Baptiste paused for effect and looked directly into those adorable eyes. It occurred to him that the huge sky out on the prairies was just such a penetrating blue.

Then he went on. "Tourangeau could see no one on top of the hill. He beached his canoe and started up the hill with great apprehension. The first thing he noticed that was unusual was something shiny beside the path. But when he came closer he saw that it was a knife gleaming in the sunshine. Then what he saw sickened him with horror and fear. The knife was sticking out of a man, one of the Canadians. A very brave man, Torangeau, he kept on, not knowing what he might find. The closer he got to the fort, the more the horror of what had happened became clear to him. His four Canadian friends had been stabbed many times. Finally inside the fort was the factor's body, mutilated and already decomposing. He was sickened by the smell and the buzzing of thousands of carrion flies circling around the corpse. There was nobody alive to tell him what horrible thing had happened to start all this carnage and destruction. Only later did he find out from the Metis woman who had tried to warn the Canadians and who had known of the circumstances of the Indian boy's death.

"Then Tourangeau thought to himself that if there were still Indians waiting about for anybody else to arrive at the fort, would he be the next victim to be knifed to death? It struck Tourangeau that he might well become that next victim of inexpressible rage. So he did what any sensible man would do. He ran as fast as he could down the hill away from the terrifying sights and the terrible stench, leaped into his canoe, and paddled as though the devil himself was chasing him. He paddled upriver to the fort where they had left their supplies only a few days before. He figured if he paddled all day and all night without rest, he had a good chance that he might reach the fort by noon the next day.

"Just as it got dark that night, really dark, and a sliver of moon was rising, he saw as he paddled around a slight promontory of the riverbank a huge bonfire surrounded by figures. He could not tell if they were white or Indian. As he drew opposite their fire, he summoned all his courage and called out to them in French. To his great relief, they answered in French. It turned out that they were employees of the forts farther up the Saskatchewan, bringing furs to what had been his fort. Poor Tourangeau paddled over to the shore, beached his canoe, and gasped out his tale of horror, shaking with terror. You can imagine how that great crowd of men felt. Believe me, there are many tales like that to be told of what has to be endured in order to bring out those fine fur pelts."

Marie Anne was utterly lost in a world of dangers and of bravery beyond what she had ever imagined. She was enthralled by the pictures she had seen so vividly in her imagination, which kept popping back into her mind.

Finally she turned to Jean Baptiste and murmured, "How very brave you are to live like that for five whole years."

Jean Baptiste smiled back at her. "It's not like that every day, you know, or there would be nobody left to return and relate any of the experiences we have all gone through. There would be no stories if no one survived to tell them." He laughed.

"I am so glad you are the one who has come back to tell us about these astonishing happenings," Marie Anne said shyly. She felt herself melt, as though all her bones had turned to jelly under the penetrating gaze of Jean Baptiste.

"When the party is over," he whispered to her, "may I have the honour of walking with you to your home? I just want to make sure that no Indians come stalking out of the forest to do you harm."

When it was time for the guests to bid Josette and her husband a hearty goodnight, Marie Anne and Jean Baptiste were the last to leave. Josette flung her arms around her sister, kissed her on both cheeks, and whispered, "I do believe my dear sister is going to have a chance at real happiness."

Marie Anne's eyes were sparkling, and it was not just the glow from the fire and afterwards the sudden gust of cold air which made her cheeks so rosy. She gave her arm to Jean Baptiste and dropped her eyes with sudden shyness as together they went out into the crisp November night.

Josette watched them go, and as soon as her husband had closed the door for the night, she embraced him. "Oh!

I do so hope Marie Anne will have an opportunity to marry and leave that gloomy old presbytery, kind as they have always been to her," she added.

The young parents barred the door and went, arms entwined, up the stairs to their sons' room to peer into the two cradles. They watched in deep contentment as the two healthy little ones slept peacefully and soundly. Then they too undressed and, after their prayers, climbed into bed together. Josette felt well pleased with herself and her matchmaking schemes.

When Marie Anne and Jean Baptiste arrived at the doorstep of the presbytery, Jean Baptiste took both her hands in his.

Marie Anne raised her eyes to smile and whisper, "Goodnight," and Jean Baptiste raised her hands, bowing down to kiss them gently.

At that, the young people parted, Marie Anne to slip into the presbytery to find that once more the housekeeper had left a candle stub burning for her. She picked up the candlestick with one hand and lifted the other to her lips at the spot where Jean Baptiste had kissed it. How she managed to make her way upstairs to her little room, she hardly knew, her heart was thumping so quickly and her thoughts were in such a jumble of excitement and eagerness.

Jean Baptiste, meanwhile, sang heartily all the way home.

CHAPTER 3

The winter passed in a rosy glow for Marie Anne. Sometimes when she was attending to her tasks in the presbytery, she would forget where she was entirely, her mind given over to the growing attachment she felt for the returned hero. Time and again when she was mending and ironing and standing over the steaming wash kettles, or kneading dough, or chopping up carrots and turnips for the priest's dinner, her eyes took on a vacant, happy stare as she repeated over and over to herself the little signs that this freedom-loving voyageur was indeed ready to put his adventurous life behind him and settle down.

Madame smiled knowingly. Marie Anne's bright eyes and her growing habit of singing the melodies of the voyageur's songs that Jean Baptiste sang for her, together with a sort of glow that seemed to envelop her, gave it away. Madame was truly sorry to think of the probable outcome of this attachment. After all, she had spent years at the end of her useful life preparing a new housekeeper for the incumbent of St Sulpice, and here it was all going for nothing. Yet she was truly happy for Marie Anne. She had become very fond of the wet, dirty-faced child of eleven long years ago, and there was no doubt about it, Marie

Anne did well at whatever she turned her hand to. She had become an excellent helper, wiry and strong. Marie Anne's smiles and her obvious excitement, her singing and her sparkling blue eyes, indeed the whole improvement in her appearance, touched the old lady's heart. How many times had she watched Marie Anne capably and skilfully taking charge of other women's babies, thinking to herself that it really was a shame that the girl did not have her own little family.

"What lucky babies they would be," she had often thought, "if they had Marie Anne for a mother."

Jean Baptiste was a patient but determined wooer. Their first kiss took place on a starry frosty evening in mid-February. It was bitterly cold, but Jean Baptiste asked her if she would come riding with him in his sleigh. Marie Anne paused only long enough to ask Madame if she could be spared for an hour.

Madame nodded her consent with her eyes twinkling. The whole village was talking about the romance of the dashing young seigneur and the Gaboury girl from the presbytery.

Jean Baptiste lifted Marie Anne into the sleigh as easily as if she were without weight at all, wrapped her carefully inside a couple of bearskins, and off they went into the moonlight. The bells on the harness jangled prettily, the only sound in the world it seemed except for the rhythmic clop-clopping of the hooves of Jean's horse and the occasional squeaky sounds of the sleigh's runners on the hard-packed snow in the intense cold. Countless thousands of stars filled the entire sky, giving enough light for Marie Anne and Jean Baptiste to see one another clearly. The river was iced over and Jean drove the sleigh out onto it, giving Marie Anne a view of Maskinongé she'd never had before.

At first she was a little afraid. "What if the ice should give way?" she was thinking to herself.

Jean Baptiste saw the tightening of her mouth and the little line of worry on her forehead. He laughed his great hearty guffaw and took the opportunity to fling an arm around her shoulders to draw her closer to him.

"There's no danger of falling in," he whispered in her ear. "This ice is thick enough by now to take horse, sleigh, us, and a couple of houses along with it. Have you never been out on the river like this? It's quite a sight, isn't it? You get the feeling that you are the only one on earth, and it's all mine. I love it."

Marie Anne grinned back at him. It was exhilarating, and her heart raced with excitement. They snuggled closer and closer together with the bearskin tucked in over their knees and up to their chins. Marie Anne felt full of warmth and happiness, and once she got over her initial trepidation, she wanted the sleigh to go faster and faster, to feel the wind against her face and to see the shoreline of Maskinongé go racing past.

"This is wonderful, Jean," she said, turning to him, her face alive with joy.

They looked at each other shyly for some moments. Jean held the reins in one hand and slowly brought the other up to Marie Anne's chin. Marie Anne closed her eyes and thought to herself, "Now at last, I think I know why I was born." At that moment, Jean Baptiste bent his head down to her and gently kissed her mouth.

"You are my little white princess, my snow queen," he said huskily and kissed her again, a long lingering kiss this time.

If choirs of angels had burst straight out of the stars and flown down to serenade them, Marie Anne could not have felt more exalted.

By this time, Jean Baptiste's horse had figured out that he was really the one in charge of the sleigh and its contents, and so it was appropriate that he choose the route: the easiest path through the covering of snow, no climbing over drifts, just a slow easy walk back to his snug stable.

Jean Baptiste kissed her again. They were both breathless, even taken aback at the passionate response they had each of them felt.

The horse slowed down to a dawdle. "No point at all in straining myself," he figured. "That Jean doesn't seem to care whether we are going anywhere or not."

Jean held Marie Anne in a bear-like hug as close as could be managed with the constrictions of the fur robes and layers of warm woollen clothing on them both.

"Marie Anne, I've made you mine. You are mine. I never thought it would happen to me like this, but here I am, Mademoiselle, your obedient servant. Will you do me the honour of naming our wedding day?"

Marie Anne giggled.

Poor Jean was somewhat taken aback. "You don't take me seriously? Marie Anne! Everyone in Maskinongé is asking my mother, and I expect yours also, when is the wedding day to be, and you don't take me seriously!"

She nestled her nose into his neck and felt almost unbearably happy. "I'm so happy, Jean, truly I am. Forgive me, but I feel so happy. It's like flying into the sky like the angels do."

"Well, my dearest little one, I hope you don't. I want you down here on earth for a long time. And you haven't answered my question. Will you do me the honour of becoming Madame Jean Baptiste Lajimoniere?"

Marie Anne giggled again. Jean Baptiste could certainly be a convincing grandson of a count with all the gracious manners of the salon rather than the rough survival of the trapper, she thought.

Simultaneously, they turned to one another, and despite the furs and the bulky clothing, Marie Anne felt his body stiffen against her. An intense longing she had never known before surged through her, and she bent her head back for his passionate kiss.

"Now I know without a doubt why I was born," she thought, "to be Jean's wife and to bear his children. Oh, Jean Baptiste, you dear man."

His voice interrupted her thoughts. "Dearest one, I am not a patient man, and you have yet to answer my question. For the third time, when are we to be married?"

Marie Anne wriggled with delight. "You forget, dearest Jean. You must first seek permission from Maman, even though I am sure she will consent."

"Well then," persisted Jean, "when I have the consent and approval of your mother, what day are we to be married?"

Marie Anne snuggled and wriggled against him. "How strong he is and how gentle," she thought. "Yet how courageous he has been out there in those deserts and living with savages. What a wonderful man. How lucky I am. And he loves me, I am sure he does … but he hasn't said so, not in so many words."

She leaned back in his arms. "Jean Baptiste Lajimoniere, do you love me?"

Jean was truly surprised. "But of course I do, and with all my heart, my darling one. You must know I do."

"Then please say so, even though I have to get you to admit it."

Jean Baptiste threw back his head and roared with laughter. The horse was so startled from his private musing he figured he had better pick up his pace and head for home in a warm stable.

"I love you, I love you, my dearest. Now how about our wedding day? When is it to be?"

"In the spring, as soon as we can, would be nice," murmured Marie Anne. "I cannot leave Father Vinet's household until Madame has found another assistant. We can't be married in Lent, of course, but right after Lent as soon as you like. Eastertide would be a lovely time, I think, an early spring wedding. What a beautiful time to be married!" She sighed with contentment.

Madame Gaboury's consent was readily given. "The son of the richest man in the diocese, a squire no less, descended from good stock, a title too, so everyone says," Madame Gaboury sighed with pleasure and satisfaction.

Of even more importance to Madame Gaboury and Marie Anne's brothers was that the Lajimonieres held good land. Jean Baptiste's brothers had been well looked-after with land and shares in the various family enterprises, and naturally it was taken for granted that Jean Baptiste would be allotted good land with water frontage and plenty of bush.

"Who would have thought our little Marie Anne would find herself such a fine catch of a husband, and at her age and no dowry? And his wild oats are sown. That's always a good sign in a young fellow as restless and as eager to be off to see the world as Jean Baptiste was," Madame Gaboury mused to the rest of her brood as she tied on her bonnet and prepared to go first to her mother's home and then to the village with her news.

She was proud of Josette for her handling of the initial stages of the courtship. Many a time, she had worried about the sunny-natured daughter shut up in the presbytery all those years. It had seemed the right thing to do at the time, but now that Marie Anne had grown into a slender young woman, lithe and strong, she had had misgivings about her decision – not that she would ever let Marie Anne know. Sometimes it had seemed to her that her daughter was indeed a little chagrined by her peremptory banishment to the presbytery, and she traced the subsequent coolness between them from the day she had stalked off to work in the priest's home.

"But now," Madame Gaboury thought, "she will make Jean Baptiste a good wife, and she looks happy."

The rest of the winter passed in a happy daze for the bride-to-be. Another fatherless girl was quickly found, and Marie Anne took pleasure in acquainting her with the niceties of caring for the priest's domain as well as the heavy labour involved.

On the appointed day, 21 April 1807 – an unusually warm day it was, with a soft breeze from the south and sunshine warm enough to make the snowdrifts cringe – a radiant bride fulfilled Josette's prophecy, in the same blue gown that matched her eyes, and was joined in holy matrimony to the man everyone said was the catch of the entire district. Marie Anne's mother, her brothers and sisters together with their spouses, and a little army of small children were all present. There were aunts and uncles, a sprinkling of great-aunts, and even a great-grand-uncle. As for Madame Tessier, although she had become quite frail, she was determined to be present and to recall for everyone's benefit the night the bride was born. With Lajimoniere relations as well, it was a large assemblage that arrived at the Lajimoniere home after the Mass for feasting, dancing, and singing.

It was one of the happiest and grandest parties that Maskinongé had ever seen, and more than one young man was emboldened to approach the demoiselle of his choice in the midst of the bonhomie. The villagers commented to one another that when all was said and done, it seemed as though their prodigal son had returned a responsible young man and come home where he belonged at last, and now marriage with the capable Gaboury girl would be sure to settle him down.

A large room on the second floor of the Lajimoniere house was set aside for the newlyweds. It was two rooms really, now that a partition had been built down the middle so that Marie Anne and Jean Baptiste could settle into a modest parlour all their own as well as a bedroom. Their meals were taken with the entire Lajimoniere household.

Although Marie Anne helped out with some of the kitchen tasks, it seemed very light to her after her responsibilities in the presbytery. The pleasant arrangement was only a temporary one until their own house on land that Monsieur Lajimoniere had designated for his son could be made ready for them.

The first week of their marriage was a time of sheer bliss for them both. Madame Lajimoniere was delighted with her gentle and willing daughter-in-law. Jean Baptiste seemed to have turned into a tamed and cuddly big black bear. Monsieur Lajimoniere felt entirely relieved that at last the handsomest, tallest, and strongest of his sons should have put his waywardness behind him.

"Mind you," he grunted to his wife, "he could have chosen a younger bride. Twenty-five years old this coming November. She is not a young girl. Sixteen or seventeen at the most is the age I would have chosen for him, but still, Marie Anne seems to have taken him in hand, and for that I am grateful."

Father and son worked out the details of Jean Baptiste's patrimony and the part he would play in the running of the large tract of land belonging to the family as well as the numerous business enterprises, the sawmill, and the grist mill among others. Jean Baptiste was quick to grasp the details of his father's affairs. It was arranged that the newlyweds would move into the house that was already going up on Jean's allotment before spring sowing got underway. For the immediate future, Jean Baptiste would busy himself readying the farm equipment and making plans for what would be his first crops.

Then it happened.

Jean Baptiste stood up to his knees in melting snows, mending a cedar fence, happy to be using his great muscles outside in the crisp spring air. He stood up straight and looked around at the fields all neatly fenced, just as his were. There were bare patches here and there, left where the wind had flung snow into drifts in the hollows and by the fence lines, leaving other patches barely covered. Now the bare patches were becoming larger each day.

Suddenly Jean Baptiste knew, as surely as he loved Marie Anne more deeply than he thought he could love anybody in this world, that fenced-in areas and guiding a horse or an ox behind a plough for the rest of his life was not for him. Riding a horse, yes, in the hard chase of a buffalo hunt, but walking behind a plodding beast and fenced in on all four sides, no, it certainly was not for him.

He couldn't stomach it. Except for finding Marie Anne, he realized with a pang that he should never have come home. His heart, although it belonged to his dear helpmate, was aching to be back in the freedom of the unlimited lands of the prairies. He leant against the fence and covered his face with his hands. It was in both a kind of despair and a growing sense of vitality that Jean Baptiste knew that his place was back in the west with his friends and the exhilaration of the chase.

He pictured his closest friends, his hunting companions Jean Belgrade, Chalifou, and Paquin, and wondered how they were faring. Right now, he thought, they would be having the greatest feelings of satisfaction as they were preparing their winter's catch of pelts for the factor. He could feel the lustrous skins of fox, of ermine, and of mink that the wives would have scraped and made ready for the annual bargaining trip to a post.

Most hunters allied themselves with either the North West Company operating out of Montreal or the Hudson's Bay Company operating out of York factory far to the north on the shores of Hudson's Bay. The North West had long been the favourite of the French Canadians, but the Hudson's Bay traders were expanding their trade farther and farther south. Their prices were a little better for the furs.

Jean and his friends decided to become free traders in order to be able to bargain and perhaps pit one price against a rival post. Now Jean realized how much he had missed the companionship of his three good and trusted friends, and he realized too all at once that he had not known how much he had missed their life together until the reality of the repetitious life of a farmer had suddenly hit him.

He shook his head and tried to throw off the feelings of intense longing to be back on the open prairies. But he could not, and looking again at all the fences surrounding him on every side helped him to make up his mind.

He had to go back – either with Marie Anne or, if she would not come with him, alone.

He felt again the prickles on the back of his neck when the four friends had gone out together to check on their traplines, not knowing if they would be murdered in their sleep or massacred fighting against bands of Indians on the warpath. Sometimes they had fought alone, sometimes they'd had to fight and yell as fiendishly as their sworn friends, a band of Crees, against Blackfeet or Dakotas.

"What has become of Belgrade, Chalifou, and Paquin, all married to Cree women?" he wondered. "They all travelled and lived and hunted and made babies out there in the north-western countries with Indian wives. It's not an easy life to be sure, but it's a good one, and with Marie Anne along I know that it is where I belong. Besides, she has asked me so many times to tell her about being out there; perhaps it won't be hard to get her to come with me."

By the time Jean Baptiste arrived back at the Lajimoniere household for the evening meal, he'd had time to sort it out in his mind. He was going back to the world he loved, the freedom of life on the prairies, and he devoutly hoped he could persuade his bride to go with him.

All through the evening meal, Marie Anne looked at him curiously. There was something different about him, something she could not quite put her finger on. She did not like to question him in front of the family, wisely deciding that if there were something he had to tell her, she would know about it sooner or later.

When at last they had bade the rest of the family goodnight and were alone together in their bedroom, Jean began, haltingly at first, to try to tell Marie Anne of his real feelings for the life of a hunter and trapper.

At first Marie Anne could not trust her ears, but gradually she began to listen, really listen, to her husband's dilemma.

"I'm not a farmer," he kept saying over and over. "I can't tie myself to these fields, this little piece of land. I must go back to the prairies where nobody owns land. It's just there, and everybody lives from it and on it. Oh, there are a few skirmishes here and there when two different sets of Indians both want to hunt over the same areas. But can't you see, my dearest, that it's the greatness of the land, the expanse, that has caught me, and I must go back. You will come with me, won't you? We can have a good life together out there, I promise you."

It was late into the night when all the rest of the household was fast asleep that Jean Baptiste and his bride of one week continued to thrash out the problem.

"To go together to the desert country or to stay at home," went through Marie Anne's mind as she held her beloved close. "How can I choose? I love him so, but the western deserts are so far away from everything I know."

Jean Baptiste had made up his mind. Just before he rolled over and fell sound asleep, he announced that his mind was set. "I'm going. Alone if need be, but I hope with you, dear love."

Marie Anne was caught in a dilemma she was utterly unprepared to face. It was true that she loved to hear tales of the unknown western countries. But to go there and live there herself … "Could I do it? Could I make my way in the wilderness?"

No woman had ever gone out with a voyageur husband. It had never even been considered.

"And what of Maman? How would she feel? Would I ever be able to return and see my sisters and brothers again?" Marie Anne lay awake for hours with questions coming and going through her mind.

Both the Lajimonieres and Madame Gaboury were outraged. The very idea of Jean taking Marie Anne to live among savages was impossible. What on earth was he thinking about? Surely he'd had enough of that rough life, risking his life time and time again. Did he intend to risk his wife as well? The arguments went on and on.

After a couple of days of violent discussion on both sides, Marie Anne, who had been helping her belle-mere and the two little maids to hang the feather bolsters out in the spring sunshine and give them a good shake, quietly excused herself and walked alone to the presbytery of St Sulpice.

"It's a help," she thought, "to be in the quiet presbytery."

After bowing in prayer to the Virgin, imploring her aid in this decision, Marie Anne sought out Father Vinet and laid the problem before him.

"What shall I do?" she begged the priest.

Father Vinet thought for a few moments in silence. "Your place is by your husband's side," he told her, "provided you believe that you have the physical strength to live in a very harsh environment, much harsher than anything you have known. You will not have the comforts of your faith. You will in all probability not see your mother and your family again. There will be no church for you to attend."

He paused. "But," he continued, "if you truly love Jean Baptiste and you think you have the strength to follow your husband, you must go."

Marie Anne thanked him and walked very slowly and thoughtfully up the hill to her new home. On an impulse, she turned and trudged the long path to her mother's house instead.

"I have come to tell you, dear Maman," Marie Anne announced slowly and quietly, "that I am determined to go with Jean Baptiste to the fur countries. Father Vinet helped me to see that it is not just my duty to my husband, but it is truly where I want to be." She smiled happily at her mother. "I love Jean Baptiste with all my heart, and if he thinks that

I will be able to withstand it, why then it must be so. After all, he knows what the life is like out there."

Madame Gaboury burst into tears and held her daughter close.

"Maman," said Marie Anne when her mother's sobs had lessened a little. "Just think. This must be what your grandmother felt when your mother left France to come to the New World."

"I suppose you are right, my dear Marie, but it does not ease the pain in my heart," her mother replied, trying in vain to stop her tears.

"Jean came back once, Maman. Perhaps he will want to come back again, and then you will see what a good life we have together. And just think of it, I shall be the very first Canadienne to go into the country where the furs come from."

Madame Gaboury dried her eyes at last. She could see that there was nothing she could do to get Marie Anne to change her mind. And in to her practical old head, the thought came too as to what Marie Anne would do if she stayed behind and her husband returned to the western countries alone. Would she be welcome as the married but deserted wife in the Lajimoniere household? Hardly. Would she be welcome back in the presbytery? Hardly that either. She would end her days sitting alone or by one of her brothers' or sisters' fireplaces, a maiden aunt who was no longer a maiden.

Madame Gaboury bowed her head. "You are a grown woman, Marie. May you ever feel that your decision is the right one."

Mother and daughter kissed one another fondly, and Marie Anne walked slowly back to the Lajimoniere house. Jean Baptiste met her on the road.

"Where have you been, my dearest one? We have all been so worried about you. You just seemed to disappear."

"I told you that I felt I couldn't make up my mind about such a big question, Jean." Marie Anne grinned up at him. "So I've been to see Father Vinet to ask him what he thinks about me traipsing off into unknown lands with you. He agrees with you. He told me to go with you, provided I think I have the strength."

"Oh! My dearest little wife." Jean Baptiste embraced her with tenderness and kissed her in full view of the villagers who happened to be about and who looked on with shock in the case of the ladies and amusement in the case of the men. "But what do you think? Do you think you can stand it, and do you really want to come with me? There is no going back alone, you know."

"Yes, yes, and yes," answered Marie Anne. "For better or for worse. I'm coming."

Jean Baptiste picked her up and carried her up the walk and into the house. "We are going! We're both going!" he bellowed to the entire household.

"You are a brave woman," Madame Lajimoniere told her. "Try to bring him back at some time not too far in the future. I should like to see my grandchildren, even if they behave like savages."

"They won't," laughed Marie Anne. "I promise you that, and I'll do my best to remember your request. They will all repeat their Ave Marias and Pater Nosters like good young Christians. Now I shall have to start gathering together linens and blankets and all the things we shall need out there."

Madame Lajimoniere sighed. "I shall be happy to help you prepare for this most tremendous journey."

"Wait up, ladies," cautioned Jean Baptiste. "Marie Anne, do you realize that you will be living with no more goods than you can carry? Or pack onto a horse or two? No sheets. No bedding. We shall be using buffalo hides for blankets and tents and our mattress will be made of evergreen boughs or just a couple of hides. No pewter finery for dining, no washing up the pottery for us. Do you still want to come?"

Marie Anne and Jean Baptiste faced each other solemnly for a moment. She looked into Jean's eyes and said softly, "If you want to share your life with me, I am prepared to share mine with you. So be it. You mean more to me than bed sheets and pewter platters."

Madame Lajimoniere shook her head. Young people these days were hard to understand.

CHAPTER 4

Now that she understood that a bride's chest filled with linens, such as her sisters had taken with them to their new homes, was not feasible for her new life in the western deserts, Marie Anne began to feel some trepidation about what she had promised. But together with her quite natural wondering about the wisdom of her course of action, there was also the underlying excitement of something new and untried. It was an exciting prospect for a young woman raised entirely within the precincts of Maskinongé to be setting off into unmapped territories.

"I must be a wanderer at heart too," she thought, "although I never realized it until now."

Jean Baptiste was relieved at her outwardly happy acceptance of the great changes that were about to occur in her domestic affairs.

"We shall be as free as the birds in the air," he told her. "No heavy luggage. No things we don't need. We will be happy without them. No fences for as far as you can see, and the country is so flat you can see as far as a few days' travel sometimes. You wait until you see how huge and blue the sky is. I swear it's bigger there than here in Canada."

Madame Gaboury had another concern. "What happens when …?" began her every sentence.

"Do not concern yourself over me, Maman," Marie Anne answered her queries. "Jean will know what to do no matter what happens. It isn't as though he hasn't been there already."

With that Madame Gaboury had to be content, but thinking back to her own difficulties in childbirth, ten times over, she thought she had good cause to be concerned.

As soon as transportation on a small fishing vessel was available going from Maskinongé to Berthierville, first through Lake St Pierre, really a wide portion of the St Lawrence, and then a narrow passage taking advantage of islands in mid-river, and at last Berthierville, the newlyweds were off. On the day they sailed away from Maskinongé, Marie Anne and Jean Baptiste had been married for exactly two weeks to the day. The couple stood in the stern of the little boat and waved goodbye to their families. Everyone came down to the dock to see them off.

Josette flung her arms around Marie Anne. "I hope, oh how I hope this will all turn out well," she whispered into Marie Anne's ear. "I never thought that bringing you and Jean Baptiste together would mean you going so far away."

Marie Anne hugged her sister. "Don't feel you did anything wrong. It will all be for the best, and maybe in three or four years Jean will want to come home once more."

The two young women looked at each other for some moments. "I hope you are right," whispered Josette. "I shall miss you so much."

"Come, dear one. Our adventure begins, and the boatman is waiting." Jean Baptiste put one arm around

Marie Anne and with the other clapped his brother-in-law and his brothers on the back.

"Good hunting, and come back before you are an old man," his brother said, flinging an arm around his shoulder.

Jean Baptiste kissed his mother's hand and then embraced her in a bear hug. "Come back, come back," she was able to say through her tears, "and bring my dear *belle-fille* with you. God bless you both."

The boatman raised the sails, which billowed in the breeze. One of the Lajimoniere boys gave the boat a push, and they were off.

Marie Anne's eyes were riveted to the shore at Maskinongé. She kept gazing at the spot where they had embarked until all she could make out was the steeple of St Sulpice growing smaller and smaller, and then a promontory cut off her view entirely. It was to become a picture in her memory that brought tears as well as sighs of pleasure for the rest of her life. Swiftly the small vessel carried them down the Mastigouche, running in full spate with the spring runoff as well as its usual current.

Marie Anne clung to Jean Baptiste. It was, after all, her first experience of being on the water, and the speed of the craft with its sails up made her uneasy. After the very last glimpse of Maskinongé, she turned to see where she was going, and the wind rushing past her raised her spirits. By the end of their little voyage, she had decided that she quite liked the feel of gliding over water. The sun shone and made sparkles on the waves as they sped along. Jean Baptiste held her close and laughed at her earlier fears.

"There will be lots more like this, you can be sure," he told her. "Feel the wind in your face. Feels good, yes?"

Marie Anne admitted that it was cheering. Responding to Jean's mounting excitement, she laughed when a particularly boisterous wave hit the side of the boat and splashed her.

"That's my Marie," laughed Jean. His obvious approval of her reaction warmed her, and she snuggled happily in his arms.

"Duck down," shouted the steersman. "We'll be putting about in a moment. When the boom wings over, little lady, lie down flat on the bottom of the boat. See, like that," he said as the sloop put about and the sails filled once more on the other side. "Now we are in the narrows. Soon we will reach Bertierville. How far did you say you were going?" he asked.

"All the way to the western countries," shouted Jean Baptiste, "but right now, I'd say as far as Lachine to meet the company boats."

The fisherman shook his head. Surely he had not heard correctly. He couldn't believe that a woman, and a pretty one at that, would try to go out to the wilderness of the voyageurs' country. He would have been even more astounded if he had known that the pretty woman was off to be a trapper's wife, a real *hivernante*, and was to live the life of an Indian squaw.

At Berthierville, they found themselves in luck. A half dozen or so young men, anxious to be off to fame and fortune and the excitement of trading furs, had persuaded a fisherman to take them as far as Lachine, where the men could be signed on by the North West Company. The young aspiring hunters were happy to welcome the Lajimonieres as fellow travellers. They looked forward to getting all kinds of valuable information on what they could expect from Jean Baptiste, a real veteran, but to say they were surprised that the lovely Madame Lajimoniere would be coming along too would be putting it far too mildly. Jean Baptiste told them that although he would sign with the North West Company – the Nor'West as it was called – in order to get paid for his voyage out to the fur country, he was determined to remain an independent trapper, trading with either of the fur companies and getting the best price.

"I and my wife are going to stay in the west over the winter, real *hivernants*, not the *mangeurs de lard*, 'pork eaters,' the term we give to the men who return to Lachine each winter," he told them.

Most of the *mangeurs de lard* were men learning and hoping to become bourgeois – clerks in charge of trade goods used for barter for the prized furs. After a few years, if they showed promise, they would be sent out as *hivernants*, men who remained in the various forts over the winters. Their dream was eventually to be sent as managers back to Montreal. Many came to love the western country as much as it had captivated Jean Baptiste and remained out in the lonely forts for the rest of their days.

The company owners, the managers in Montreal, made fortunes out of the lustrous pelts, which they shipped off to England or to the continent. It was the fashion at the time for new peers created in England, when they appeared at court functions, to wear sumptuous fur-lined mantles. In France, the reigning monarch and his courtiers appeared at official functions and coronations wearing long robes lined entirely with ermine trapped in their winter finery, white except for the little black tip at the end of the tail. The bearskins were prized for busbies, the towering, hot, and heavy headgear worn by many a British regiment of guards. Beaver skins were important to the gentleman's hat trade. Large sweeping brims to be brandished in courtly bows, often with a feather or two, was the European fashion. The market, in short, was highly favourable for the company owners and shareholders who were not apt to penetrate farther west than Montreal, where they could enjoy a sophisticated social existence. There was no chance for the trappers to become rich men or even to lead a life of ease on their retirement. Few of them lived long enough to retire, and most realized shortly after arrival that voyageurs were not ever going to become wealthy. It was the thrill of getting by on their own and answering to no one in authority that drew them and captured them.

A life of ease and pleasure held no attraction for Jean Baptiste. The mist on the rivers early in the morning sunshine, the brilliant blue sky, the huge expanse of grasslands and prairies, living by his wits and trading the furs he trapped and shot – that was the life for him, and now it was going to be better than ever with his beloved wife by his side.

He loved the challenge of chutes, saults, rocks, storms on the water, and riding for days on end in search of buffalo. Each day on the water, his spirits rose higher. The closer the travellers got to Lachine, the louder his singing became. Marie Anne was infected by his boyishness, his delight at returning to the west.

"It's a wonder you ever left," she told him.

"Why, to find you, of course," he replied, grinning at her.

The would-be voyageurs chimed in on the refrains of his songs and were eager to take full advantage of their luck and to learn from this old-timer. At Lachine, Jean Baptiste and Marie Anne put up overnight at a small and not-too-clean establishment where they were lucky to be accommodated in a room to themselves. The place was crowded. It was early May, the busiest time in the year for the North West Company to sign on voyageurs and *mangeurs de lard* for the trip by trade canoe to Fort William and beyond. A large crowd of young hopefuls had gathered.

Marie Anne was entranced by everything she saw and curious to know about every facet of her new existence. "It's no wonder farming on his father's lands didn't have appeal for Jean," she thought to herself, "after he has known such a life as this with all the camaraderie and the anticipation."

As soon as they understood that Jean and Marie were man and wife, married in the sight of God in church, the men treated Marie Anne with respect, although there were many shaking their heads behind her back at what they considered Jean's folly.

"We have only just begun our trip, my darling," said Jean, gathering her up in his arms. Marie Anne felt protected and secure.

Like the voyageurs, the trappers, and all the Canadians, Jean Baptiste and Marie Anne were strong in their faith. Before they turned in to bed each night, both got down on their knees to pray. Marie Anne looked with love and devotion at her medal, a special present from Father Vinet. Husband and wife both told their rosaries, as did all the voyageurs each day they were in Lachine, although some of the men became a little lax in their devotions the farther away they were from church and weekly Mass attendance.

After their usual prayers one night, Marie Anne turned sleepily to Jean and murmured, "I pray that I shall always have the strength to be a good wife to you wherever fate takes us."

"You will, my love. I know you will," replied Jean huskily, and together they climbed into their bed. It was the last night Marie Anne would know the luxury of a bedstead and a linen sheet for many a long year.

On the day they were to proceed, as soon as the first streaks of sunlight wakened the birds, the men of the expedition were up and about, busily loading the big company trade canoes with the year's needs in the way of supplies for the men stationed at the forts and the goods to be traded to trappers in exchange for the winter's rich haul of fur. There were a few knickknacks, black pepper, sugar, coloured beads, ribbons, red flannel, and various sorts of finery to dazzle the Indian ladies and make them encourage their menfolk to bring in extra pelts.

Finally the flotilla got under way, and all paddled to the westernmost point of Montreal Island. There the canoes were beached, and every traveler made way to the church of St Anne. Mass was said, confessions were heard, and each devout voyageur prayed to St Anne, the mother of Mary, for help and protection on what was always a trying and perilous journey. It would be the last time that any of them would be able to attend Mass until either they returned to Lachine on the trip down from the west with the precious furs or, as in Marie Anne's and Jean's case, until priests arrived in what was referred to as the western deserts.

Marie Anne was to think to herself many years later that all in all, it was just as well she could not have seen into the future at that point, or she might well have faltered in her resolve and begged Jean to ship her back to Maskinongé.

After the Mass, Marie Anne had her medal blessed by the priest of St Anne's. An extra blessing, she felt, would be a good thing, as all blessedness had to last for gracious sakes only knew for how long.

The men made their way quietly back to the canoes. The young ones, the first-timers, were especially subdued. That they were actually leaving on the great adventure and that there could be no turning back made everyone more thoughtful than usual. But when the boats had rounded the point and all eyes turned to the west, spirits rose again, and the songs and the rhythmic pull on the paddles banished their second thoughts and gloomy fantasies.

The managers had made it plain to Jean that they did not relish having Marie Anne, wife or not wife, as a passenger. She would be taking up space that could be used for trade goods, and there was the matter of providing extra provisions for her. Jean made it equally plain that he was not prepared to sign on if Marie Anne were not to accompany him. The managers weighed the pros and cons. A man of Jean's experience and leadership qualities was too valuable to let go with so many greenhorns signed up, so Jean won his point. Still, the managers insisted that he would be entirely responsible for Marie Anne, and that fights and unpleasantness would not be tolerated no matter how unsettling it would be for the other men to have a white woman along.

Jean stepped up to the managers and towered over them. "Your remark does you no credit," he said with clenched fists and eyes flashing. "Madame, my wife, will be well protected by me."

Jean turned and left the office and found Marie Anne waiting for him outside. "You are coming with me, my good wife," he said in a firmness that gave notice to all voyageurs within earshot that this lady would be travelling to the western fur country and that she was to be treated like a lady – his lady. Woe betide any rash young man who forgot it.

Accordingly, Marie Anne was assigned a place on top of the cargo in Jean's canoe. She had to sit with her legs drawn up underneath her and remain still for hours at a time so as not to be responsible for anything untoward in the way of rocking the boat and perhaps even causing a tip-over. As soon as the flotilla arrived at a place of portage, Marie Anne had to get herself down from her perch, out of the canoe, and out of the way as the packs were assigned to the carriers. Shouldering the one sack of baggage she was permitted to bring with her and lugging it over the portage, she did her best to keep up with her canoe mates. She soon learned to move quickly. There was always good-natured rivalry between the canoes about reaching the portage and unloading first, so as to be first away and first back in the water at the other end. Jean's canoe often won the race, so Marie Anne had the spectre of being run down by a following party to keep her scrambling to stay out of harm's way as well as not to delay Jean and his companions.

Although the Canadians – French-speaking, all of them – were a gallant lot, chivalrous and polite to their lady passenger, they made it clear that nothing must interfere with her canoe's position in the races, or French gallantry might wear thin enough to collapse. If this were to make Jean ashamed of her or uncomfortable with his canoe mates, Marie Anne knew it would cause unpleasantness. She learned to dogtrot with her pack on her back. When brambles and brush tried to hold her skirts back, she just yanked herself free and kept on trotting.

"A far cry from a dainty walk from the presbytery to the fish market," she told herself and giggled. The presbytery seemed like a dream existence to her now. "It's a good thing my pretty little sister can't see me like this."

Marie found the portages around the Long Sault arduous, even though it was a relief to stretch her legs after being still for hours at a stretch. But that was only the beginning. The Ottawa River had many a portage, and Marie Anne had to learn to clamber over rocks – some of them huge and slippery – and slosh her way through marshes. Her boots were unequal to the struggle and soon gave out.

Under the guidance of a friendly Indian woman who showed up at one of the campsites, she learned to mend the boots as best as possible. Basswood bark was torn into thin strips and used to bind the sole to the upper in a makeshift mending operation. Marie Anne tucked some extra strips into her sack for future needs.

Day followed day on the long trek, and there were no further adventures, only gratitude each night for food and rest at the end of another day's travel. Marie Anne and Jean both repeated their prayers together before snuggling up, and Marie Anne noted how many of the other travellers, seemingly rough fellows some of them, did the same. The young couple now married for just less than a month was too exhausted to do more than cuddle briefly and fall into deep slumber, the sleep of the physically exhausted.

It was fascinating to Marie Anne to watch Jean Baptiste wrap his belt, the woven *ceinture fleche*, around and around his middle each morning. "It's not to be fashionable," he told her. "It's for safety's sake. Saves a lot of bad bellyaches."

Marie Anne marvelled at the size and weight of the packs. "How much do they weigh?" she asked Jean.

"Each load weighs exactly ninety pounds," he told her. "A voyageur is expected to carry three loads at a time. Some of the men like to show off their superior strength and heft up to five at a time. That's four hundred and fifty pounds, but they'll regret it later."

Although he was the tallest voyageur of the entire crew, he took his packs three at a time and that was that. "Trotting along at the smart pace we keep, and the going so rough, the rocks slippery, tree roots to trip you, no, it's better to be sensible."

Eventually the flotilla reached Sault Saint Marie without mishap and rested there for a few days while some of the trade goods were unloaded and added to the company factor's stores. The year's supply of goods, food, and ammunition for the use of the factor and his employees, was received with many signs of gratification. They had run out of tea and insisted on having a real lady join them for their first sip of the new crop.

"What would happen if we had met with unfriendly Indians or a bad storm had prevented us from ever coming to Sault Saint Marie? What would have happened to all these men?" Marie Anne turned a worried face up to Jean's.

"That's a risk we all take," he said gravely. "It's best not to think about it. Think of our grandparents back home. They had to face as much danger from the Iroquois, the Indian raiders, as we do, and how about the ones who first left France? They lived to bring up our parents."

Marie Anne shook her head and tried not to think of the enormity of the risks they were all running. "Doesn't do to brood," she said to herself and went off to join the factor's Indian wife in gathering green shoots for the next meal.

Before they set off once more, Jean drew her aside. "Hang on tight for the next part of the journey. Whatever you do, don't rock the boat. Now we enter the great Lake Superior. It's as big as all the land we have passed over, and the storms can be fierce and the waves gigantic."

Marie Anne nodded and took a deep breath. She straightened her back and climbed resolutely onto her perch.

Jean smiled and glowed with pride. "She has courage, that little wife of mine," he thought.

The canoes hugged the north shore and made good progress. They stopped once again to unload supplies at a fort called Michipicoten but did not linger. The weather was too favourable not to take to the water again as quickly as possible. The flotilla, a smaller number of canoes by now, crept further along the north shore until it reached Fort William, a large and up-to-date fort by the standards of 1806.

There was high excitement on their arrival. There were even musket shots fired as though the travellers were visiting royalty. The Nor'Westers in the flotilla produced feathers, streamers, anything to decorate their hats. Marie Anne was captivated, and one of the men lent her a scarf to wave gaily. It was a festive welcome.

All the paddlers were ready for a few days' rest, although none would admit to weariness. Each man kept his sore arms and shoulders and any other discomforts to himself. There was such a spirit of bravado that no one would admit to a lack of courage or stamina.

One of the paddlers had scraped a leg painfully on a jagged rock when beaching a canoe at a campsite between the Sault and Michipicoten. Marie Anne insisted on dressing the bleeding mess with crushed leaves of the fireweed, padding it with moss and wrapping the bandage round with birch bark, tied in place with strands of her basswood strip. The man's wound healed quickly and cleanly.

"Where did you learn that, my clever wife?" asked Jean in amazement.

"When you were busy with the factor and that cargo, I made friends with the factor's wife. She was caring for an employee of the company that way, and she showed me what would be good for wounds. See? I can be of use on this trip after all."

Jean smiled at her with pride. The men looked at her with new respect.

"I think there is a lot more for me to learn from women who live out here in this country already, and I'm going to do my best to see how they manage."

Marie Anne had such an expression of seriousness about her that any misgivings Jean may have had about her presence gave way entirely. Marie Anne was rather wryly amused to realize that from being an object of some awe and resentment, she had now been accepted and even adopted as a sort of mascot, a bringer of good luck. For as the voyageurs all pointed out to one another, who could remember so peaceful a crossing of the treacherous Superior?

Around the campfires every night, the voyageurs bragged about the extraordinary dangers they has encountered successfully and told stories to illustrate their toughness and bravery. Marie Anne loved listening to these sagas, but at the same time she kept her fingers tightly around her precious rosary and her medal.

She noticed that many of the men did likewise, and not just the newcomers hearing the tales for the first time. Many a story did she hear about the size of the waves and the fury of the storms on Lake Superior. She felt extraordinarily thankful and lucky to have been spared the worst of the storms. There were times though, with water washing up on top of the cargo and soaking her thoroughly, that she had shivered in fright and gone over her prayers again and again. The cairns on the shore that had been pointed out to her did nothing to calm her fears. They were markers to remind travellers of past disasters when a whole canoe was swamped or overturned and the crew and cargo never seen again.

The veterans claimed that there had been no real storms to speak of and suggested with their characteristic gallantry that perhaps it was the fair Madame Lajimoniere who had brought them fair winds and good passage. Many of the first timers, the *mangeurs de lard*, would be turning around at Fort William after they had unloaded cargo and reloaded with pelts for the return to Montreal, stopping to pick up more furs at each fort on the way home and wishing they had the luck of the plucky Madame with them.

At the fort, Marie Anne encountered some of the rougher elements of voyageur and *coureur de bois*. These men had not been east for some years and were naturally entranced by the sight of a white woman, and a young and pretty one at that. Some made rather obvious and most unwelcome advances to her. Jean Baptiste had only to come quickly to her side and indicate that she was his church-married wife, and her gallants retreated without any more trouble. Jean's height, strength, and reputation made it advisable to back up as gracefully and as quickly as possible. Possibly the stare from now icy blue eyes in a head held high had a role in it as well.

Marie Anne on her part showed her devotion to Jean Baptiste shyly but openly. Trappers and voyageurs smiled at the couple, an entirely new experience in the western fur country; and some, it must be said, smiled with more than a little envy. They were all in agreement, however, that none of the possible brides they could recall from faraway Canada would have come with them, and they marvelled at the sight of Madame and Monsieur going arm in arm to their tent to bed.

With surprise, Marie Anne realized one sunny morning that she had been travelling exactly one month. It had seemed to her as though she had been moving through the wilderness for weeks and weeks, but checking with the factor, she found indeed that it was only the sixth day of June.

CHAPTER 5

For a whole week, Marie Anne had had time to look about her at the fort as well as rest up from her strenuous month. She found it a relief to have her feet on dry ground for a change and not to carry all her possessions on her back wherever she went. She tried not to recall how very far she was from Maskinongé and the comforts of her old life. Whenever she found herself being a mite nostalgic for the accustomed ways, she reminded herself that she was married to the best man in the world, and wherever he led she was prepared to go.

Fort William was the largest of the North West Company's forts west of the St Lawrence. The factor had even brought a spinet over from his home in Scotland, and in the evening Marie Anne could hear him playing airs from his homeland. China dishes and portraits could be glimpsed through the large open windows of the main meeting room of the company's staff, all out of bounds to the voyageurs and *coureurs de bois*. A few Indian women worked inside the stockade, cleaning up the factor's quarters and scrubbing pots in the hot kitchen and outbuildings. From time to time, the smartest would graduate to serve as helpers when the need arose in the small building set aside as a hospital.

One of these, a Chipeweyan, smiled at Marie Anne and indicated that she would like to be friendly. In Marie Anne's eyes, the woman was certainly ugly. The three black tattooed stripes across her cheeks gave her a repellent appearance, but her eyes were warm and her air of self-composure, Marie Anne realized in shock, came from her position as the wife of the factor's assistant.

The woman pointed to the sad remnants of Marie Anne's footgear and shook her head. Then beckoning and smiling, she bade Marie Anne sit down on the hospital steps, indicating that she would be right back and that Marie Anne was to wait there for her. In a few moments, she returned with small pieces of buffalo hide, a knife, and strands of buffalo sinew stretch out so finely that they could be threaded through the coarse needle she produced. Marie Anne was fascinated. The Chipeweyan measured Marie Anne's foot on the hide and, with great care, cut out what she turned into a moccasin all in one piece.

"Now," she seemed to be saying in her sign language and with a lot of encouragement in her gestures, "stitch like mine. Do you understand? Can you do this?"

The black eyes watched intently as Marie Anne took a stab and pricked her finger. She tried again, and slowly the piece of hide took on the shape of a foot. The Indian wife found it hilarious that a grown woman did not know how to make a pair of foot coverings. Between Marie Anne's struggles and the Indian's amusement, the two women began to understand one another and have a few good laughs together. Marie Anne frequently checked her work against her friend's moccasins, but she found the hide very tough and hard to pierce. She had considerable trouble making the gathers as small as the ones on her new friend's footwear. The Chipeweyan continued to encourage her, help her with the hardest parts, and find entertainment in the whole operation.

"I must be doing something right," thought Marie Anne. "At least it's giving this woman some amusement, and I desperately need something better on my feet."

When the slipper part was finished, ankle pieces were cut, and again Marie Anne looked carefully at her new friend's feet to see how the pieces were to be stitched on to make a shield around the leg. She could see at once how the ankle piece was a brilliant way of keeping the ever-present mosquitoes from gorging themselves on her ankles. In the winter, the shield would be useful for preventing snow from dropping inside the moccasin, she figured. Filled with admiration for her friend's help, Marie Anne thought to herself that another day she would get her friend to show her how to make leggings from the soft pliant doeskin like the ones her new friend was wearing.

"That must be how she protects her legs from getting bitten," mused Marie Anne. "I must try to find out all I can from her."

When Marie Anne had finished her stitching and tried on her moccasins, she marvelled at how comfortable they were. "Now," she said, pointing to the pretty beadwork designs on the Chipeweyan's moccasins, "I'm going to get my husband to get me some of those little beads from the company store."

The factor's assistant had no idea what Marie Anne was saying, but she did understand what Marie Anne had in mind as she nodded her head up and down, smiling broadly, obviously proud of her pupil's grasp of the task. "Maybe," thought Marie Anne, I can see how she does it, and I'll make my new boots as pretty as hers, with roses and those handsome zigzags. I have a lot to learn out here in my new homeland."

As if reading her mind, Jean Baptiste came over from the other side of the parade ground by the factor's store. He looked on with beaming approval at Marie Anne's abilities to fit in with the ways of the Indian women.

"You are doing well, p'tite," he said with a huge grin. "And now I suppose you would like to do some fancy work on your stylish new dancing slippers. I know just the place to go to get you some very pretty beads. Would Madame prefer blue to match her eyes, or perhaps a little of everything, since all the colours of the rainbow are so particularly fashionable this season?"

Marie Anne laughed in delight. The wonderful man she loved so deeply seemed to know just exactly what she was thinking. He could be one of the most tireless paddlers, as strong as anyone she had encountered on the entire journey, one of the noisiest when they gathered around the fire at night to sing and swap stories, yet here he was, the charming gallant, bringing her a nosegay of columbines or the wild roses that had just come into bloom and that had so glorious a scent, and at the same time admiring her moccasins, calling them dancing slippers indeed.

"No sooner said than done," he declared, and off he went back across the square to the company store. By the time he had returned, Marie Anne had the ankle shields stitched in place and was wiggling her toes in her new finery.

"I'll have to return the needle to that friendly woman," Marie said as she started sorting out her beads.

"Yes, dear, you will. And here are some extra beads and some needles, both the heavy and the bead kind. A present for your instructor is quite in order and always welcome."

That was a lesson Marie Anne was never to forget.

Within the week, the stores delivered by the flotilla that had brought Marie Anne and Jean Baptiste to Fort William were sorted and redistributed into smaller units, the trading stock for each of the smaller forts that stretched almost all the way to the Pacific Ocean and northward into an immense region known as the Northwest Territories.

On the morning of the day of their departure, Marie Anne was astounded to hear Jean making a shout that startled the birds out of the trees. She ran down to the dock to see what could be happening. Could Jean have fallen into the river? She found him in the midst of three men, all shouting, laughing, and whacking him on the back.

Jean's three closest friends – Belgrade, Chalifou, and Paquin – had all decided to strike out for themselves and bring their furs to Fort William rather than rely on the factors at Fort Gibraltar or Pembina. A fine reunion was going on when Marie Anne walked down to meet them. The three *hivernants* thought they had bade goodbye to their cheery pal for the last time when he had left them the previous late summer. Although they were delighted at his return, there was no word for their astonishment at seeing him again, and they had some catching up to do. They had never even considered the possibility that they would see him again.

When Jean introduced Marie Anne, three jaws dropped in unison. Marie Anne greeted them politely and charmingly, and still they were dumbfounded. So pretty a woman coming out here – what in God's name was Jean thinking? What had the factor thought about it? Jean had to admit that the factor had been as astonished as they. No lady had ever come out to the fur country before, and no other female either.

A few other *hivernants* who had come no further east than Fort William especially to meet the flotilla were not quite as friendly as Jean's friends, even after they had recovered from their shock. Jean shrugged and stared them down. Marie Anne stayed close to Jean, and both were relieved when some of the men who had come west with the flotilla spoke up for the pretty Madame who could pull her weight and dress a wound or two as well. Still, there were mutterings of what was the western world coming to with women barging their way in and changing everything.

Next day, the flotilla of *hivernants* and various clerks of the company packed the smaller canoes – about fifteen feet shorter than the forty-footers, the Montreal or *canots du maitre*, that had brought them through the rough passage of Lake Superior – known as *canots du nord* or north canoes. They set off with the usual ceremonies of farewell, flags waving, pennants on the canoes, streamers on the canoeists' hats, and a volley of musketry aimed up into the air, which never ceased to bring howls and prolonged barking from all the dogs at the base.

Jean's spirits rose high with excitement and anticipation as each day brought them closer to what he thought of as home: the immense stretches of empty land, the good hunting country.

"How keen he is to get back to the lands he loves so much," thought Marie Anne. "They must be truly wonderful."

She was feeling a little lost herself and lonely for the companionship of a woman friend. The Chipeweyan and she had begun to strike up a warm and understanding friendship. Now that she was back in the exclusive company of men, she felt the strangeness of her position more than she had ever been aware of in the initial stages of the journey. But she held her head up and affected not to hear or understand when remarks were made about a petticoat bursting in on a man's world.

"I'll show them," she promised herself. "No matter what it takes, I'm going to live in the fur countries and make Jean proud of me."

The trip across the open water of the north shore of Lake Superior had been without serious incident, except for two storms that had terrified Marie Anne but did not bother the boatmen unduly. She still shivered when she thought of the crosses and cairns pointed out to her, monuments placed high on the rocks overlooking the spots where less fortunate travellers facing treacherous high seas on the huge lake had lost their lives. There were not a few reminders to make the travellers recall where others had perished.

"We have only a short run down Lake Superior now," Jean told her before they set out. "Then we have a long portage, but it's not so tricky from here to Pembina. We are past the most hazardous part now," he said as he kissed her in full view of all the men and deposited her lightly on top of the cargo.

Bright and early on a beautifully warm early July morning, the men and their supplies started out for the hard travel to reach Fort Gibraltar at the point where the Red and the Assiniboine Rivers converged. Although not as dangerous as the last part of the trip to Fort William, it was still arduous. The first carry-over, Grand Portage, was, as Jean had promised, long and tiring.

As day followed day, Jean recounted the names of all the landmarks on their route, starting with Hotter des Terres, which as the name suggested, meant a hard scramble up a height of land that left Marie Anne breathless and puffing, her cheeks flushed and her side aching with a stitch, although she was not going to admit it. Then came Lac Mecane, Lac du Bois Blanc, Lac la Pluie, Lac des Bois, Portage de Rat, Portage du Bonnet, Bas de la Rivière, Lac Winnipeg or Ouinnipique, then down the Rivière Rouge to Rivière Assiniboine.

Marie Anne was impressed by the way all the men knew their way. It all looked just green to her, but it had been a well-travelled route for years now, they told her, and it seemed as though they had all memorized a map of the bends and turns that looked much alike to her.

On the many short portages, Jean frequently carried four packs. It seemed he grew stronger and more impetuous the closer they got to Pembina. Most of the men carried only three at a time, but occasionally a voyageur would want to make sure that all his companions realized his greater strength. Only a few tried to heft five at once, a dangerous weight to carry even with the belt, the *ceinture fleche*, yards of woven wool about eight inches wide wound round and round their abdomens. "Just someone trying to show off," Jean told her. "Better by far to stay healthy than strain yourself and get a hernia."

The four friends sang as they paddled. Two of their companions each paddled stern and the other was set at the bow, poling and keeping a lookout for rocks, shoals, and deadheads – fallen trees that glided along just under the water's surface that could rip the fragile canoes apart.

As usual, Marie Anne was ensconced on top of packs wedged in the middle of the canoe. Now it was even more important that she sit motionless for hours, like some sort of elegant cross-legged statue. At least that is how it appeared to Jean. With relief she realized that by now she was so accustomed to this mode of travel that she could remain seated cross-legged for hours with no support for her back without losing all sensation in her legs, as had happened in the first days of the journey. Again, Marie Anne had to prove herself by staying well out of the way when the loads were being placed in or out of the canoe.

After a few days of travel, with Marie Anne showing her customary eagerness to help with food preparation, Jean's friends began to accept her. Eventually, she endeared herself to the entire company with her gentleness and her smiling good nature.

Jean was both proud of and relieved by the way she was adapting and the way the men had accepted her. Far from resenting her, midway into the trek they had begun to welcome certain small niceties that had crept into their routine. It was not unusual for her to be saluted with a couple of wild flowers when she reached the end of a portage. She always thanked the donor and tucked them into her hair, which was becoming more and more fair, bleached by the sun.

Upon their arrival at Fort Gibraltar, it did not take the *hivernants* long to unpack the supplies destined for the fort. With a considerably lightened load, the paddlers of Jean's flotilla convinced him they could manage the *canots du nord* well enough without him for the five days' paddle up the Red River to Pembina. Jean Baptiste was urged to take an Indian canoe, a light one about twelve feet long, and have a little wedding trip alone with Marie Anne. After a great deal of guffawing and backslapping, Jean agreed.

Accordingly, Jean and Marie Anne set off alone together for five days of blissful tripping with no freight, no portages, and only their own necessities.

"This is the real start to our life together, my dear wife," Jean whispered. "We will build great fires each night and sleep under the stars. My dearest, you have shown me you have all the strength and wisdom in the world, and I'm so proud of you, my love. Now I want you to know why being off and alone in this glorious land has woven its spell on me and will on you too, I hope," he said wistfully.

Together they set off once again, with yet another factor shaking his head and scratching it in wonderment at the same time. Unknown to Jean, each factor they had encountered so far had thought that this brawny young adventurer used to have more sense than to bring a little fair-haired doll, even a determined doll with a glint in those striking blue eyes, out here to a land heretofore reserved for Indians and their wives and a few white men, most with Indian women, but certainly none with a white woman.

CHAPTER 6

Marie Anne had learned how to handle a paddle while she and Jean Baptiste were staying at Fort Gibraltar. Now she was able to show off her new skill and set a smart pace in the bow of the small Indian canoe that was taking them up the Red River. The natural rhythm of paddling she found soothing and satisfying. Kneeling to paddle as she had been taught made no strain whatsoever on her back. On the first morning out, to her great joy, she thought she might have felt a slight movement inside her.

"Why, it's true," she thought. "I've been wondering and hoping, but now I know my baby has come to life." She turned to Jean to share her news.

Jean whooped like an Indian party of one on the warpath and bent forward to kiss the back of her neck, and then thought better of it. A sudden lurch, and they both laughed with high good spirits but agreed to delay any physical contact until they beached the canoe.

"I'm having a baby, not a fish," said Marie Anne, grinning at Jean with the impish twist of her mouth that he loved. Turning round to business, she set an easy natural stroke in the bow.

Marie Anne had every confidence in Jean's ability to handle what seemed to her to be a tiny fragile craft. After what she had been through to reach Fort Gibraltar, the immense angry waves of Lake Superior when she thought the big canoes would be swamped, she refused to let herself imagine what it would be like to be there in a little twelve-footer. After those long days of sitting motionless, wedged in between or on top of the trade goods, she was glad it was just the two of them paddling together to their winter home. Everything conspired to make her feel the greatest sense of joy, anticipation, and contentment.

All around them, the birds sang. Such beautiful little creatures – birds she had never seen back in Maskinongé. It was so good, she said to herself, to get away from Fort Gibraltar, with those trappers coming in from the upper countries to pick up their supplies, and now to be alone with Jean in the wilderness.

Most of the trappers were not like her Jean, she mused. There was something about him, a gentility that set him apart and gave him a leadership quality. Besides, he was at least a foot taller than most of the *hivernants*, for the most part short men and proud of their shortness, claiming their short stature made them better paddlers.

Outside the stockade, the fort where the hivernants and Indians camped, there had been a lot of drinking of hard spirits, more drunkenness in fact than she had thought existed in the world. What a relief it was for her to get away from the leering glances of some of the Canadians. The Indians were simply curious about her. After all, it was the first time they had ever seen a woman who did not have dark brown skin and black hair.

"But even if the trappers had not seen a white woman for years," she told herself, "that was no excuse for the way they looked at me and tried any silly excuse to get me away from Jean's side." She shrugged her shoulders and paddled right on without breaking rhythm. "Anyway, they all seemed to have plenty of sleeping partners with the Indian girls. And the trading about in sleeping partners was shocking." Marie Anne dug her paddle into the water with a splash.

One of these days, she decided, there should be a priest in every fort to keep them all in order. She wondered if she should bring up that idea with Jean. Maybe she would, but not just yet. Better to let it rest for the present.

Listening to the birds' cheery songs, she felt happiness all the way through her body. Her Jean Baptiste had made all those trappers know with just a word or a gesture that she was private property – his snow-white princess, as he called her. She felt cherished and content.

Jean brought her out of her reverie with a shout. "Paddle hard, p'tite. Keep an eye open for danger. That's your job while I steer."

The canoe was caught in an eddy, and it took a strong arm on the stern paddle to bring the bow around to get past the submerged rocks and then head the little craft back into the current again.

"That's Fort Douglas we just passed," Jean called out to her. "Last post of civilization until we reach Pembina. Not far now."

"But we do not stop, Jean. Why?"

"That's the Hudson's Bay Company post, dear heart. Fort Gibraltar was the Nor'West post, you remember? I'll trade with either one, whoever makes me the better deal on my furs, but I don't trade with both the same day, and anyway I have nothing to trade with them today."

Jean laughed at his own joke. Even the birds seemed to pause in their songs to listen to his great guffaws.

Each day they had paddled in a southerly direction up the Red River. Each night they had found a sheltered place to camp, quiet and safe from intruders. Sometimes they made their evening meal from their store of dried meat. Sometimes Marie Anne caught a fish and grilled it on a stick as she had watched and learned from the Indian women at all the forts and encampments they had passed.

The first night they camped together all alone under the stars, Jean hugged her and told her she could cook a fish better than any Indian wife.

"This is what I came all this way for," Marie Anne thought to herself. "This is what I dreamed of. I do think I have the strength to live out here as Father Vinet advised me." She patted her stomach. "And the little one as well."

Aloud she said, "You know, Jean, when I lived in the presbytery, I used to get so tired of scrubbing out those pots after three mealtimes a day." She giggled and observed, "No pots for me out here, and only two meals to cook for. No pots at all to scrub. Just a piece of buffalo hide all stitched up and greased for a pot. Then, if you burn it, poof! Just throw it in the fire and catch another buffalo."

Jean laughed. "There are advantages out here all right, and I'm glad you see it my way." He pulled a couple of thick logs and a tree root onto the fire – "Just to say 'stay away and goodbye, and don't any of you wandering beasts disturb my darling, my mother-to-be. We don't want you joining us tonight.'" Turning to nuzzle her ear, he whispered, "Even if it makes you feel too hot and the smoke stings your eyes a bit, a fire warns off animals. It helps to keep the mosquitoes off, too."

Marie Anne made a little passage in the buffalo robe for air to get into her nostrils. Her head and all the rest of her body were completely encased in buffalo robes, even though it was July and hot all night. Still, somehow, a mosquito found its way up her nose. She scratched it down quickly and covered her hand again.

"They make such a buzzing sound when they all wake up together in the evening and torment us," she said to Jean. "There must be as many mosquitoes around us as there are stars in the sky."

"Maybe more," he whispered. "Sleep well, my dear little mother."

Marie Anne was often to look back on her five days of tripping up the Red River to Pembina as one of the happiest times of her entire life. She thought she had everything she needed for complete happiness: a man she loved and who loved her, who looked after her with tenderness and in good time would be a good father and proud of his family. Of course she missed the routines, the church bells, going to Mass, everything clean and fresh and sweet-smelling in all three homes she'd had in Maskinongé.

"But the birds everywhere! How beautiful they are, and how their singing makes up for church bells. Jean is right. The sky out here does seem bigger and such a glorious blue. And what a pleasure to roll out of our buffalo robes at first light to watch the sun come up – and the sunsets, the incredible sunsets, the whole sky pink and rose and even green. It's like having a window to peep through into heaven."

Marie Anne fingered her rosary and the precious medal she wore around her neck. "Everything will work out. I know it will."

It was mid-July when Jean Baptiste beached the canoe, picked Marie Anne up in his arms, and carried her across the beach to set her down in her new home, Pembina.

It was not much of a place, to be sure, just a very small trading establishment as these forts go, with a small staff headed by a Scotsman, Alexander Henry, who spoke no French. Its one claim to fame was that it had been built where the Red and the Pembina Rivers meet, and so it was a convenient place for hunters to converge. It had not been enlarged much since its inception in 1797, when an established Indian encampment was first transformed into a fort of sorts by a Canadian named Chaboillez who had traded with some Crees on a once-a-year basis. A few years later, the rival Hudson's Bay Company set up a post nearby, but the French Canadians still preferred the Nor'West fort run by Chaboillez. The Crees were happy to trade with anybody, and both companies were well aware that Crees took to the prairies with bartered goods and, acting as middlemen, traded out on the plains for furs. Their mark-up on the white man's goods was enormous.

Marie Anne met the five or six trappers who made Pembina their winter headquarters. The trappers, the factor, his assistant, and a small band of Crees made up the entire population. For most of the trappers, it was just a convenient place to cache their furs before the annual trip upriver to Fort Gibraltar.

The other Canadians, Jean's hunting companions, had all taken Cree wives. Arriving before Jean, Belgrade warned the others that Lajimoniere was back with a white wife – young and a real lady. Again there was astonishment and disbelief that Jean Baptiste would do such a thing; it was unthinkable. The Indians were eager to see this extraordinary creature from a different world. The welcoming group of Crees was fascinated by the white skin (lightly tanned as it was), the blonde hair, the blue eyes. Jean's friends had not begun to do justice to the novelty of her appearance.

Marie Anne smiled shyly. The wives of Jean's three closest friends smiled back tentatively. They were not sure at all what to make of the pale woman in the strange clothing. The moccasins and leggings they could understand, but the skirt with another worn underneath – that struck them as strange indeed. They circled round and round her, taking in every detail of this curious being. But they were enchanted by her beauty and eventually began to make tentative gestures of friendship, encouraged by their husbands.

It was not long before Marie Anne had made three good friends. Madame Belgrade, Madame Chalifou, and Madame Paquin became her closest companions. Marie Anne's by-now obvious state of pregnancy brought the women together in sympathy and in the unspoken understanding that all women have for one who is about to give birth. Slowly the women came to understand one another, with much pointing and giggling. The Cree wives laughed and pointed at Marie Anne's clothing. Marie Anne in turn was quick to observe that her friends' leggings and shifts, made of the softest deer hide, were more practical than her bulky skirts and bodices over her swelling stomach. She was so keen to make friends, and the three wives were so delighted with their exotic new acquaintance, that in a very short time they had worked out their own way of communicating: a combination of hand signals, smiles, shy giggles, and a word or two more each day.

The three Cree wives took pleasure in initiating Marie Anne into a whole new way of keeping house. "So that's what you call a hide teepee," she thought.

The teepees were made of buffalo hide stretched over poles, with a hole at the top to let smoke and steam escape and with an ingenious arrangement of buffalo-hide flaps to catch the wind and prevent the smoke from re-entering the teepee. The women taught Marie Anne how to make a new bucket out of buffalo hide, lacing it with sinews and then greasing it with buffalo fat so that it would hold water and could be suspended over a fire that served as a cook stove.

Marie Anne thought rather ruefully that here she was learning the housewifely arts over again for the third time in her life. But still, she was grateful for the new skills she was learning. Her new doeskin shift with its jaunty fringes she found much more comfortable than her old bodices, and the shorter skirt gave her much more freedom of movement. The new little life must have welcomed the change of clothing as well, as it became far more active, kicking and lunging without the bothersome tight belt on the old skirt to push against, much to the joy of the mother-to-be.

The Cree ladies had planted squash and bean seeds earlier in the summer when their husbands had gone off to the prairies for the early buffalo hunt – the one that yielded the softer calves – before their trip to Fort William. Marie Anne helped them with weeding and watering and felt herself accepted in the small community.

Towards the end of August, when Jean and the other men went off together to the prairies once again for the summer hunt – the one that produced the hides and meat they needed for the long winter ahead – Marie Anne found herself busy from daybreak to late afternoon helping to harvest squash, beans, and whatever was edible growing roundabout. Although a species of onion grew wild, the Crees ignored it. The flavour did not appeal to them. They took care in showing Marie Anne just how the various parts of the harvest should be stored. Corn and turnips were brought in as well. Seeds were dried and pounded, and then mixed with meat and fat for pemmican, the staple food of all the plains Indians. Berries were gathered, and what was not eaten at once was dried and later would be added to the pemmican.

Marie Anne recalled Jean telling her back in Maskinongé that anything and everything went into pemmican, even worn-out moccasins. She had laughed heartily at the time, but now she was wondering whether maybe he had not been making a joke. Almost all the fish they were catching were smoked and dried in preparation for the frozen months ahead.

The four women laughed a great deal together, and the first month of Marie Anne's new existence passed pleasantly and very busily. Her friends found her medal and her rosary beads of great interest. They could not understand why she did not festoon the rosary around her hair as an ornament. It was so pretty. Why keep it hidden in a pouch around her neck? When Marie Anne finally got the idea across that it was something sacred and not to be used lightly, her friends shyly brought out their own possessions, their totems, a very important part of the beliefs of the Cree people. They tried to make her understand.

"When you are young," one of the women told her, "in a dream you see something. Boys see eagles sometimes. Sometimes a girl sees a beautiful feather, something like that, and you know that you will have protection if you keep this symbol with you always. When you awaken, you search for what you dreamed about, what your dream really means. When you find it, you know that the feather or whatever you looked for is yours, truly yours, and that the spirit of what you have found will take care of you. Sometimes the dream is the same one your mother had. That means a lot."

"What does your totem mean?" the women wondered.

She tried to explain but couldn't. All the Cree words she had learned were for things, objects that could be seen or touched. She had no words in Cree for faith or for her religious beliefs. Each woman stored away her sacred object in a secret place inside her shift, and they all ran down to the water together to cast a line and hopefully catch something to cook for the evening meal – perhaps even to add to the line of drying carcasses.

Another Indian woman joined them with her young child. She sidled up to Marie Anne and gave her a present of some berries she had gathered. Then she smiled and pranced about, indicating that she wished to become Marie Anne's close, dear friend. Marie Anne drew back. It seemed odd to her that an Indian should suddenly be so forward. She'd had to wait patiently for friendly overtures from the wives of her husband's friends.

Madame Belgrade took Marie Anne aside. "Take care," she said quietly, shaking her head and making a go-away gesture with her hand to the newcomer. "She does not wish you well. Do not eat or drink anything that she gives you."

"Why not?" asked Marie Anne.

"You mean you haven't noticed her, always trying to get your husband's attention, skulking around behind him?"

"Yes, but what of that? She wants to be friends with us both, I think."

"No, no," and Madame Belgrade looked impatient. Once again this white woman surprised her. Could she possibly be such a baby? "You must be on your guard. Your husband has not spoken to you about her?"

"No, he hasn't." Marie Anne suddenly felt apprehensive and shivered. "Please tell me. What is it that I should know?"

Madame Belgrade took Marie Anne's hand in hers. "Listen to me."

Marie Anne turned away from her friend. She had such a sense of foreboding, of fear, of something without a name.

"Look at me," said Madame Belgrade. "I have to tell you something. You have to know. Your husband used to live with her before he went back to the eastern countries you came from. They were married here and lived together for three years. No one believes that her child is his, for when he was away on his trapline, she stayed here as most of us do in the winter catching season, and she took another man into her teepee. When your husband got back here to Pembina, the other man bragged about it to your husband, so Lajimoniere ordered her out of the teepee and told her never to come back. He would not speak to her. He did not speak to her for a whole year, and then he went back to your home. Now she wants to get him back again all to herself. The other man left before your husband, and we don't know if he will ever come back. That's why she tries to get your husband back. I have heard it said around that she means to get you off your guard and then offer you some tea made of a bad bark, a poison. She said that once you are dead, she will get your husband back to herself again."

Marie Anne sat down suddenly in a heap. She covered her face with her hands and tried not to burst into tears before these stoic friends, but it was useless. She howled.

She was certain that her heart was broken. Suddenly a big black cloud had come over the sun, and her whole world was crushed into a muddle of black and grey. She was frightened, angry, and disgusted all at once. She felt betrayed, and tears trickled down her cheeks in two rivers of agony.

According to everything she had been taught, nobody ever married again while the first spouse was still living. It was unthinkable. It was a sin, an unforgivable sin. Would God punish Jean? Was her marriage a true marriage, or would her baby be born out of wedlock, a bastard? Would God punish her for conceiving a baby in sin? What would Father Vinet advise now if he knew? Her thoughts came and went in a jumble. Never in her life had she felt so alone.

"If only I could talk to Josette," she thought. "No, I couldn't. How could I face anyone in the family, in all of Maskinongé for that matter?" She howled and rocked herself back and forth in complete misery.

The Crees were surprised and bewildered. Hadn't Lajimoniere proved to her over and over that she was his one love? The past was past.

"I had to tell you," said Madame Belgrade as gently as she knew how. "You must know about her. It is better so. But don't think badly of Jean. All the Canadians take wives like us. A man cannot stay alone, living as we do. Who will dry his meat for him? Who will make his moccasins and lace the sinews around his snowshoes? A man's wife plants corn and the other seeds we grow to mix with meat for pemmican while he is out seeking the buffalo. And where would any of us be without buffalo? It's our food and our protection from weather and our robes to keep us warm at night."

"But why didn't he tell me about her?" wailed Marie Anne, and her tears started up all over again.

The other women looked at each other in consternation and bewilderment. This was a reaction they could not understand. Lajimoniere's first marriage was over and done with, wasn't it? So what was all the fuss about?

"No, no. Listen to me, little white Madame," said Madame Belgrade. "Now, no more tears. I think he had forgotten about that woman so much that he had better things to talk to you about." She wiped away at Marie Anne's tears with a rather dirty finger. "No tears," she repeated. "I think it is bad for what you hold inside you, yes?" She patted Marie Anne's stomach.

Marie Anne tried to smile back at Madame Belgrade, but it didn't look like much of a smile. Madame Belgrade very shyly patted her on the arm. It was a gesture of real and loving friendship.

"You are right, dear friend," whispered Marie Anne. "But I can't bear to face Jean. Please, you tell him about …" and she curled her lips in disgust "… his wife."

"No." Madame Belgrade made the word sound like a threat. "You must. He must first know what she is trying to do to you." She took Marie Anne gently by the arm and led her to her teepee.

Marie Anne rubbed her eyes with the fringe of her shift. What was to become of her she couldn't imagine, but it helped to have Madame Belgrade's good sense and kindness with her in her loneliness.

As the two friends walked together up the bank to the encampment, Marie Anne said, "You are my friend. In my home, friends have special names for each other. I shall call you Amie, and you must call me Marie Anne or just Marie, if you prefer."

Madame Belgrade tried out her new name several times until she pleased herself that she was saying the word exactly as Marie Anne had done.

Jean Baptiste looked grave when she told him about the encounter. "You must believe me," he kept saying, trying to hold her close to him.

She struggled free, rigid with anger.

"Marie Anne, believe me, everyone takes a helpmeet out here. Many of the clerks have gone back out east or to their homes in Scotland and just left their wives here to manage, the good Lord knows how, and without cause. They tell them they will come back to fetch them and their children, but they never do. But I had good cause. Just look at her child. A redhead. Nobody in our family has red hair. You know that. But the Orkney man she took into my tent was a redhead. I could have killed him, but I didn't want to do such a thing. A man needs a wife, and you are my own dear wife married to me in the sight of God. It takes two, you know, to stay warm all night long when the wind comes howling across the open grasslands." He took her cheeks in his hands.

Marie Anne closed her eyes. She couldn't bear to look at him.

"Didn't Madame Belgrade, your Amie, tell you that I ordered the woman to get out of my teepee, and that we were not together for more than a year before I came back to Canada to find you, my own dearest Marie? It was a long cold year, I can tell you."

They both sat down.

"You know, dear," he went on, "she still has found no man to live with her, so apparently no one else wants her. I have a feeling that is why she really hates you so much, and it makes her dangerous to us both."

Marie Anne still had no words. She felt desolate and heartbroken. She tried to picture a child with red hair. Had she never noticed such a child ? But she could not recall anyone with bright red carroty hair. How could she ever believe a word Jean said now? How could she trust him?

"Tell you what," Jean went on. "Pembina is no place for you now with the winter coming on and that woman so close by. I shall have to be away for days and a few nights at a time checking on the traplines and hunting for my trade skins. I don't want to think of you here without me. She is a jealous woman, and believe me, an Indian's need for vengeance can be terrifying. It's not something to be regarded lightly, ever."

Jean got up and pulled the listless Marie Anne to her feet. "Come, my dear one," he said, "let us see how quickly we can strike our teepee and put everything together. You and I are going up the Pembina to Grand Camp. It's not very grand, I'm afraid, but it's far enough away that you will be safe there. I'll let Belgrade know where I am going but no one else."

They set off without a goodbye up the Pembina River about three days' paddle to Grand Camp. There was no looking back and no delaying. Marie Anne climbed into her place in the bow with a heart that seemed to weigh her down with grieving. She began to paddle as she had to, but she longed to lie down in the bottom of the canoe, cover her head, and weep. Jean tried to liven things up by singing some of her favourite melodies, but such a reproachful stare was turned in his direction, a "how can you sing when I am in such pain" look, that he soon desisted. It was a silent pair that set off for yet another new experience for Marie Anne.

"The only three friends I have in the whole world," she thought over and over to herself. "When will I see any of them again?"

That brought on more tears. Jean was nonplussed at the shaking shoulders of his once so proud and so valiant wife. He hoped and prayed that time and the new little life would bring a smile back eventually.

At Grand Camp, Jean already knew some of the Cree trappers, but there were no Canadians in the camp. He greeted his acquaintances and told them what had happened at Pembina. A tearful, sad-faced Marie Anne had to endure the stares once again of people who had never imagined such a creature. One or two of the women approached her and tried to rub her cheeks to see if underneath the fair skin there was a brown layer just like their own.

Marie Anne took what she considered unpleasant behaviour with stoicism, realizing that for her there was no other course. She was the stranger in their midst, and it was up to her to try to make herself acceptable in their society. She missed her friends more than ever, and with the few words of Cree she had learned she set to work to overcome the hostility she was encountering.

The Cree wives were not overly anxious to make friends, and without the bond of having Canadian husbands, Marie Anne felt herself very much the outsider. She dressed herself as the Cree women did, but even so, her pale face and blonde hair set her too far apart for them to accept her.

"Perhaps they are thinking there will be other white women coming out with their husbands, and it won't be as easy for them to acquire a Canadian provider as it has been," she considered, not unnaturally, as she had observed that a Canadian husband was thought of as a real catch by the Indian women she had met at Pembina and all the way from the east, remembering the wife of the factor's assistant who had taught her to make moccasins. The Canadians treated their wives rather differently than the braves, and the women enjoyed it. It was not an Indian's custom to surprise his wife with a bunch of sweet-smelling wild roses, but for the gallant Canadians it was a natural thing to do.

Jean Baptiste was tolerated and even welcomed on the winter trapping expeditions. His reputation as a skilled hunter was well known to them all, but as for that white-faced woman, who knew if she could be trusted?

Marie Anne passed a very lonely fall and early winter. She often walked by herself to find some consolation in her solitary life by observing all the changes in the woods nearby. The passage of the migrating birds lifted her spirits momentarily, wishing she could fly away with them, until she fell back into her mood of utter dejection. She gathered what she could of anything she thought would serve to make the pemmican or the store of trade tea go further, but the women never invited her to go out with them foraging the last of their harvest, nor did she feel welcome to tag along.

Occasionally, Jean would make an appearance with his skins. Their relationship was chilly on her side and hurt and bewildered on his. His consolation was the growing pile of valuable furs he was amassing. He tried his best to fathom Marie Anne's coolness but finally gave up, turning all his attention to his hunting, yet still hurrying back at every opportunity to check on his wife, both her attitude and the state of her pregnancy.

The baby was growing month by month within her, and try as she might to sleep when she was alone, she was often too disturbed, too fearful, and too cold to rest well. She did, however, have time to herself to come to terms with her position. For better or for worse, she was completely dependent on her mate. She would have to face up to her fate – wounds, pride, and all. And there was something else she faced, despite everything she had been taught about faithfulness and punishment for sinners: she loved him.

When Jean returned from a hunting expedition in mid-December, he found a subdued but far less remote wife who was coming close to term. He also realized that Marie Anne could not possibly give birth among these women who, while their hostility had lessened, were still not friendly.

"We will go back to Pembina, little mother," he announced. "We will still have to be cautious of the woman, but you must be with friends to help you when our young hunter arrives. I'm no midwife. Amie and the others will help you."

Marie Anne turned and wearily fell into his arms. "Somehow," she thought, "he does always seem to know what I am thinking or dreading. I think Jean Baptiste will always take care of me and my little one. It's all I can hope for. His strength gives me strength. And I'll say my rosary twice over just to make sure everything will come out all right. And one thing is clear to me now," she said to herself. "We cannot live out here in these western deserts in enmity. I have to learn to forgive and overlook even if I can never forget that terrible day when I found out I was Jean's second wife."

Jean gently stroked her hair and kissed her on her forehead. After a little while, she looked up at him. There were tears in her eyes, and to her astonishment she noticed tears on his face too. They looked at each other for a long moment before Jean Baptiste bent his head down to kiss her.

"Thank you, my dearest wife, for coming back to me," he said with a huskiness she had never heard before.

CHAPTER 7

According to Marie Anne's reckoning – and she had been most careful to make a mark each day on the skin side of her buffalo robe, her calendar – her last show of blood had been just the week before her wedding. She counted up again and again, and now it seemed there was not long to wait before the baby should arrive.

When Marie Anne had arrived at Pembina and knew without doubt that a baby was on the way, she wanted to know how to keep track of the days and months. She got Jean Baptiste to find out that day's date from the factor. Then she went down to the shore, picked up a stick, and started trying to figure out when the baby could be due.

Amie found her scratching little marks in the sand, rubbing them out and making more scratches. Amie was fascinated but perplexed. What was her friend doing? Marie Anne started to explain, patting her belly and making counting gestures with her fingers. Amie laughed at her friend, thinking what strange notions she had sometimes.

"Don't look at the sand," she said. "What can it tell you? Look up at the moon. It comes round a full nine times, and then you have baby."

Marie Anne shook her head. "I want to know other days too. It has to do with this," and she pulled the little doeskin bag hanging around her neck. "I want to make a little mark on my sleeping hide so I really know what day it is."

Amie shook her head. Such strange ideas this pale-skinned friend had, but making little designs on the sleeping robe, now that she understood.

"There's a flower that comes up soon after the sun is feeling good and warm. We boil up its roots and save the sticky stuff. It dries at last. Then you can wet a stick and put some on the end. With a little water or spit it makes a red mark on the skin and it won't come off." Amie grinned. "I'll give you some and you can draw pictures if you like."

Amie came back with what looked dried blood. Marie Anne looked at it and turned to Amie. "You are sure this is a flower? It looks like somebody's wound."

"No, no," Amie laughed. "It's a little white flower with large green leaves and the roots are red. It comes up after the snow goes."

"I think I know it," Marie Anne smiled. "But I never knew you could make the roots into this."

Amie replied, "Sometimes the men put it on their faces, not the white men, just us."

From that day on, Marie Anne had made a tiny mark on the skin side of her sleeping robe. She had put a circle around the eighth of August, the Feast of the Assumption, and another for All Saints Day, the first of November. Now she figured she had but a week to wait for the Feast of the Nativity, and probably a few days more for the birth of her baby.

Jean Baptiste agreed with her about the Feast Day and bade her pack her belongings into a deerskin bag she had made in preparation for the trip back to Pembina.

"We can arrive in Pembina before the Feast Day," he told her. "My, there seems to be a lot to pack this time." And he held his head on one side in the way that had always charmed Marie Anne and had not lost its attraction for her.

She thought, "There's that little-boy look about him that I have loved right from the start."

Aloud she said, "The women at Pembina taught me to make nice things for our baby, little clothes out of doeskin and a rabbit-fur sack for him to snuggle into and stay warm." She lovingly folded up each tiny garment.

Jean's eyes twinkled. "You have been busy. I thought I might be missing a skin or two. You know, I think you could settle down in the very middle of a desert and make a comfortable home out of it. I'm finding out all the time what a lucky fellow I am. I hope and pray I never do anything again to hurt you as I have done. I don't want anything or anybody ever to come between us again for the rest of our lives. I love you so much, my Marie."

Marie pulled his head down and kissed him, the first kiss in many a long month that she had freely given him. "Father Vinet told me to come out here with you if I thought I had the strength. I see now he meant more than strength in my body. As long as you love me, I will have strength enough."

"You know that is forever, my dearest little wife," he whispered and gathered Marie Anne into so bearlike an embrace that the baby kicked in protest.

Jean laughed that great ringing laugh of his in highest glee and Marie, rubbing her nose into his chest, realized what a long time it had been since she had heard that wonderful sound and how much she had missed it.

She thought to herself, "So I'm not the first woman to lie with him. That's something I just have to accept, I suppose." She paused in her nuzzling. "Anyway, he didn't know me then, except for dowsing me with water all those days ago when I had to go into the presbytery. But that doesn't count. He loves me now. I know he does. And a wedding in a church is a real wedding in the sight of God. A lot of things are different out here, and that's how it is."

A heavy load seemed to fall off her shoulders. "I'm Jean's wife, and soon I shall be a mother, the mother of his baby. That's what counts."

She straightened up and smiled at her husband. "What's done is done," she resolved to herself, "and there's no undoing it. Let's think about what's coming. It's not easy to forget what you don't want to remember. That must be how it was for Jean, and I haven't been kind to him all these weeks." She leaned back and grinned her old loving ear-to-ear grin.

"Let's finish packing up," she told her husband.

"I have a better idea before taking down the tent." Jean gently drew her down onto the furry buffalo robes.

"Jean?" Marie Anne longed for him, but had to ask, "What about the baby?"

"I'll be careful, sweetheart," Jean whispered as he eased her under the topmost skin.

Although Grand Camp was not much of an encampment, at least in size, Pembina was not much of a trading post. It could hardly be called a fort at all. The trappers with their Cree wives and their Metis children lived outside the barracks with the Indians. The factor at the Nor'West Company post was a nice enough fellow, but his only interest was in trading furs for trinkets, the odd piece of red cloth, beads, and a bucket or two to the ladies – as well, of course, as the ammunition and tobacco that the men required. In short, he was eager to make as much money as he could in the shortest possible time so that his worth might be recognized and he might be sent to a more important post and eventually live like the rich owners of the company in Montreal. He was the last person in the world to realize that his ambitious dream was just that: a dream.

All the way to Pembina, Jean insisted that Marie Anne ride on the travois pulled by his dog team as he ran alongside, his snowshoes making a soft *slush slush* noise behind her. "No mushing for Madame on this trip. I don't intend to have my son born out in the open."

The trip was swift and easy. Jean Baptiste could get the teepee up and down in as good time as anyone in the western country – "as fast as a couple of flicks of a buffalo's tail" was his way of putting it. As for fires, he had a bright blaze going in no time at all when they stopped for the night. They met with no adventures, no wolves to harass the dogs. The weather was ideal, bright and sunny. Marie Anne lay back in the travois and dreamily watched the tails of the dogs waving like bushy feather dusters. It was a beautiful sight.

After their reunion, they both felt pleased with each other, as well as the weather. It all seemed to be a good augury.

The three Cree wives were delighted to welcome Marie Anne back. They were also pleased to see that whatever differences there had been between the white couple were all put aside. They seemed as loving as before, perhaps even more so in a slightly different way. Jean was not so ready to treat her like some fragile doll but more as his real partner, an observation they all noted with approval.

Marie Anne too had changed. It was subtle but there it was, the friends observed to one another. She seemed to stand taller. There was camaraderie between her and Jean now and less of the hero-worshipping that had puzzled the women. After all, he was a man like other men, and not like that invisible one who had something to do with that string of beads she was so fond of. It was good, they agreed, whatever the change was.

"I have a surprise for you, dearest." Jean turned to her as he was setting up their buffalo tent and she was busily rearranging her things and the baby's. "Tomorrow evening is the Eve of the Nativity, as you know, and the factor makes a special time of it. We will sing quietly together on the eve, but on the day itself there will be a feast for everyone. We all gather for the fun. We make an orchestra! Yes we do. The factor's iron pots get to be our drums, and we have the jolliest time."

Coming home from the Christmas singing, Marie Anne and Jean Baptiste walked hand in hand through a fresh fall of snow. Even without a moon, it was easy to see their way, as the stars were so bright. "Which one was the star to the stable?" Marie asked.

Jean shook his head. "With so many to choose from, it must have been a wonderful sight."

Christmas night was given over to merrymaking as Jean had promised. "Not much like the party my parents gave for me back in Maskinongé where I first got a glimpse of you, is it?" Jean shouted to her over the din.

"But it's really fun, Jean. The dances are so comical, and the women look so solemn and dignified as they prance about. Everyone is so merry, and it's the first time I've had a look inside the factor's log house."

The factor's brandy made a great contribution to the party atmosphere. All present, from those too old to go out hunting again to the papooses and toddlers, had a glorious time.

The rumour running around the Nor'West camp was that the factor at the Hudson's Bay post had delivered a white baby to an Orkney girl who had fooled everybody into thinking she was a boy. The girl, they said, had followed her Orkney sweetheart out to the west by way of the York factory on James Bay. She had been deserted and then "befriended" by another Orkney man who advised her to dress as a boy while she searched for her first sweetheart.

The factor was astounded to find this young lad, an apprentice, requiring his services as a midwife – and on his own hearthrug in his own private quarters. The baby, a boy, arrived on Christmas Eve, they all said.

The rumour turned out to be true, and Marie Anne was asked as a joke if she would like to prevail upon the services of the Hudson's Bay factor. She replied that she would rather take her chances with their own factor if need be, but that she was happy to be in the hands of her friends. Someone even asked her if she was sorry that her baby would be the second white baby born in the west, not the very first.

She didn't bother to answer that one. "This is no time for jokes" was her explanation, and the Lajimonieres moved their teepee closer to the Belgrades.

After the excitement of the Christmas party, Marie Anne settled down to wait with Jean in their teepee for the coming of the new life. Upon two or three occasions, Marie Anne tried to persuade her husband to go for short trapping trips, just an overnight, but he refused to do so. Marie thought she had until the end of January by her reckoning before the baby was due. Jean tried to work things out on his fingers.

"No," he said. "It's closer than you think. I'm sure of it. Madame Paquin thinks so too, by the way you are carrying the baby so low. She has had quite a few babies herself, so she should know something about it. Anyway I'm not leaving you until I am sure you and my little hunter are both doing well."

Marie Anne's friends sided with Jean. "That baby will make up his mind very soon now," said Amie one fine bright and cold afternoon.

Marie Anne smiled. She had been feeling very drowsy all afternoon, and for the first time found that some pemmican, dried but yet a trifle greasy in the stew, was not agreeing with her.

Amie took charge. She politely but firmly persuaded Jean Baptiste to go and visit her husband or the factor or even Mr Henry over at the Hudson Bay post. What about Mr Henry? Rumours turned out to be true, and Alexander Henry had been chief attendant at the unexpected birth only a few days before. It was the first known birth of a white baby in the west, but Marie Anne would have the distinction of giving birth to the first white baby born in a teepee – and the first legitimate one.

Arrangements were quickly made as Marie Anne continued to feel drowsy and queasy. Madame Chalifou brought moss she had been collecting for the baby's use and comfort. The three friends began a vigil.

On January 5 in the year of our Lord 1808, in the evening, Marie Anne felt the first attacks of labour pains. Her friends held her hands and bade her sit up and bend her knees. They proved themselves to be kind and experienced nurses. Madame Paquin brought food for the other two, and all three prepared themselves to spend the night with Marie Anne if need be. Labour pains came and went, but no baby followed.

Eventually, a weak January sunshine cast a little ray onto the balsam bough sleeping platform, and the women looked from one to another.

"She has been labouring all the night through," their glances said. "She has had enough. She can't be expected to keep on like this all day and into another night."

"It is time," said Amie to the other two.

A shadow passed across the teepee's opening. Madame Chalifou got to her feet and went towards the opening of the tent, raising its flap and making a shooing gesture with her free hand.

"No, Jean Baptiste, we have no news for you. Stay away, and this is the last time I tell you."

The flap was lowered most decisively, and Jean wandered off, miserable and full of thoughts that were quite new to him. Should he have brought Marie Anne out here? Was this wilderness living too much for her? Should he have listened to their parents? He came back to the teepee despite Madame Chalifou's warnings and paced up and down like an animal on a chain.

"You are quite right," said Madame Chalifou to Amie when she had settled herself down again. "A first baby is always the hardest to bear. We'll have to quill her."

Marie Anne looked at the three in alarm. "What are you going to do to me?" she sobbed.

"Nothing bad, and it won't take long," answered Amie, wiping away some of the trickles of perspiration on Marie's forehead.

Madame Paquin went off to her own teepee and selected a quill from the goose wing she used to whisk out the worst of the dirt from her home and sometimes to paddy whack her smallest when they persisted in getting in her way and endangering themselves and her cooking arrangements. She carefully bit off each end of the quill and inserted a little black pepper she had gott from the trading post. Then she hurried back to Marie Anne. Amie took the quill from her and gently inserted the pepper-laden end up Marie Anne's nostril. "Sniff. Sniff hard," she said. "Sniff."

Marie Anne took a deep breath through her nose, the pepper did its work, and she sneezed hard several times. Her baby daughter was born in short order, pink and perfect.

"Do you always do that to women trying to give birth?" Marie Anne asked her friend some time after the baby's impetuous appearance.

"No, no," said Amie. "That's only for when the baby cannot make up its mind to come out, and the mother seems to get weaker and weaker and still nothing happens, so then we have to make it happen."

"I'm so grateful to you all," said Marie Anne, grasping her friends' hands. "I don't want to think about what might have happened if you hadn't known how to take care of me."

Amie smiled shyly. "Now you know what has to be done to help someone else in the same bad position."

That closed the incident. Marie felt closer than ever to her friends and grateful for their knowledge of survival.

Jean Baptiste inspected his daughter with awe. "She is so beautiful," he said huskily.

"Of course she's beautiful." Marie Anne beamed up at him. "Look at her. She has your looks, brown hair, brown eyes, and a dimple on her chin. I want to call her Reine. Since she was born on the Feast Day of the Three Kings, that makes her a queen surely."

"You are my queen, and she is our princess, but you are right: her name day is such an important feast we should call her Reine. Reine she is, and we will make the sign of the cross over her and name her even if we have no holy water and no priest to do it for us. Are you sure you don't want to call her Marie Anne? Your mother gave you her name."

"No, I don't," Marie snapped. It surprised her that she could yet feel some bitterness about her mother's banishment of her to the presbytery.

She still felt some weariness after Reine's birth. The Cree ladies found it hard to understand. They were usually up and doing right after a birthing, even as protracted a one as Marie Anne's; nothing momentous about it to their way of thinking. Marie Anne knew in her bones that she needed rest, however. She cared for little Reine as though the child were a royal queen on a throne. She went through vast amounts of the moss her friends had recommended. She wanted her little one to be as sweet and clean as the linens in Father Vinet's presbytery. Remembering long lines of white squares on clotheslines back in Maskinongé, Marie Anne thought the moss was an admirable way of tending to the baby's needs.

"At least there is no business of heating water over an open fire and rinsing the cloths and then hanging them out on a line," she thought with relief. "Just gather the moss and when it is used, throw it out. A very satisfactory solution."

She laughed to herself too as she recalled her mother's home and her grandmother's and all the fussiness that had gone on at the presbytery about starching linens and washing them in boiling water and everything just so. She thought of the long washing lines and bed linens back in Maskinongé on every woman's clothesline and the struggle to get the washing pinned to the line in freezing cold weather.

"And here's Reine, the fairest baby in all the world, with moss for her nappies and a rabbit skin for her blankets. She's really going to think she's an Indian."

Marie Anne was blissfully happy with her bonny wee daughter, and her strength soon returned. The trust and love between Marie and Jean returned with a deeper sense of commitment to one another. Their marriage had faced an unsettling situation, but now each felt they were really together in a stronger bond of union than before. Some of Marie Anne's romantic notions were giving way to a realization that she had nowhere to go except at Jean's side.

"I just have to accept what happened and go on from here," she decided.

When word got around the camp that Marie Anne was poorly after her birthing, Jean's Cree wife thought she would make herself available again. It was considered a coup to have arranged a marriage – native style to be sure – with one of these handsome gallant foreigners, and she had no intention of giving up without doing her utmost to break up Jean's new attachment. Jean Baptiste had a couple of noisy run-ins with her and finally got the message through. She seemed to have no male relatives who wanted to stand up to Jean on her behalf. Her alliance with him was over and done with, and he had no intention whatsoever of having anything to do with her again.

Although she was angry, she at last had sense enough to know when she was defeated. As for her child, no one was ever sure who the father was. Jean repeatedly pointed out that red hair was unknown in his family. Then it came out that it was her parents who were instigating a good deal of the trouble because they thought Jean might demand back some of the presents he had given them as the bride price in the Cree fashion. He assured the parents that this was not the case, and furthermore, that Marie Anne was his one and only wife and that the ceremony, a sacred sacrament in his culture that had made them man and wife, was one that bound them for life. The parents told the woman to leave Jean alone or there would be trouble with all the Canadians and that her best course was to try to find herself another man if she could. There was no point in waiting around for the redhead to return. It was more than likely that he had gone across the great water they talked about and forgotten all about her.

When Reine was about three weeks old, the three friends decided it was more than high time Jean joined them on their hunting and trapping business. The winter pelts would now be at their silkiest. Jean Baptiste felt content that Marie Anne was surrounded by friends and that there would be no further trouble, at least for a while. Marie Anne found her days so full of joy in caring for Reine that although she missed Jean greatly, she had plenty to occupy her mind and her hands. Her Cree friends found it perplexing and puzzling that she used so much moss on her baby, even as they marvelled at the little girl's white skin and rosy cheeks.

Marie Anne was not to know that her friends, Crees that they were, belonged to the tribe that the other tribes of the Plains considered a dirty bunch, the dirtiest of all the tribes. Perhaps it was because they were still adapting from the ways of the forests, their traditional hunting ground. To the ways of the Plains, that made them seem so to the other tribes. Marie Anne noted her friends' standards, loved them for the people they were, and kept her ideas of good housekeeping to herself.

The short snowy days of winter gave way finally to long hours of sunshine. The snows evaporated day by day, and green spears sprouted everywhere – new grass, new shoots, budding trees, the first of the spring flowers. The earliest of the migrant birds returned and sang as sweetly to Marie Anne's ears as when they had enchanted her the preceding summer. Geese, ducks, and pelicans all flew over them in great waves of honking and wing-beating in a desperate rush to get to their nesting grounds. The first spring flowers meant that the trapping season was over, and the trappers would be returning with skins. Then the wives would have regular scraping bees so their mates could present the skins in the priciest condition at the store. Everyone would converge on the fort's stores to get shot powder, sometimes blankets, tea, and a host of dainties, the glass beads perhaps, that the traders would be bringing from Montreal.

Marie Anne picked a bouquet of the first of the wild spring crocuses and held them up for Reine to see. She laughed in delight and hugged her baby when Reine squealed with pleasure at the pretty sight and stretched out a little fist to try to grab them. She slung Reine into the papoose on her back and stretched both arms up to wave to the great Vs of geese overhead straggling and weaving, sounding as though each one had a different idea about the route.

"Now I know how the *hivernants* felt when they greeted us last year," Marie Anne thought. "Now I can call myself an *hivernante*, the very first *hivernante*."

She stood as tall as she could and waved her greetings to the noisy hordes. "Welcome back home," the *hivernante* called out to them. The baby, wide-eyed at what was going on, waved both her tiny hands, all she could manage in the confinement of her papoose. Marie Anne turned her round and kissed her.

"That's right, my precious. Let's both welcome back the travellers."

CHAPTER 8

The real spring was at long last breaking out. A couple of late blizzards with shrieking winds and snow drifting across the timid green shoots had dampened everyone's spirits, but now the crocuses were popping up everywhere. Marie Anne took the greatest delight in picking armful after armful of the lovely little mauve flowers growing wild all around them. Reine loved to play with the petals and scatter them, gurgling happily as they floated off in the wind. She was now a bonny four-month-old, happily observing the retreating world from the vantage point of her papoose on Marie Anne's back.

Marie Anne's friends were enraptured by the light brown eyes and soft curly brown hair like her father's, and Reine in turn was enchanted with the whole vast world opening up to her. Moss for her diapers was a taken-for-granted thing by Reine. She had no way of knowing that in her mother's culture, it was quite unknown. One concession Marie Anne made to her own upbringing was to keep her baby sweet-smelling and clean. It meant keeping an eye peeled for a fresh batch of moss whenever she left the teepee, but she took pride in keeping her baby and the papoose fresh. Her friends shook their heads and thought her ways took a lot more effort, but if that was her way, so be it.

Marie Anne was still very careful to keep a good distance from Jean Baptiste's country wife. She still felt uneasy and a little threatened, which made her more protective of Reine than she would have been otherwise.

By the end of the third week in May of 1808, Marie Anne was beginning to wonder if something untoward had happened to her husband. The four Canadians had not returned from their early buffalo hunt. While she had every confidence in Jean as a hunter and the best possible provider, she sometimes imagined terrible things, accidents, ambushes by unfriendly competing hunters, all sorts of mishaps on his lonely forays. Perhaps it was an angry bear that had attacked him. They were known to be hungry and vicious-tempered just after their winter's hibernation. It was not unknown that a skirmish with a band of strange Crees or even Sioux might end in bloodshed and death. She felt herself to be vulnerable in the extreme. One afternoon, she got down on her knees to pray for Jean's safe return, taking out her precious medal, twice blessed, and telling her beads.

Suddenly there was a commotion of dogs barking, stamping horses, and the ringing deep voice she loved.

"Here we are. Bad pennies always show up." Jean flung aside the tent flap and gathered Marie and the papoose together in a bear hug of triumphant return.

To Marie Anne's questions, he replied that hunting was so-so, not too bad but not great. "It's not as good as it was six years ago when I first came out here. You know, maybe there are getting to be too many of us hunting down the same weasel. Maybe all that stuff in the factor's store has something to do with it. It seems that the more goods the factor gets to dazzle the hunters and their wives, the bigger the pile of furs the hunters bring in every season. The hunters want to get their hands on stuff that's pretty but they don't need. It's wasteful."

He led his horses over to the corral, having first untied the travois with its load and slung his muzzle loader over his shoulder. "Not too much to trade, but enough for us all to get by," he told her. He ruffled the little brown curls on Reine's head and gave Marie Anne another hug. "Have you had any interference from that woman?"

Jean Baptiste did not want to spoil any part of his homecoming by mentioning his former Cree alliance by name. He knew that there was still a little sore spot deep down inside Marie Anne.

"Just a little, but not enough to make me really scared of her." Marie Anne put the best face she was capable of into her reply. Nothing must mar their reunion. "You can be sure though that I've kept my eyes on Reine every moment."

No point in telling him that the woman had offered her some tea leaves, "good for cramps in the stomach." Marie Anne had imagined they would be, but good for her rival's stomach, not hers.

Jean Baptiste turned sharply to see if he could read more into her words. His eyes had no mirth about them, and he drew Marie Anne down beside him on a tree stump, their familiar seating arrangement.

"When we were out in the bush together, Belgrade, Chalifou, Paquin and I, we talked a bit about what was going on here with that woman. We figured I could never be sure of getting entirely rid of her. She may not be saying much or doing anything to alarm you at the moment, but she was ready to kill you once out of sheer jealousy. I am afraid she is the enemy of us both. We all figured that no one will be able to tell when she will plot some kind of vengeance, and that's not something to live with."

Marie Anne looked at him intently. To Jean, those blue eyes seemed bluer than ever in the late afternoon sunshine, but to Marie Anne, his eyes were full of concern – concern she had been trying to put out of her mind.

"It's time we moved on, dear wife," he announced. "Paquin has agreed to come with us, as well as Belgrade and Chalifou. Their families are coming too of course. We figure that the hunting should be a whole lot better farther west in the upper countries, and we all agree that woman will bring us trouble sooner or later."

"Where are we going, dear Jean?" The upper countries sounded foreboding.

Jean smiled to reassure her. "To Fort of the Prairies. It will be a great journey that will take us all summer long, dear love."

Jean lifted the papoose off Marie's back and extricated the chubby little one from her nest of softest doeskin and rabbit fur.

"You are going for a long lovely ride," he told his cooing daughter. "We are going to find the mighty Saskatchewan River and paddle for many days, far, far to the west and north, and to one of the biggest forts in the whole western countries. Now what do you think of that?"

Reine beamed a wide toothless grin.

"You know, you are right," he said to Marie Anne, "she doesn't have your looks. But I certainly see a look of my family, with her hair just like my mother's. She has your wonderful smile though. It shouldn't be too hard to find a suitable husband for such a beauty when the time comes."

"Why, Jean Baptiste!" cried Marie Anne in mock horror. "She's only a baby. We won't think of such a thing for years and years to come."

Jean laughed and kissed them both.

"How will she marry without a priest to bless her?" Marie asked.

"As you said, my love, that is a bridge for crossing many years from now."

"Exactly how far to the west are you planning to take us all, Jean? Where is Fort of the Prairies? Is it farther than, say, from Fort William to Fort Gibraltar?" Marie Anne started mentally adding up the paddling days on her fingers.

"Well," began Jean Baptiste, "let's see. It's like this. If you think of how far it is from Fort William to Fort Gibraltar and then add a couple of days' paddle, that will take us to Fort Cumberland. Now from Fort Cumberland up the Saskatchewan to Fort of the Prairies, well, I'd say a little farther than from Fort Gibraltar to Fort William."

Marie Anne's jaw dropped. "You mean we don't run into danger falling off the edge of the world?"

Jean laughed again. "No. No, dear wife, I am not going to let you fall off the edge of the world. We don't even see what they say is the route to Cathay or China or whatever they want to call it. We go a long way west, but we still don't get to the Far East and the great sea that divides us out there."

"How do you know we won't get lost and fall off?" asked Marie with horror in her eyes and a tremor in her voice.

Jean Baptiste held the baby in one arm and threw the other around Marie Anne's shoulders. "Because, my dear one, your loving husband has already been there. Three summers ago, I went up the Saskatchewan as far as Fort of the Prairies. You will see. It truly is bigger than Fort Gibraltar, and you will love the open prairies. It's beautiful here, but wait until you see that whole huge world under the biggest sky you can imagine. It makes you feel as if you are the only person on earth. You love the sunrises here. Wait until you see the Northern Lights flashing up and down the whole sky. And buffalo! Oh, so many of them. It's a good life we shall have out there."

"I thought it was beautiful here," said Marie Anne a little sadly. "It just seems that we are going such a long, long distance from home."

Jean stroked her hair. "Well, it's true, it is a mighty long way from Maskinongé, dear, but this is our home now, and our friends are coming with us."

"What does Amie think of going so far away from her people?" she asked him.

"She and the others are quite content to pack up and go," he told her. "Amie came with us three years ago when Belgrade and I went to Fort of the Prairies. Moving about doesn't really bother any of the ladies. They are used to it. Whether they come back to where they were for last winter or not doesn't bother them. I think they rather like to be on the move. Quite different from Maskinongé, isn't it?"

"Well, I suppose I have to get used to packing up and moving around too," Marie Anne said a little wistfully.

A momentary picture of a pretty small house with a thatched roof, a small fenced area with chickens, perhaps roses in a garden and geraniums in the windows slipped into focus. She shook her head to get rid of it. "I could use some of those geraniums around here though," she thought. "We need something to keep away the flies."

It took a scant two or three hours for all four couples to strike their camps and load the canoes for the long trek to the western Hudson's Bay post, Fort of the Prairies. No time for lengthy goodbyes. All of a sudden, they were on the move.

"Like gypsies," Marie Anne thought to herself.

The entire company of four voyageurs, their wives, children, dogs, and all their belongings, as well as three or four days' worth of provisions, sorted themselves into two large canoes. With a strong man at the bow and stern of each one, the little company of adventurers set off up the Red River on the first lap of a journey that would take most of the summer. The horses were sold, as there was no convenient way to take a horse in a canoe. The men figured on buying new mounts after they had reached their new hunting grounds. Everyone but Marie Anne was in holiday spirits. She turned to the east and bade her homeland a silent farewell. It wasn't long, however, before her natural high spirits took over and she joined in the gaiety.

Their first real stop apart from brief overnight camps was at Fort Gibraltar for the important business of trading their winter's hunting spoils for their necessities and whatever else the ladies could inveigle the men into bartering. Bolts of scarlet wool and the little multicoloured glass beads for ornamenting clothing always caught the fancy of wives who accompanied their husbands into the stores. Once they had chosen beads, they needed needles and cotton thread to go with them. The beads, they felt, were prettier and much easier to sew than the porcupine quills they had known previously. Collecting quills, dying them, and then working with them was much more arduous than threading a thin sharp steel needle, and as for making sinew fine enough to go through the pretty beads, well, what a waste of time.

The three Cree wives were adamant about adding these delicacies to the load. Marie Anne watched with amusement the bickering between the couples and thought the tobacco the men considered a necessity weighed more than a few beads.

"Who is going to carry that stuff?" the men asked.

The wives all chorused that they had been told they were travelling by river all the way and there wouldn't be long portages across difficult terrain. They were reminded that going by river did not necessarily mean there would be no carryovers. The men pointed out that they would be paddling down the Saskatchewan and for sure there would be rapids. In the end, the ladies won, and blankets and beads were part of the trading. The men shrugged as if to say, *the things women would rather have than important stuff like tobacco.* By the time they embarked, all were well pleased with their new possessions.

Marie Anne could see that this was the life that Jean loved so deeply – packing up, heading off into new territory, making ready to take on whatever he encountered and the buffalo hunts. He was truly a restless spirit, and she had to admit that his enthusiasm was infectious. One part of her longed for the settled life, the serenity of going to church each week, of making her confession regularly and being surrounded by her own people. The other half exulted in freedom and fresh experiences.

"How will I put these two longings together?" she asked herself again and again.

Watching the rhythmic sweep of his arms and shoulders up in the bow as they swept down the Red River mesmerized her into dreamy contentment.

"He always has to feel himself free," she thought. "He wants me to share this sense of being able to pack up in a moment on what seems to me sometimes a whim and go off goodness knows where. It has its bad moments, but all in all, it's a good life. I suppose that I shall never get to see the St Lawrence River nor ever see St Sulpice on the Mastigouche again. I wish I could know what happened to Josette and the others, and Maman, but there it is. I'm here now, for better or worse. Jean says one of these days there will be farmers and herdsmen settling this great beautiful country around Fort Gibraltar. He says there will be churches or at least a chapel with a priest. Well, I don't know about that. It seems too much to hope for. Perhaps it will come to pass in my lifetime, perhaps not. It would be a blessing to have Reine properly christened with holy water, though. In the meantime, I'm going to have to see about some fresh moss for her the first moment I get my feet on dry land."

Marie rocked Reine, who was letting the whole world know she was uncomfortable. "Jean," she said finally, "let's all sing and distract her before we have all the children howling and the dogs raising a ruckus."

Indeed, it was just this life that appealed so strongly to Jean and other young French Canadians. They had all turned their backs on farming back east in response to an urgent need to test themselves without restraints of church or society. Not that they had abandoned their faith. The Metis children of Jean's friends had all received the sign of the cross on their foreheads as newborns, and the men all carried rosaries. They were none of them eager for riches. They knew that the life of a hunter would never make them rich. That was for those who were content to spend their lives back east. To be on the move, to depend on their own skills, and to provide for their wives and children – that was the life.

Jean Baptiste in his turn reflected as his paddle dipped into the water and swung up gracefully in an easy satisfying movement repeated over and over. Marie Anne had adapted herself well to the ways of her Cree friends. He felt no compunction whatsoever now about taking her so far west and to an area as remote from civilization as it was possible to get. She'd adapted to the Cree wearables, the deerskin sleeveless shift and the leggings. She didn't seem to be pining for her billowy woollen skirts and the white linen aprons she had started out with a year ago. He pondered for a moment on what both mothers would say if they could see her in her Indian get-up and grinned. He wondered what she had done with her white underclothes and those aprons.

"Probably torn up for the baby," he figured. Then he remembered that Reine had started out her life completely outfitted like all the Metis and Indian babies around. It was a puzzle, but he stopped thinking about it. "She probably has things stowed away somewhere," he thought, turning his full attention to setting a smart pace in the bow.

Marie watched the shoreline scudding past. She thought she could recognize some landmarks. "Was it really only last summer?" she kept asking herself. To her, it seemed as though it must have been in another lifetime that she and Jean had paddled to Pembina so light-heartedly. She cradled Reine in her arms and began to sing one of the songs that her own mother had sung to her and the younger ones such a long time ago and so far away. It was a song about a young girl, Therese, about to be married and leaving her dainty bedroom with lace at her dressing table to become a married woman. "Therese is seated in her chamber, in her chamber of a girl," she began, but her throat caught and she could not continue. The memories came flooding back, of roses and cornflowers in her mother's garden, the very bushes that her great-grandmother had brought from across the sea from Normandy, and the smell of fresh-baked bread straight from the bake oven in the garden, brought into the house in triumph on a long-handled spatula.

"Once you have tasted that bread," she thought, "you never lose your taste for it, and the wish to smell it and eat it follows you. Ah well. If I can't taste bread, at least I have corn and squash and beans. And Amie has shown me how to plant them and take care of them. I would never have thought of planting a corn seed together with a little fish, but Amie says that is the way to do it to make the corn grow tall and give lots of cobs. I suppose we will have to wait until next season to get a garden in. I hope we can get a share of the harvest, wherever it is we are going."

It took only two days of paddling to reach the first fort. The wives, children, and dogs were glad to have a short time to get the stiffness out of their legs from the very cramped quarters of the canoes. They were piled on top of each other and the household goods. It would be a relief to get rid of the added burden of furs. It was the end of May when they arrived in the factor's store at Fort Gibraltar. Even though his new supplies had not yet arrived, he was glad to see them and able to take care of their most pressing needs.

When he heard where they were headed, he couldn't help making his surprise obvious. "You mean you are taking Madame Lajimoniere, such a lady, to Fort of the Prairies?" he asked incredulously. His amazement showed on his face. "It's such a long hard pull, and there are many places where you will have to portage around rapids, you know."

"Yes, I do know. I've been there already," said Jean with more than a little annoyance. "My wife lived through the journey up from Fort William, and those portages are more rugged than anything she will face out to Fort of the Prairies."

"But Madame was not carrying a baby last summer. Surely that makes a difference, doesn't it?"

"She'll be all right." Jean picked up his ammunition and his tobacco and strode out of the store.

He had no intention of giving his reason to the factor, and he did not intend to hang around and be told it was not wise to take her across such a vast space. He hadn't come to the west to listen to an older man talk to him like his father.

The factor came down to the beach to see them off. He waved goodbye and called out good luck. He had wondered many times how the pretty Madame Lajimoniere was going to make out in her first winter, and here she was looking as pretty as ever with a baby on her back. He shook his head at what seemed to him an unbelievable incongruity – the dainty Canadienne dressed in Indian fashion chattering freely in Cree to the other women.

Marie Anne waved back, wondering if she would ever see Fort Gibraltar again, or if she would ever have the opportunity to travel east again. "I thought I had cut my last link with home when we left Fort William, and now we are cutting off the last link with Fort Gibraltar. I wonder how far this Fort of the Prairies really is."

She felt inside her shift for her medal and the rosary in its pouch. It gave her courage, which she badly needed as the fort receded in the distance.

The factor stood on the shore watching them go. He wondered if he would ever meet that courageous, remarkable lady again. Shaking his head and wondering what the world was coming to, transporting white ladies off to the far west, he went back to his domain to see if he could get his bookkeeping to come out reasonably well enough to satisfy the inspector fellow he could expect any day next month.

After they'd left Fort Gibraltar well behind them, the little company paddled up the rest of the Red River to its mouth at Lake Winnipeg. Marie Anne looked longingly to her right, the way back to Fort William, but her attention was soon taken up with keeping the lively Madamoiselle Reine from scrambling about the canoe. She was an inquisitive child, and Marie Anne knew only too well how important it was that the exuberant and self-assured little mite not be allowed to be so playful as to tip the canoe or encourage the other children and the dogs in any lively games.

The two canoes hugged the western shore as they kept a sharp eye out for the entrance into the much larger expanse, the main body of Lake Winnipeg itself. Then Marie Anne realized that the lake she found so enormous was in reality only a bay in the southern end, a small bag of water hanging down from an immense inland sea. The four friends made good time with no serious problems or surprises. The weather was kind, with only a gentle breeze to ruffle the water. Even though it meant a longer day's paddle, they hugged the shoreline, going deeply into many a bay.

All four women were subdued after they turned into the great expanse of Lake Winnipeg proper. For all of them, it was a leave-taking from the familiar. The Crees were a little apprehensive about going so far from their people, despite what Jean had said about it to Marie. Amie and Marie looked at each other fearfully, although Amie was trying to be a stoic. She had no tribal connections where they were going, and she had no illusions about being welcomed into the western encampments. At least she would be far to the north of one of the traditional enemies of the Crees, the Dakotas, but nothing she had heard from her father's people about the Bloods, the Blackfeet, and the Sarcees – to name only three of a host of independent and quite differing sets of tribes – made her happy to meet them. Customs, language, all were so different from what she had known. There were even Crees who had migrated to the plains so many years before that they no longer felt a communion with the Crees of the Woods from whom Amie was descended.

As the spirits of the men rose to the challenge of what they felt in their hearts would be a better life, the women became more concerned. Each one tried not to mention it either to each other or to the children, and particularly not to their menfolk. Amie's two young toddlers, a boy and a girl, were having a particularly happy time with something new to peer out at from their tight places, surrounded by hides and with the dogs curled up in their laps, snoozing their way across the water.

Each evening after a long day's paddle, the party would agree on a likely campsite, beach the canoes, and set up tents. Dogs and children tumbled out onto the beach and raced about, getting underfoot. No one minded the confusion; it was part of the Indian woman's way of child-rearing. If a small one were hurt, he or she simply raced to the nearest mother for suckling or general sympathy. Marie Anne watched and realized that there was more of a general bond between mothers and children than the strong bond of a mother only for her own offspring that she knew.

"That is one thing I don't think I can ever feel at home with," she thought. "My baby is my very own and mine alone."

The women's first task was to gather evergreen boughs to make a comfortable mattress and more for a flooring if the weather looked as though it might rain. The men, after unloading the canoes, went into the bush to collect saplings to be used as poles to keep the tents up. Then the packs were unrolled and the hides that had been packing material became the walls of their shelters.

Experience had taught them all that a teepee should face east to keep out the prevailing wind, which blew from the west. A firepit was dug in the centre of the tent so that the smoke should go straight up through the open space at the summit of the poles. A flap of hide was positioned at the top of the tent to deflect smoke and send it into the wind to prevent it from settling downward back into the shelter.

The women gathered anything edible that they could find: berries, seeds, even a wild onion, which they did not enjoy at all but which all the Canadians thought improved the flavour of the stew. All was added to the hide pot simmering over a campfire, making everyone's nostrils quiver. The men were always on the lookout for fresh meat – a deer, perhaps an antelope, or even just a rabbit. Bird nests yielded eggs, not always the freshest. Pemmican was carried and used only in case the hunting was poor. Whatever was on the menu, it was the women's job to cut the meat into thin strips and lay it on top of the packs to be used as the next three or four days' provisions. First the meat was smoked over the campfire, and then the next day it was laid out to dry and turned frequently. The heat, the sunlight, and the glare from the water soon turned what to Marie Anne seemed something repugnantly smelly into jerky, which was the staple of their diet. She tried not to think about the flies.

Each night, the travellers built a huge bonfire on the beach to ward off mosquitoes as well as prowling animals. The men refused to think of the possibility of encountering a band of hostile plainsmen. The farther they travelled west from the usual hunting grounds and the lands that the Cree wives felt familiar with, the more apprehensive the wives became. Amie tried not to let Marie Anne know of her fears, but the two women were in such sympathy that they both knew the other was trying not to show it.

When the men were not too exhausted after their day's paddling, they swapped yarns around the fire. It was a time they all enjoyed together. Marie Anne was to look back on that summer with happiness all the rest of her life.

No matter how many times she had heard the yarns before, Marie Anne was enthralled. She thought back to the days back in Maskinongé when she had listened to

Jean, the returning hero, spinning his stories. Here she was living right through the tales in the very places where they had happened.

One night, Belgrade recounted the adventures of a factor in a small fort on the Saskatchewan. It had taken place during the time that Jean had left for the east, and Belgrade was sure it would be a new one for him. It concerned a factor, who had played a trick on some Blackfeet out on the Saskatchewan.

"On the Saskatchewan," thought Marie Anne in alarm, "that's where we're going. And they say it is such a long way up the river to the largest fort in the northwest. I hope we get to where we are supposed to be going."

She thought of Jean's insistence on the need an Indian feels for revenge and shivered. Again she fingered her medal and prayed to St Anne to get them safely past any angry tribesmen seeking to wreak vengeance on any whites they came across.

"At least this Fort of the Prairies is a big one with, Jean says, a strong stockade around it." She shivered and prepared to listen to Belgrade's story. "If this is what Father Vinet meant by strength, I'm going to have to get rid of my fears and make the best of it. There is nothing else to be done."

"This factor," Belgrade started in, "he was alone with just one servant in the fort. Everybody else had gone. Some had gone to take supplies to a neighbouring port. The rest of the clerks had headed off to the plains to get a fresh supply of meat."

Sure by now that everyone was hanging on his words, he continued, "Well, a band of Blackfeet camped just outside the stockade. They had finished up all their liquor and were feeling pretty full of high spirits, and as you know, most Blackfeet would rather trade than go hunting themselves – the traders and raiders they are called – so they figured that with the factor almost alone, they might have a little fun and scare him into giving them liquor, never mind a trade. Then they figured they could keep the party going all night and then some if they felt like it. They figured they might just hit him for some tobacco at the same time.

"So they went up to the gate of the fort and knocked to be allowed inside. You can be sure there was a lot of yelling and whooping and banging. Enough of a racket to waken the dead, I'd say. Well, the servant woke up first. He went to the gate and opened a little wicket to see what in thunder was going on. Scared half to death he was, but he ran to wake up the factor. He told the Blackfeet he would have to ask the factor for the keys to the gate.

"Now the factor was already in bed, and he wasn't about to get himself up in the middle of the night and put his clothes on just to receive a band of pretty drunken Blackfeet. He sent the servant back to the gate. Opening the wicket just a crack, the servant gave the factor's instructions.

"The factor is already abed, and you will have to wait until tomorrow to come back and let him know what you wanted," he said as the factor had instructed him.

"At that, you can believe there was a real outcry. It must have been bloodcurdling. Those Blackfeet can make a terrifying din when they go on the rampage. So the servant shouted to them he would have to wake up the factor again and see if he would let him have the keys so he could let them in."

Belgrade paused while Jean dragged another piece of wood onto the fire. The sparks lit up a circle of attentive faces.

"In the meantime," he went on, "the factor heard the racket and he got up plenty mad. He was ready for anything. Now on either side of the gate, there were two towers that had loaded cannons in them, and the two towers stood, oh, maybe fifteen, eighteen feet above the ground. The factor told the servant to take the cannonballs out of the cannon but leave the powder. Then he told the servant to wait for his signal, and they would each fire off the cannons together.

"Now the Blackfeet figured that since they outnumbered the factor and his servant, they had nothing to fear, so they were lounging around waiting for the gate to open. Suddenly, both cannons went off with one beautiful roar. It was a much bigger racket than the party of Blackfeet had made, you can be sure. The Blackfeet leaped up into the air and took off so fast their feet never touched the ground until they reached their camp. I guess they sobered up in a hurry too."

The men all broke up with laughter.

"There's more," cried Belgrade. "I haven't reached the end of my story yet. The factor yelled, 'Stop, stop. I have yet another shot that I want you to hear.' But those Blackfeet, they just went on running as straight as an arrow flies."

The four men thwacked their thighs and roared with enjoyment of the joke.

"Did they come back?" asked Paquin.

"Not that I ever heard of," answered Belgrade. "I guess they would be back later to trade, but they haven't tried to get another supply of free liquor as far as I know."

The men continued to laugh and refill their pipes and then stare into the fire in contentment. It was a huge joke, a great trick, and the factor had certainly won. The women all looked at one another, trying to keep their expressionless faces from displaying the dread in their hearts and a sense of foreboding.

Jean Baptiste got up once more to throw more logs on the fire along with some brush to make the flames higher yet into the night sky. It seemed almost a silent act of defiance to all the perils that lay around them in the shadows.

Marie Anne slipped her rosary through her fingers and prayed with extra fervency. When she put her rosary back in its little pouch, she looked up at the sky, so full of beauty, so speckled with uncountable stars. The sky was so peaceful. Why did that word *vengeance* keep running through her head? Why couldn't these human beings all around her feel some of that peace and live together without bloodshed?

The travellers took themselves off to their tents, making sure the dogs were tethered and that all the children were accounted for and sound asleep. The firepit in each tent was put to use to act as a smudge pot to help keep mosquitoes at bay. Soon the only sound in the camp was the odd crackle in the campfire and a whimper or two from a dog having a dream.

Marie Anne lay wakeful for some time with Reine cradled in her arms next to Jean, who was snoring contentedly.

"Please, God give me the strength I must have for Reine's sake." She repeated her heartfelt prayer until she too drifted into sleep.

CHAPTER 9

As soon as the sun rose the next morning, everyone set to, rolling their equipment into the tents and then into the canoes and generally going about their tasks with light hearts. They even tried out some of the songs that Marie Anne had been teaching her friends, songs that she had sung as a girl back in the east. The partial translations from French to Cree sometimes altered the sense of the song considerably, but the women enjoyed themselves, and the Canadians often joined in with their deep voices making some pleasing harmonies, a veritable choir in the wilderness.

Still hugging the shore of Lake Winnipeg, the little company made a leisurely trip. They knew they had plenty of time to reach Fort of the Prairies by late summer in time for the later buffalo hunt. In the meantime, game was plentiful all the way. The biggest inconvenience was the hordes of mosquitoes. Each night the huge campfire was supposed to act as a preventive to keep the ravenous little monsters at bay. The fire smouldering all night in each tent was an additional attempt to discourage them. But as though each insect had an internal alarm system to rouse them all simultaneously, the whining noise of thousands of tiny predators made life miserable for them all as soon as it was dusk.

"That firepit may be a discouragement," said Marie Anne one morning as she stretched and scratched, "but to the little beasts, I think our fires are simply a challenge."

Jean laughed. "You wouldn't be saying that if we hadn't made a fire. You would have been gnawed to the bone," he said and kissed her on a particularly ugly swelling on the end of her nose. "It will get better soon. This mosquito season will end in a few days, you'll see, there won't be as many of them. Remember last year on our way to Pembina?"

As each day's paddling took them farther from Pembina, Marie Anne felt a mingling of relief and regret – relief at putting the Cree woman out of the picture and regret at getting so far from Maskinongé. On several nights, she talked it over with Jean after the camp had settled and Reine was safely asleep between them.

About his first wife, Jean reassured her again and again. "She can't possibly follow us all this way with a child and no protector. How could she manage by herself? The boy isn't big enough to carry a canoe of the size she would need. He is too young to hunt by himself. No, she can't possibly follow us."

"But what if others like us want to strike out for Fort of the Prairies? Couldn't she come along with them?"

Marie Anne did not really think of this as a possibility, but she had to hear over and over again from Jean that it was so unlikely, there was nothing to worry about. Gradually the spectre of what Marie Anne saw as her rival dwindled, and with Jean's repeated assurances that she would never see the woman again and neither would he, she began to put the whole shocking incident at the back of her mind.

The regret she felt at getting farther and farther away from her family, all the familiarities of Maskinongé, was harder to manage. She tried not to mention it to Jean. He didn't seem to understand her bouts of homesickness at all. Over the course of the summer, Marie Anne forced herself to accept the reality of the Cree wife and rid herself of her rancour at what she still thought of occasionally as Jean's deceit in not preparing her. Accepting the growing distance that separated her from her loved ones was harder to bear. Much as she had come to love Amie and be grateful for her friendship, there were more than a few moments when Marie Anne stood by herself facing the sunrise with Reine in her arms, wishing with all her being that she could chat away with Josette.

Jean observed her more than once standing like a solitary statue. If he realized that she was homesick, he said nothing. There was nothing he could do about it, and Jean — the impetuous wooer, the high-spirited companion, the successful hunter — was not given overmuch to introspection.

According to custom, the party stopped mid-morning for their breakfast, the first of their two meals a day. The menu was no different from the evening meal except that not as much was eaten. At one campsite, after Marie Anne had breakfast ready, she carried Reine over to the rock they had selected for their dining table. A bouquet of wild roses, freshly picked for her, lay in front of her place. She picked them up and buried her nose in their fragrance. Amie came over to admire them.

"That's one of the reasons we love our Canadians so." She sat down beside Marie Anne and bent over to have a sniff. "A Cree man would never think to present his wife with a bunch of flowers."

"Do the other Canadians do little things like this for their wives?" Marie Anne held her nosegay up for another sniff, revelling in the sweetness.

Amie giggled. "Oh, they do. At least all the ones I know do. Canadian men are so different from our people. Canadians all wear a totem around their necks like you do."

Marie Anne realized she was referring to the medal the priests had blessed for her. That these men who had married women of quite a different faith still remembered their own gave her a feeling of comfort. That somehow there would be priests sent out here to minister to all these children born of baptized Christian men was Marie's firm resolution.

Week followed week, and the little company made slow and satisfying headway up the west side of the lake. It was so huge they could not see the opposite shore. To Marie Anne, it was like being on the edge of the world, except that out beyond where she could only imagine it was the world she had left behind. How often she wished she could hold out her bonny wee *voyageuse* for Josette's and the housekeeper's admiration.

By keeping in close to the shore, they often paddled into deep sheltered bays, some of them with reeds. Then the lead canoe would come to a stop and both would glide along silently looking for ducks and their nests. The children turned bright attentive eyes into the reeds, and it was often a young one who first pointed out the duck with her ducklings while the drake tried frantically to draw them away. To be aware of all the living creatures, their habits, their sources of food, their behaviour – this was something of great importance to all the women. It was part of their childhood, and they were determined to have their children learn their Indian ways.

The weather seemed to give the travellers a blessing, with fair winds and day after day of brilliant sunshine. The mosquitoes were at their worst at night, but the hours of darkness were mercifully short, for though ultimately they were headed west, their journey was taking them far to the north.

At the passage between Lake Winnipeg and Cedar Lake, Belgrade pointed out a new post. "Must be Hudson's Bay Company. It's a bit too far north to be Nor'West territory, and I think maybe I see an English flag."

"You're right, Belgrade." Jean raised his hand over his eyes to squint into the distance. "No, I'm not sure. It could be Nor'West colours. One of these days, those two are going to meet head on, and I hope I'm not caught in the middle."

Paquin shipped his paddle. "With the English moving farther south every year and the Montrealers getting farther and farther west all the time, it's bound to happen."

"Look!" shouted Belgrade. "It *is* the Nor'West flag."

"All the better reason to trade with whichever company we happen to be near and get the best deal," said Chalifou.

All four grunted in agreement. Independent trappers they would remain. Jean Baptiste took a long pull on his pipe and looked thoughtful. These forts coming along, each season it seemed, would spell trouble eventually – but for now, each man hoped to be able to pit one against the other and drive prices up.

As they had all the supplies they needed and were in the habit of hunting for daily requirements of meat, there was no need to stop and put in at the small fort. They waved as they passed and headed directly across Cedar Lake. At the end of the next day's paddle, they stopped briefly at the Pass, a Hudson's Bay fort at the mouth of the Saskatchewan. Again the factor was aghast at the sight of a pretty white woman. He watched, astounded, as the little party of travellers started the long haul up the North Saskatchewan River.

Perhaps it was the Pass factor's astonishment at seeing a white woman that made Belgrade decide to go ahead with Paquin and play a little trick on the Indians at Fort Cumberland, their next rest stop. The Belgrades and the Paquins set off together first and made the Chalifous and Lajimoniere promise to give a day's handicap.

Marie Anne was thoroughly apprehensive of Belgrade's tricks. Sometimes they were great fun, and sometimes she felt he went too far. At the moment, she couldn't imagine what he had in mind. After all, they had promised to stay together.

"What could he be up to now?" she said and turned to Amie.

Amie grinned but said nothing.

When she, Jean, and the Chalifous arrived at the camp two days later, she soon found out that Belgrade had been up to his tricks and no mistake. At first Marie Anne was utterly charmed by the reception she was getting from all the Indians, no matter to what tribe they belonged. There were smiles and dignified greetings from everyone whenever she so much as glanced at anyone. As she climbed out of the canoe, she found the entire encampment jostling and pushing to be the first to bid her welcome. She felt extremely self-conscious and sure that something was wrong. When she contrasted this reception with her experience at Grand Camp, she knew that something was definitely odd. She felt as though she were some kind of deity. There were speeches from the leader begging her to be kind to them, and gifts were pressed on her. Amie was obviously ill at ease and would not tell Marie what was going on.

After an entire week, the Indians were still begging her to accept gifts of all kinds. It was embarrassing. Marie Anne felt uneasy as well as mystified. She went off in search of Belgrade.

"Jean Belgrade." She stood in front of him and barred his path. She was annoyed, and it was plain from the tone of her voice that she was quickly becoming angry. "Jean Belgrade, what is going on? What on earth have you told the Indians here about me? Tell me at once what all this bowing and showering me with gifts is all about."

Belgrade laughed, but he cautioned her not to sound angry. They were conversing in French, as neither was anxious to have the Indians eavesdrop. They needn't have been so cautious, however; at the first angry words, the onlookers disappeared as if by magic.

"It's time to explain," he said. "But first, I wanted you to have a grand reception."

"Whatever do you mean, Jean Belgrade?" Marie Anne stamped her foot. "You have never shown that sort of consideration to me before. What have you done to make all these people afraid of me and treat me like the Queen of France? Why are they all so eager to please me? Am I supposed to give them gifts in exchange? Because as you very well know, I don't have anything I can part with."

"No, no," Belgrade said, looking a little sheepish about his prank. "When I arrived a day earlier, I told them a white-skinned woman was coming. Mind you, they had heard something about it. They have a way of getting information around, and quickly. I've never figured out how they do it. But I've seen it happen too many times to think it's all just a lucky hunch on someone's part."

"Belgrade," said Marie Anne in a low-pitched voice filled with determination that had an icy edge to it. "What have you told them?"

There was complete stillness. Marie Anne had the eerie feeling that the entire population had made itself invisible behind every tree and shrub. She hugged Reine more closely to her than ever.

"I'm sorry, Madame Lajimoniere," Belgrade began, and Marie Anne could see that he meant it. "It was only a joke, and I never meant to upset you. Since they had an inkling that a white woman was coming, I could tell that they were very curious about you. They wanted to know if you were good or bad. How white was white? How should they speak to you? Should they be careful? Was it necessary to keep the children out of sight? Would you harm them? It was a perfect set-up for my little joke. So I tried to answer their questions, and I told them you were good but that you had strong power, very strong, strong medicine, and that all you had to do to kill someone who displeased you was to frown at them. I figured I was safe, because you don't frown. So you see, everyone has tried their utmost not to upset you or insult you, even unknowingly." He grinned. "So now you know why they are all so anxious to get you to smile at them."

Marie Anne shook her head. "That Belgrade," she thought. "Who can stay angry with such a fellow?" Aloud she said sternly, "You and your tricks. When will you ever learn to stop playing your famous tricks? Now I'll have to go around with a perpetual smirk on my face, or they will know that you tricked them as well as me."

In spite of herself, she broke into a chuckle. She still felt a bit put out, but Belgrade was such an amusing friend that she could not really stay angry with him for long.

As soon as she laughed at him, the entire body of campers appeared again as if by magic. The tense moments were over, and the bowing and smiling started all over again, with Marie Anne playing the part that Belgrade had forced on her. Jean Baptiste had been in on the joke from the start, of course, and now he made the surrounding woods ring with his hearty laughter.

The men all smiled, and the women tittered with relief at the outcome of the contretemps; they could not follow it in so many words, but the gist had been plain enough. The powerful white lady was on friendly terms with them all again. No one thought to question why Belgrade had not rolled over dead at her outburst. Perhaps the medicine did not apply to white men. Even without her spurious credentials of magical power, Marie Anne was something quite miraculous, with her golden hair and those piercing blue eyes.

While they were making up their minds to pack up and leave before the dazzling welcome had lost its attractiveness for their hosts, another Canadian arrived at the fort. His name was Bouvier, and most unusually for a hunter, he showed up by himself and without a wife, children, or dogs. The four men took to him at once, and even though he seemed a rather solitary fellow, they enjoyed his conversation. They decided to ask him if he wished to team up with them. After some consideration, he thought he would join them. He had been alone for so long that at first he was not sure if he wanted to be so close to women, babies, and dogs. One bitch even had half a dozen wriggling sucking pups to keep her canoe in a perpetual state of watchfulness. But it seemed to make sense all round. Their two canoes were certainly crowded. Bouvier's canoe, while small, would carry another paddler and be handy for separating toddlers who got into the occasional bout of fisticuffs – and perhaps a dog or two as well, for the same reason.

It was arranged.

Accordingly, after a week of holding court and being the uncrowned queen of the fort, Marie Anne set off with her companions, who had enjoyed the prank at first but were now heartily sick of all the attention the white lady of power had been shown, and headed up the mighty North Saskatchewan River bound for Fort of the Prairies.

CHAPTER 10

Feeling rested and refreshed after their adventure at Fort Cumberland, the travellers now in their three canoes paddled and camped their way up the North Saskatchewan, now turning north, now winding south, following its course but yet always making headway to the west. The weather remained hot and sunny.

By late July, the mosquitoes, as Jean had predicted, were not as troublesome. It became the travellers' habit to make the evening stop when the sun was still high in the sky so they could make camp in broad daylight. The women prepared the evening meal. After they had eaten, they had time to relax and lie out on any rocky promontory to take their well-earned ease after a full day's paddling and a good feed of fresh meat or fish and whatever fruits they could find.

How they looked forward to enjoying the nightly spectacle – the sun setting into the far horizon after painting the entire sky with shades of red, pink, mauve, purple, and even shafts of green. Each evening the shifting shades of glorious colour combinations made a different picture. It was a time of contentment, a time for friendship, a time for bits of small talk between the men and the women. Amie's sense of fun kept them laughing, and Belgrade was obviously very much in love with his witty young wife. Some evenings, they lingered until the soft and deepening dusk gave way to starlight and silence – a silence occasionally broken by the eerie call of a wolf or a lonely coyote in the distance.

On a few nights they had been treated to the spectacle of the northern lights, so brilliant, so unbelievable. Then sleeping children were wakened and carried out of the teepees. Lying down on their backs, the children gazed with awe at the sight, marvelling at the swiftly forming and reforming shafts and curtains of vivid reds, greens, blues, and whites streaking up and down and then encircling the sky.

Each morning they roused at first light, and although there was much work in breaking camp, all the travellers paused from time to time to watch the glow of sunlight catch now one treetop, now another. The sunlight catching the waving motion of the grasses in a slight breeze never failed to delight Marie Anne.

As Marie Anne told and retold her children many years later, never had she imagined a sky so huge, so much bigger than back in Canada, and so deep a blue. What wonderful clouds, she told them, so magnificent sailing across the sky majestically. She and Amie imagined all sorts of cloud pictures of strange animals, canoes laden with travellers, fantastic castles. The cries of the coyotes always sent shivers up her back – not the long lonely howls of the wolves, which thrilled her, but the haunting shrieks of something in the direst pain, the most imploring screams. Jean did his best to assure her that the coyotes were not in pain, merely serenading their beloveds, but Marie Anne found it too preposterous that such anguish could mean a protestation of love to any creature. It reminded her too poignantly of the sounds from the barn back in Maskinongé when her father slaughtered a pig

The days followed one another in a hazy, lazy succession of pleasure. The nights followed one another under the friendliness of thousands of stars, with the occasional little cries of small wild animals that alerted the dogs and the chittering of birds as they settled for sleep. Then after the moon rose, the lovesick coyotes would give their raucous serenade. Marie Anne loved it all. She particularly loved the orange lilies growing everywhere and the sudden whirring of grouse wings when they unknowingly disturbed a nest. There was so much to observe and enjoy.

One evening the little band made their camp rather later than usual. They'd had a full day of laughter, of outrageous jokes in which even the taciturn Bouvier had joined. They had sung, gathered berries at the day's first meal stop, and allowed the children to paddle and splash about in a protected cove. Instead of camping at the normal time, they had elected to press on a bit. The shadows lengthened before a likely spot for an overnight camp came into view. They tied the canoes to some willows growing along the shoreline. The men found plenty of deadfalls that made an easy task of getting a great bonfire going at the foot of a slight rise in the ground.

More tired than usual after so long a day, the four old friends relaxed around the fire with their backs to the river. The wives busied themselves with preparations for supper and for making the camp ready for the night. The children were either safe on their mothers' backs or close underfoot.

Bouvier seated himself on the other side of the blaze with his back towards the hill. All five men were swapping yarns and generally enjoying their rest and their pipes.

Suddenly there was a terrible scream.

Bouvier called out in agony for help. There was a split second of silence as each man sat up alert. Confusion followed as the mothers instinctively huddled with the children and the men shouted to Bouvier that they were coming, grabbed their muskets, and got a ball of shot from their pouches in one continuous movement. The bonfire sent its flames and smoke in a whirlwind so that no one could see what was going on. Whether it was a war party of hostile braves or some other kind of ambush no one could be sure, but the men rushed to the defence of their families.

Racing around the bonfire, to their wide-eyed astonishment and horror, they stared unbelieving at the sight of poor Bouvier being dragged up the hill by a sow bear followed by two cubs.

Canny as they all were about the woods and the plains, it had never occurred to any of them that a bear would attack a man surrounded by other people at night, so close to a roaring blaze. Their principal reason for making such a huge fire and keeping it going all night even in the heat of summer was to discourage foraging beasts, as well as the ubiquitous mosquitoes. The sow bear held Bouvier in one claw and struck him repeatedly in the face, trying to knock him senseless before tearing him to pieces.

Jean Baptiste was first around the fire. He ran as hard as he could, chasing the bear and yelling at her, trying to frighten her into letting go her hold on Bouvier's neck. The bear turned, straightened up, and releasing her clutch on

Bouvier's neck, growled and clawed Bouvier's face again and again. She was angry and vicious. Realizing suddenly that she had to deal with a number of attackers only made her vent her rage unmercifully on poor Bouvier with increasing strength

Jean came up behind the bear. He beat her furiously with the butt of his musket, hesitating to shoot her even at point-blank range. There was so much milling about with others hurling rocks, so much movement and everything happening so fast, he was afraid he might shoot Bouvier by mistake.

The dogs, although chained, were frantic to get into the rescue mission. The women were bent on getting control of the dogs and maintaining control over the children, who were screaming hysterically. Everyone yelled in fury or in terror, and the women did their share of rock throwing at the two cubs running to the safety of their mother.

Bouvier's screams were the most terrible, the most frantic sounds, pleading with someone, anyone to be merciful and shoot him. "I'd rather die by a shot than be gnawed to death! Shoot! Shoot me, for mercy's sake! Shoot me!" he screamed whenever his mouth was clear of the murderous claws.

At last Jean thought he saw his chance. The sow reared, and Jean got her on her rump. At the explosion and the resultant shock and pain, she let go of Bouvier, who fell bleeding into the pine needles on the woodland floor. Instead of gathering up her cubs and beating a retreat, however, the bear was more angered and crazed than ever. With a bloodcurdling yell, she turned and reared at Jean. His shot had missed a vital spot. She was in pain from the wound and more on the warpath than ever.

Marie Anne watched in absolute dumb horror as the beast lunged at Jean. She knew that in shooting the bear at point-blank range, Jean had taken a tremendous chance, because his musket held only the one shot that had penetrated her rump. It was an act of true bravery.

Now Jean made a dash for the canoes where he had another musket stowed. Stampeding down the rise past the fire with the bear in pursuit, he leaped into his canoe and had barely picked up the gun when the bear flung herself at the canoe and all but tipped it and Jean over. She was set to clamber into the canoe, seize this interfering creature, and finish him off. Somehow, Jean got his second musket loaded and ready for the final shot, whether for the bear or for himself he was not sure. Certainly if he did not get a vital spot this time, he would have no chance for a second attempt.

The canoe lunged from side to side, this way and that.

Jean stood up in the wildly rocking boat and faced the bear standing upright, taking aim at what he hoped was the beast's chest. With the tip of his musket almost buried in the bear's fur, he pulled the trigger. This time the bear collapsed spread-eagled across the canoe, which tipped and sent Jean backward into the water.

The cubs, watching the goings-on from the top of the rise, turned and fled.

As soon as it was obvious that the sow bear could do no more harm, Marie Anne with Reine in her arms, hurried off to where Bouvier was writhing in agony. Although she had been shaking with terror, now that the only sound was poor Bouvier's groans and his pleas for mercy and to be shot, her instinct was to run to him and try to help him.

The bear had clawed his face from his chin to his hairline. Both eyes had simply disappeared, clawed clear out of his skull. His nose was an open wound, and it was hard to tell his face from the back of his head. Running back to the camp, Marie Anne handed Reine to Madame Chalifou, who was trying to restore some peace among the children.

Marie Anne untied her little bundle of precious savings – the last of her linen petticoats. She tore it into strips, and Amie went down to the water to fill a bucket. Together the two women went back to attend to Bouvier, assuring him that he was not dead and that no one was going to let him die by himself out in the wilderness. It was not possible to leave him all alone, they told him. Together they washed away the blood and pieced the torn flesh in place as gently as they knew how, but his wounds were deep and blood gushed without stopping.

Marie Anne took it upon herself to be his nurse, care for him, and dress the wounds as well as she was able. Amie was only too willing to help all she could. The four men insisted that he would be no burden to anybody and that he was to continue with them to Fort of the Prairies. To leave a man to die alone in the bush, then to be gnawed to the bone by predators, was unthinkable.

It was a fitful, wakeful night for the travellers. Bouvier tried not to groan, but Marie Anne and Amie both heard him and went to see if they could do anything for him.

"In the morning," Amie told Marie Anne, "we will go and search for a flower I know of. I hope it grows here. We will crush the leaves and lay it on his hurts. It is a healing plant. It will help him. And then we shall put moss on the top of the leaves, and on his arms we can make the same healing and then tie birchbark around to help him from paining himself."

"Yes, that's what's needed, Amie," replied Marie Anne in a whisper so as not to awaken the children. "That's better than my petticoats. Now that he will never see again, we must remember to help him feel and find his way. How terrible to be forced to live in darkness all the rest of your life."

When morning finally arrived, Bouvier once again begged them to shoot him and bury him wherever they were.

The men refused. "And have some wild animal come and dig you up again after our burial efforts? A waste of our time! Not on your life. Never." It wasn't much of a joke, but they were determined to get him to the fort.

When Amie spied the plant she needed, Marie Anne cried out, "Why, that looks a lot like a plant I knew back home! It's called night willow, and I never knew you could use it on a wound." They gathered what they hoped would be enough to last for at least a day and a night.

A couple of *hivernants* and even a factor or two had been known to have practiced medicine at one time before coming out to the New World to seek fortune, or perhaps had run away from an unpleasantness, or so it was said. They all hoped that with luck such a one might be found at Fort of the Prairies. After all, it was bigger than Fort William, they reminded one another, and besides, it was a Bay fort, and sometimes there were old salts from the British navy at their forts who knew a bit of medicine. There was to be no more argument about it. Bouvier was going to Fort of the Prairies with them and that was final.

Madame Lajimoniere and Madame Belgrade would be his attendants. After all, there were no more portages – perhaps a few carryovers, rapids here and there. They could easily carry him anywhere, they told him. To leave a friend in the wilderness was unthinkable, they told him again and again.

At first light, as was their practice, the travellers packed up swiftly and took their leave of a campsite no one ever wanted to see again. No one could bear to look up at the rise where the ground was still red with Bouvier's congealed blood. Putting last night's ordeal out of their minds and as far away as possible, both in reality and in retrospect, was the first and most important task of the day.

It was a subdued and chastened group that set off for whatever help Fort of the Prairies might hold for Bouvier and for them all. Even the dogs were glad to be off. They hopped to their appointed places in the canoes with no bits of playfulness, no last little games of "catch me" that normally had children and dogs in turmoil. Their tails were tucked well between their hind legs. The children were wide-eyed and silent.

Bouvier's canoe was made fast to Jean's. Marie Anne paddled stern, really little more than steering, so that she could keep an eye on her patient. Occasionally one of the other wives would swap to give her some rest. It did slow down the cavalcade somewhat – but mercifully, as Jean reminded them, they were going with the current.

Their passage was uneventful from then on, and they were spared any more living nightmares, but they all had a greatly increased respect for Madame the Black Bear, especially if she were accompanied by her cubs. Gradually, everyone began to shed some apprehensiveness, and by mid-August, on one of the loveliest late summer days, the travellers reached their destination.

They made their canoes fast at the company wharf, and with an enormous and palpable sense of relief, women, children, dogs, the invalid, and the men disgorged onto the wharf. With their feet on the dry land of what they hoped would be their headquarters, Marie Anne, the four friends, and even Bouvier, with a great deal of assistance, knelt down and gave thanks in the way their church upbringing had taught them by repeating their prayers together out loud.

Finally safe at the fort, Marie Anne put the last of her longings and reveries to rest. There were too many barriers, too many bridges crossed, and too much to do to think about Maskinongé and its comforts.

Bouvier lived to tell the tale of his encounter with the sow bear as best as he was able to tell anything with his speech so badly impaired by a crooked, vivid red scar where his mouth had been ripped open. He was, of course, blind and badly crippled, but thanks to the gentle and persistent care given him by his faithful nurses, Marie Anne and Amie, he spent the next ten years of his life at Fort of the Prairies.

CHAPTER 11

The end of August meant the grasses of the plains had ripened to a rich golden colour, that the ducks were meeting together and perhaps putting their flight plans in order with much quacking for their great migration south, that the pale green leaves of the birches and caraganas had become dried and yellowed and whispered in the breeze, and that a great many of the songbirds had already set off for more hospitable wintering grounds. The nights were drawing in, and it was up to the women to make preparations for the long months of cold ahead.

As soon as they had settled themselves in at Fort of the Prairies, the four women were hard-pressed to make up for lost time after the summer travels and go together out of the fort to search the surrounding terrain for berries, seeds, late fruits, wild turnips, and squash. Marie Anne gathered wild onions, but her Cree friends turned up their noses at them. They were fit only to be bartered with the white men at the fort, they told her. Marie Anne laughed and insisted they were good eating. Everything they had collected was dried either in the sunshine or over the fire and added to the pemmican sacks. The men made their plans to go for a short buffalo-hunting expedition, to take just what they and their families needed for meat for the winter.

Then it was the job of the ladies to receive chunks of raw meat, boil them, dry them, and smoke them. When there was finally no danger of the meat putrefying, they took the stone-hard chunks and beat them soft, adding rendered buffalo fat. This mixture was in turn mixed with the ingredients the women had gathered, and the result was stuffed into buffalo side sacks. The recipe varied depending on what was available, and hopefully it would be enough to last over the months when the ground was frozen and snow-covered.

The women gathered various plants, leaves, roots, and barks to be stored for future use as medicines. One of the young Paquins needed constant watching over a persistent cough. Madame Paquin kept a store of hemlock bark handy and frequently burned a portion to make a tea infusion for the child. It was a common remedy for coughing – so common, indeed, that its popular name was "old Grannie." Every spring Madame Paquin gathered Jack-in-the-pulpit, cooked the roots over hot ashes, and administered that in a tea to clear the child's phlegm.

They received a warm welcome from James Bird, the factor, who made it obvious that it was a great pleasure to have them at the fort. It was two years since he had last seen Jean Baptiste and smoked a pipe with him. There was catching up to be done. The best part about the newcomers for the factor was the appearance of Marie Anne. He had heard the usual rumours about a white-faced lady coming up the Saskatchewan, but he was genuinely astonished that a gentle beautiful woman had actually made her way thousands of miles across the middle of the continent. He was pleased and happy to have such an unusual guest in his fort, and with a white baby as well.

He found it hard to believe his good fortune in having such additions to his social circle, and he could hardly stop cooing at and paying court to Reine. That Jean Baptiste's wife and her colleague had been such stalwart caretakers of Bouvier astonished him even more. He was filled with admiration at the way the ladies had cheerfully taken on a task that would have appalled and sickened many a man he could name.

Mr Bird insisted that the Lajimonieres take up residence inside the stockade. He refused to consider the outside area a suitable position for the Lajimoniere family surrounded by Indians, Metis, and the *hivernant* hunters and their families. Jean tried to tell him that he and Marie Anne had always camped outside with the Indians before and that putting up his teepee with Indians surrounding him was what they both expected. Marie Anne glanced around, and it was her turn to be astonished at the sizes of the various encampments surrounding the fort on both sides of the river. The camps belonged to a goodly number of different tribes, not all of them living in peace with one another. In truth, she was heartily relieved when Mr Bird prevailed upon Jean to camp within the stockade. She and Amie set about making friends with Mr Bird's wife, an Assiniboine.

Although as a factor of the Hudson's Bay Company Mr Bird was not supposed to consort with the "natives," he like the others had taken an Indian woman to be his "country wife," as they were known. The country wife usually stayed back in the country when the men were posted home to England or Scotland. The North West Company factors were not so instructed, and as many of them were Canadian, their children were acknowledged as their legitimate offspring and were known as Metis. Marie Anne had quickly become aware of how many more Metis there were who spoke French as their second language than English. The children of the Bay factors and their staff often had the thick Scottish burr of their Orkney fathers as well as French and Cree words, giving them a distinctive way of speech.

Mr Bird was shocked at the condition of Bouvier and astounded that Marie Anne and Amie together had been able to nurse him so successfully. It now seemed more than probable that Bouvier would survive his ordeal and that his wounds would close over and heal in time, although he would be hideously scarred and crippled to the end of his life.

Bouvier was the most concerned. "How do I repay you good people, and you especially Madame Lajimoniere and Madame Belgrade, for the care you have taken of me? But what is to happen to me now? I am quite useless. I still think you would have done me a service by shooting me that night. I cannot hunt, so how can I live?"

Marie Anne and Amie both reached out together and took hold of a hand.

"It was God's will that we were able to help you and that you are recovering. You must never say such things again." Marie Anne took his hand in both of hers. "You are alive. How could the blessed saints and God himself not care for you?"

Amie was mystified at Marie's profession of faith but said nothing.

Mr Bird stepped in quickly. "There is always plenty of work to be done around here. Others can go to the forest and the plains for hunting. Others can gather the wood we need. But we have needs inside the fort itself. You can make us a few chairs and counters for the stores. That's something we need more of. We could do with a table in the company's dining area. I would appreciate a wooden bedstead. If you would take on carpentry jobs, we can keep you busy for a long time to come. I can put you on our rolls, so your food will be provided, and of course we will find you a place to sleep.

"There is no hurry for you to start," he went on. "Get your strength back first and find your way around. Get your bearings."

Bouvier turned his head towards the sound of Mr Bird's voice. "If I can honestly pull my weight, I'd be proud to serve you and the company," was all he could bring himself to say.

Mr Bird was as good as his word. As soon as he was able, Bouvier started in to work as the fort's carpenter on the payroll and as a maker of sturdy simple pieces of furniture. As it was obvious that Mr Bird was used to having things go his own way – he was, after all, the factor – the three Lajimonieres set up their teepee inside the stockade. There was a good possibility they might take over a log lean-to later.

Marie Anne unrolled her buffalo hides for the tent walls. She felt a slight regret at Jean's refusal of the lean-to, saying only, "Perhaps when winter sets in, it might be easier to keep ourselves warm."

Jean was not keen to try it.

Marie Anne shrugged her shoulders. "It might be a good deal colder here than Pembina," was her only comment. She continued to herself, "We'll have to wait and see what happens. There's just no way Jean wants to take up living inside a sturdy wall with a roof."

She was learning to be philosophical about Jean's reluctance to have any part of an existence that reminded him of back east and luxury. Now that she was becoming used to life as a semi-nomad herself, she could understand why he never wanted to return to the society they had both been brought up to respect. She was learning to love this life too, most of the time.

The Chalifous and the Paquins made their camp outside the stockade, as they had done together in previous years, and set about to make new friends and to be accepted amongst these western Cree. However, it was arranged that Belgrade and Amie with their children should, like the Lajimonieres, live inside the fort over the winter. Amie felt as relieved as Marie Anne. It was true that some of the encampments were Cree, but it was a branch of the tribe unknown to Amie, and she did not feel at ease with them as yet. She was not at all sure that she and Belgrade would be accepted by them simply because she was eastern Cree – a Cree of the Woods and not Cree of the Plains.

Amie was expecting her third baby sometime in the darkest part of the winter. She and Marie Anne had become ever closer and dependent on one another following their experiences shared over the summer, and she was pleased that her friend would be close by when her time came.

Amie and Marie Anne were soon put to work helping with the various tasks of nursing in the hospital, a rather grand name for a small draughty log cabin. Not only was it thought advisable for them to continue in their ministrations that had been so successful with Bouvier, but their reputations as tenders of the sick was so well established, it was enough for them to be left with a number of responsibilities.

When the two friends realized that the filthy bandages they found on the patients had first to be boiled in a heavy iron cauldron, and then scrubbed with harsh homemade soap rendered from buffalo fat and ashes from the fireplaces, and then rinsed in hot water, wrung out, and spread outdoors to dry, they both agreed the old Indian ways had more to recommend them than the laborious white man's. So off they trudged together to look for healing plants before the frost did its damage. They were often seen disappearing into the bush together with a willow basket to hunt for sphagnum moss and the night-willow herb. In the course of their wanderings, they often came across a number of plants that Amie recognized as having favourable uses.

One afternoon, as the two were filling their willow baskets with herbs to be dried for winter use, Amie turned to Marie Anne and said, "I feel better now about being away from the others. We can make good use of these plants, and I like helping out."

Marie Anne agreed. "And you help me so much too, Amie. I think we work well together."

Mr Bird insisted that both women dress in white woman's clothing while they worked in the infirmary.

Amie was nonplussed at what this required, but Marie Anne helped her stitch up a woollen skirt. She constantly tripped over the almost-floor-length skirt, and the sleeves of a linen shirt constantly got in her way. Along with a shawl and an apron, this made them, as Jean Baptiste put it the first time he caught sight of the two in their fancy get-ups, "ladies fit to be found in any gentleman's salon." Belgrade joined in and agreed with him, and Marie Anne laughed at his compliment.

Amie, for her part, was mystified at the whole affair, but if the white people required her to go about like this in return for a safer bed in which to lay her little ones and the baby she was carrying, so be it. "I'm not about to start an argument on the subject," she reasoned, "and I can still laugh at myself in this clumsy skirt. I find the shirt itchy, but Marie Anne says it will get better after it gets soaked in water a few times. Doeskin leggings make far more sense to me, and neither of us has given *them* up. We wear the white woman's get-up only around the infirmary or in Mr Bird's presence."

It was not only the Cree people she had never heard of that made Amie apprehensive. Fort of the Prairies, strategically situated to attract hunters from north, south, east, and west, and with its accessibility on the Saskatchewan, had become a meeting place for many tribes, some of them quite new, strange, and of extraordinary appearance to all the wives of Jean Baptiste's friends. Their superb horsemanship and their eagle-feathered headdresses, which trailed down their backs and even dragged along the ground behind them, were objects of curiosity to the Woodland Cree.

The Blackfeet were known by other tribes as raiders and traders. The Blackfeet themselves were quick to point out that the Assinniboines and the Bloods were just as apt as they to raid for a fast haul of better steeds. The Crees too were well known for their informal trading habits, much to the chagrin of the two fur companies. It was their custom to barter furs for whatever necessities and trinkets they could get in a haggling contest in the company store, and then take the trade goods out onto the prairies to find other bands who were not disposed to take the time to haul their furs into a fort. The Cree mark-ups were nothing short of scandalously exorbitant. The informal "middlemen" returned to the fort and were able to parlay their new crop of furs into yet more trading goods and spirits.

The Sarcees were in a more difficult position and were sometimes resented by the others. They had formerly made their home in the mountains farther to the west and north. Lack of game and a series of unusually bitter cold and long winters had forced them down onto the plains and farther south, where they found themselves in direct competition for hunting territory claimed by the many tribes who had been established for generations. Not everyone was generous enough to welcome ever more newcomers that put increased strain on decreasing herds.

The other tribes were of a single mind about one thing: They all agreed that the reputation the Cree had for dirt and general uncleanliness was well founded. Many were the jokes and personal remarks passed about the Cree living habits. Amie and her friends held up their heads and were silent. Marie Anne was furious when she heard the cruel remarks about her cronies.

"Perhaps some of the Crees around here are a mite casual about their housekeeping," she mentioned to Jean, "but no one can say that Amie doesn't get after her children, and Madame Chalifou and Madame Paquin too. They certainly try to keep things as neat as possible, which is not easy in a tent with the dogs as much underfoot as the children. Amie even goes after dear old Belgrade to straighten up and clean up some of his messes around the teepee.

"And anyway," she continued, "it's all a matter if degree. No one around here would pass a cleanliness test with your mother or mine, and that includes thee and me."

Jean laughed. Her remark struck him as both just and close to the mark. "I suspect both our mothers would be a bit critical if they could see us right at this moment," was his comment.

He picked up his knife again and resumed hacking bits of buffalo meat into chunks destined for Marie Anne's hide pot. Marie Anne smoothed some curls into place on top of her head and bent once more over the steaming pot, stirring carefully with her long-handled spoon, a wooden tool that Jean had whittled for her from basswood.

The Blackfeet had earned their reputation for trading. It was their custom to take the women and young with them while they went out hunting the buffalo on both the early hunt for the calves and the later one for the full-grown animals. The Blackfeet women were known as real gardeners and were famous for their crops. They collected porcupine quills and made them into decorative trappings for the objects they made for trading with the other women. Sometimes they bound the quills together with buffalo sinew to make brushes.

"No wonder they keep their hair looking so neat," observed Marie Anne. "They have real combs and brushes they have made themselves. And their moccasins are so pretty with the quills dyed and made into little tufts of flowers and leaves in such dainty patterns. Amie said she saw some lovely ones made of caribou hairs."

In no time at all, Marie Anne had acquired a comb made of cedar and a brush of porcupine quills. She took Reine down to the water, and together they had a good head wash. Then Marie Anne teased out the tangles in Reine's hair.

"She looks much more like a true Canadienne now that her topknot is clean and neat," Jean remarked.

"And so do I, in case you hadn't noticed," Marie answered as she put her hair into a thick plait that she wound around her head, fastening it with a hairpin carved out of tortoiseshell. "Now I shall need a looking glass to see how I look," she said coquettishly.

"You look fine, just like my queen," said Jean with pride in his voice. "You know, I think an occasional head wash and a good brushing do wonders for your appearance. That buffalo grease you ladies have been smoothing your heads with gets to have quite a fragrance about it."

Against the inside wall of the teepee, Marie Anne had stowed some old rolled up buffalo hides. They made something to sit on and were stored against future need. She transferred the marks she had made on the back of an old one to the back of a beaver pelt she had hung up as a sort of decoration.

This was her calendar. Each and every day since she had left home, she had made a mark on something, usually her sleeping robe, to mark another day. Whenever they had made a stop, she had conferred with the factor, contrasting her calendar with the official one. It was the only way she had to mark such important dates as saints' days and her own pregnancies.

As fall gave way to winter and the geese had long since flown away from the cold, the winds grew much stronger, snow fell in deep piles, and the two friends had to break ice at the river's edge to gather water in their hide pails. They were both most wary in passing the various Indian encampments. At the end of summer and again at the end of the fall buffalo hunt, the differing tribesmen were contented enough to accept each other, if not as brothers, at least without much bloodshed; by the depths of winter, however, it was a different story.

There was rancour about territorial rights for hunting and trapping the lucrative pelts. Hunters returning with a good haul that enabled them to tot up their "beavers," the form of money that the Bay used, could indulge themselves in a shopping spree. More and more, beavers to each hunter's credit in excess of what he needed to survive were used in exchange for spirits, usually rum or brandy, sometimes fortified wines. It was all strong stuff and helped to make small differences become the angry altercations that could be heard around the fort constantly. Fights broke out with a frequency that bordered on monotony, sometimes turning vicious enough to make an addition to the pile of corpses placed high on the burial hill behind the fort.

Mr Bird had been the unwilling and unhappy onlooker at some turbulent fights. It was his job to remain calm and in control of the combatants, an almost impossible task without a regiment of men, which he did not possess. He had a great reputation throughout the northwest as a most able factor, and no altercation of any kind was tolerated inside the fort. There were a few times when Marie Anne cowered inside her teepee. Together with Amie, she and the children formed a tight little knot, terrified at the shouting and gunfire. The two women were especially fearful when their menfolk were off on their hunting or trapping expeditions. At those times, it seemed to them both that no silky white ermine skin could possibly be worth what they were going through.

However, Jean and Belgrade were told that headquarters in London seemed especially keen to get as many winter ermine as they could. It had something to do with the court at London and the lavish way the titled folk dressed in immense robes lined with the white fur and the little black tail tip. Mr Bird thought it was probably a coronation or something that might be at hand. The men shook their heads but went off happily enough to find the pelts that were so particularly wanted and for which a good price was guaranteed.

Marie Anne and Amie always knew that once peace of a sort was restored even partially, there might be extra work for them over at the infirmary. As soon as their world was back in order, they hastened with the children clinging to them to take up their nursing responsibilities.

One cold snowy day, it suddenly occurred to Marie Anne that the Feast of the Nativity was approaching and should be upon them soon. She hastened off to Mr Bird to check her figures with his calendar and found that she was right. The Feast of the Nativity was but four days distant.

"Everyone gathers on Christmas Day in the fort," Mr Bird told her. "Of course you are expected. We all look forward to a party."

Marie Anne found herself dreading a get-together for all hands inside the stockade and in the factor's premises. Thinking back to the Christmas Eve gathering last year at Pembina, with the Canadians singing the familiar old carols, and then the feast on the day itself, with their music-making and general good-natured frivolity, she caught herself longing for the simpler ways of Pembina.

"So many more people around Fort of the Prairies and so much more drunkenness," she said to herself. "It makes the idea of a massed party something to dread."

Amie was also apprehensive. She was grateful for living within the stockade, but this had made it difficult for her to come to terms with her own people, remote as their relationship might be. Mr Bird's wife seemed unconcerned about the whole thing.

Jean and Belgrade also showed no concern. They had a great deal of confidence in Mr Bird's abilities. As it turned out, their confidence was justified. Mr Bird was far too astute a factor to let a feast-day party become a rout or a bloodbath of brawling drunken plainsmen reckoning up old scores. It was a quiet and decorous gathering for the employees of the Hudson's Bay Company and their special guests.

One week later, on the eve of the beginning of 1809, everyone joined in a rollicking Indian version of Scottish reels, and while there was plenty of grog to go round, the fiddler and the pipers kept the dances going so heartily that the revels never got out of hand. The New Year arrived in true Scottish tradition.

Then it was that Marie Anne was reminded forcefully that she had a daughter about to celebrate her first birthday on the Feast Day of the Three Kings, a festival not celebrated by the Scots at the fort. She wanted to mark Reine's day and do something special for her little one's first birthday. Reine had become a smiling chubby child, inquisitive and bright, and a darling with everybody. Marie Anne wondered how she could possibly make a present for Reine to let her know that the day was a special one. She had very few choices at hand.

Suddenly, it came to her. "Of course," she said. "I have been saying my rosary over her. I will make her a rosary all her own. She can wear it in a little pouch around her neck and as soon as she can follow me, I will teach her to repeat the prayers."

Marie Anne got out her supply of trade beads and added a few dried blueberries. She made a little cross out of porcupine needles and fastened it with some thread. Then she slipped beads, then a blueberry, more beads, another blueberry, and more beads onto a thread with the cross at its midpoint until she was satisfied she had done it correctly.

"You are so right, my Marie," said Jean when he saw what she had made. "There are some things we must never forget, and one of the most important is to make sure Reine knows her prayers and is brought up in our faith. We must make sure that Reine says her prayers each day just as we do."

Marie Anne fought back a few tears. Jean took her hand and together they knelt down and prayed. With his arm around her shoulder, he said, "We have much to be thankful for. Let us remember our blessings. We have each other and Reine as well."

"Somehow it seems easier to remember all the things we were brought up to practice when we are living under a roof and in the same place," Marie Anne said softly, glancing up at the beams of the lean-to they were now occupying. "Jean, will we ever have a roof, a solid one I mean, and of our own?"

Jean turned to her and studied her face, those strikingly blue eyes now so pleading. "Some day," he said. After a pause, he continued. "Some day I think this land will have traders on it, not only the Blackfeet and the Cree. Some day I am sure there will be settlers, white men and women, farmers, Canadians, with homesteads."

"Do you really think that?" Marie Anne was not sure whether he was imagining things or trying to make her happy, or if he believed what he was saying. "I hope so, Jean. I hope you are right. Do you really think that there will ever be a church anywhere near here? With priests?"

"I am sure of it, dear love," he said, and then responding to the longing in her face, he mumbled, "I don't know when. Maybe we won't even live to see it, but Reine will, of that I am sure."

He sounded so confident that Marie Anne was half-convinced. "I wonder when that will be," she murmured.

"In the meantime," he told her, "we must never forget our prayers."

Marie Anne sighed. "You seem very sure about all this. Have you been talking to Mr Bird?"

"Yes, dear heart, I have. It is Mr Bird's opinion that as the skin harvest is getting a little smaller each year, the company will want to bring out settlers to farm the plains. If they do not harvest furs, the lords of the Hudson's Bay Company will be looking for some other source of income, something they can sell at a profit. You can be sure of that.

"This land should be good for growing grains, if nothing else," he went on. "Look at the way the grasses come up. Besides, Mr Bird was telling me that in Scotland, where he comes from, there are many people being shut off the lands they have always farmed for generations. So sending them out here where there is so much space might possibly be what they have in mind."

"You must have been talking to Mr Bird a lot to have learned so much." Marie Anne managed a tight little smile. "It would be wonderful to think that someday our little Reine could learn her catechism properly and be married by a priest as we were. I do hope you and Mr Bird are right."

Marie Anne got to her feet and, in a no-nonsense voice, announced that she was going to see Amie. "Her baby is due any moment. She thinks it will be tonight, and as she was certainly right about Reine and me, I want to be with her at once. Please see that Reine is all right, dear Jean. And do try to get hold of Belgrade and Amie's children. Keep them away from her teepee. A birthing is no place for a father until it is over."

As good as her word, Marie Anne sat with Amie all the night through. Mrs Bird came by to see if she could help and stayed, as Mesdames Paquin and Chalifou were not welcome inside the stockade overnight. The two women took turns holding Amie's wrists and supporting her back as she sat up in her labour. With far less trouble and no necessity for a "quilling," Amie produced a black-eyed little hunter-to-be who bellowed his announcement to the world that he had joined its company. Belgrade rushed in to embrace Amie, overjoyed at the addition to his family.

Together, Marie Anne and Belgrade made the sign of the cross on the boy's forehead and christened him Jean like his father. From then on, he was known as Ti-Jean, a nickname for Petit Jean.

To Marie Anne's astonishment, Amie sat up straight, stretched her legs, and stood up. She smiled happily at both Belgrade and Marie Anne and calmly went about her morning's chores with her new little bundle, her black-eyed Ti-Jean, fast asleep on her back.

Marie Anne crept back to her own home and snuggled in beside Jean, who was not yet properly awake.

"Everything all right?" he asked sleepily.

"It's a boy, Jean. Belgrade and I made the sign of the cross on his forehead and named him Ti-Jean. They are both so happy. I hope my next one will be a boy. You would like that, wouldn't you, Jean? Jean?"

But already Jean had dropped back to sleep. And as for Reine, sleeping between them, she did not even stir. Marie Anne's news would have to wait.

CHAPTER 12

Amie enjoyed her experience as a nurse. She hadn't had time to become acquainted with the other trappers' wives, as Madame Chalifou and Madame Paquin had, but she rather enjoyed their occasional allusions to her exalted state. Both ladies were intrigued by her new clothing. The long skirt certainly got in the way when she took her buckets down to the river for the Belgrade water supply, but she learned quickly how not to trip over it on the climb back to the fort. Her two old companions and their new friends had been quick to point at her and giggle over her new airs and graces. Now she felt herself almost on a social par with the factor's wife, living inside the fort. The Lajimonieres' lean-to was close by the infirmary, and so the Belgrades put up their teepee to be handy to both.

However, when winter settled in for good and the steep path to the river was slushy and icy, both Amie and Marie Anne were happy to get out their doeskin leggings and shifts. Since the factor insisted on long skirts within the fort, Marie Anne and Amie wore their leggings and then hitched the skirts up over their shoulders as a sort of mantle as soon as they were out of range of Mr Bird's vision.

Mesdames Chalifou and Paquin were greatly entertained and brought the rest of the Cree ladies to come and watch. When the two friends reached the fort entrance, they put down their buckets and flipped their skirts back over the leggings. The other women never failed to find this hilarious.

When she thought about it all, Marie Anne could see the funny side of the situation. Josette might have giggled too, perhaps in embarrassment as much as anything, but Maman and Father Vinet's housekeeper? Oh merciful heavens! What would they have thought? Marie Anne shrugged and picked up her buckets. She couldn't help a little giggle at the picture in her mind.

"It's a different world out here," she mused as she slithered down the icy path. "And it's been such a good winter for the furs. I wonder if Mr Bird is right about their becoming scarcer. I wonder if Jean will ever think of going back to Canada."

She gripped the buckets harder and made them more comfortable on her cold hands. "Stay close by me, p'tite," she said to Reine, who was busy sliding about on the icy patch, falling down and laughing.

"What a pity to bring her indoors when she is having so much fun and her cheeks are so rosy!" thought Marie Anne. "It does me good to hear her laughing, but Mr Bird told me to keep her by me all the time, indoors and out. Doors! That old saying sounds ridiculous to me now that my door is just a flap of hide."

She turned to Reine. "Come along, p'tite. We have to go home now, and you can watch me scrape Daddy's lovely soft white furs."

Marie Anne paused. It was the first time she had used the word *home* to mean anything other than Maskinongé. "I am becoming a real *hivernante*, or maybe a real Indian woman," she thought. "But I'm still a Christian Indian woman. That makes a difference. And I'm going to have another little Christian before winter sets in again, that's for sure."

Mother and daughter trudged across the barracks square. Marie Anne held aside the buffalo skin that stood for the fourth wall of their home as well as a doorway and waited for Reine to catch up. Together mother and daughter disappeared into the gloomy dark shelter.

Working inside the hospital gave Amie an opportunity to get to understand and assess the white people's utensils. She decided that her old buffalo hide pot needed renewing. She found it more out-of-date and smelly each day. Now it became her custom just to happen to have to saunter past the factor's store at least once a day. Frequently she dropped in to look over the trade goods piled high on the shelves. What had particularly caught her eye was a large iron kettle. She came into the store to stare at it and to covet it. She determined that she going to persuade her good man to get it for her. She just had to wait for the right opportunity.

At length it came. When Belgrade came home for a few days, gloating with satisfaction at his and Jean Baptiste's recent success and while helping her clean and board his pelts, Amie decided this was the moment. She hid her old hide pot, the one that had been oiled and re-oiled, stitched and re-stitched with sinew, until it was hard to find places for new holes. It was blackened and filthy from a couple of years of hard use as well as getting battered about on the family travels.

When Jean Belgrade suggested it was time she rendered some fat for him to soften the boarded skins, she became the nonplussed housewife, unable to comprehend what could have happened to the dirty old thing.

Belgrade laughed at her. "You have been looking at those iron pots up at the store. Have you tried to lift one? Do you know how heavy those kettles are?"

Amie grinned at him in a way that said louder than words that she was more than willing to pick one up and find out for herself, but maybe not put it down again.

"*D'accord*," he said, grinning back at her. "You get your pot. Go pick it up and tell Mr Bird to put it on my account."

Jean Baptiste smiled at Marie Anne when she told him about Amie's strategy.

"I suppose you want one too, my dear. At least an iron pot won't smell the place up the way that hide does. I was going to suggest that you throw out that horror this summer, and we would see about a new one after the second buffalo hunt." He laughed and continued with a bow, "Now that we are living in the height of luxury in our own shack, you had better get one like Amie's. Otherwise you will want to borrow hers, and that spells trouble."

Amie and Marie Anne exchanged knowing grins that became chortles as soon as they had put a little distance between themselves and their husbands. They had set out a well-laid trap, and it had worked as smoothly as the snares and traps their menfolk used for the furry beasts. The pair soon came back, each lugging a large, heavy, and unwieldy iron kettle and feeling well pleased with herself.

Jean Baptiste and Belgrade exchanged a rather rueful smile, and each raised an eyebrow. "Guess who will be carrying that thing over any portages we have to make," said Jean.

Belgrade winked. "Especially if it's full of meat."

Jean Baptiste could only shrug. Lean-to living and being on the inside of a stockade was making them soft, in his opinion. But he thought it best not to make his opinion known on that score.

The two women celebrated their new kitchenware by serving up rabbit stew in the latest fashion in *haute cuisine* – rabbits they had caught themselves in their snares before the men had arrived back from their trapping. They had already divided up the skins for Amie's new papoose and moccasin linings for Reine, whose baby toes seemed to her mother to be growing every day.

On one fine sunny day, Marie Anne was sure that she heard a crow. Amie came running full of excitement, for she had heard it too. Winter seemed to have dragged on much longer in Fort of the Prairies than down south in Pembina. So it was that spring had crept up so surreptitiously they had been caught unawares. But when they both looked at the reddened tips of the birch trees glowing in the long rays of the sun, they knew that winter was surely passing at last.

"Time to be thinking of setting out on the spring calf hunt, ladies," said Jean Baptiste one morning when the earliest of the flowers, some crocuses, came pushing their way up through what was left of the rotten snow. "Winter has gone for good. At least until after next fall."

"Jean, I tried to tell you, but you were sound asleep. The night that Amie had Ti-Jean, I counted the moons the way Amie does, and now I am sure. I think we will have a little hunter for you right after the late buffalo hunt," she whispered.

Jean Baptiste let out one of his famous noisy whoops of joy, picked up his wife, and kissed her soundly in front of the Belgrades. Jean gave him a sound thwack on the back, and Amie said quietly, "I thought so."

Accordingly, Belgrade and Jean Baptiste started making their preparations. First of all, they had to trade with their Indian neighbours for horses. They were able to get good strong ones, partly of European stock, that were more highly valued for hauling skins on a travois than the lighter but faster western ponies.

This year, the two friends decided to go together, just the two of them. Chalifou and Paquin had arranged to go with a party of Cree with whom they had been living over the winter outside the stockade. Jean Baptiste and Belgrade, from their exalted social position inside the stockade, were not sure of their welcome despite their reputations for bravery and horsemanship, both skills essential on the buffalo hunt.

The women all went with their menfolk out onto the plains. For the Cree, it meant the enactment of their spiritual ceremonies in the lodges they set up for the summer months. The boys were expected to perform deeds that taxed them to the utmost in order to prove that they had the discipline to become courageous members of their tribe. It was at the summertime religious observances that the boys were suspended by long shafts of sinew through their chests and fastened to the topmost part of the sacred lodge.

The boy was swung round and round the lodge with all the members of the tribe watching. He was expected to ignore pain entirely. Only after the completion of his ordeal would he be allowed to marry and become a full member of the tribe, a brave in every sense of the word. Marie Anne tried not to think about what to her was sheer barbarism and observed that Amie was a bit chagrined at having to miss the festival.

"Festival," thought Marie Anne. "Lord, have mercy."

Amie was sad to see her friends departing without her. Chalifou and Paquin were not expected to enter the brotherhood of the hunting party in the religious observances, but they would take part in every other aspect of tribal life. Amie was loath to miss the celebrations and general festivities. They were, after all, her people.

Marie Anne could see that Amie felt a bit cut off and was saddened for her friend. She of all women knew what being totally cut off from family could mean. She was also torn to see Madame Chalifou and Madame Paquin go off on their separate way. They had all been of such great help to her in her first winter and had shown her so much kindness. Yet, with much tearing at her heart, Marie Anne recognized that the Paquin and Chalifou children, baptized by their fathers as they certainly had been, were not what she wanted for Reine to accept as the normal way to live.

"I can't become an Indian," she thought. "I'm not an Indian, and I don't want Reine not to know the difference between Indian and Canadian. I don't like to think like this. But there it is, and I don't want to try to change Amie and the others. They are Indian. The country wives of the company men all try to act as though they are white. They get their men to buy them not just beads but all kinds of fancy things, like jewellery. Even earrings. Earrings!"

Marie Anne paused in her thoughts, conjuring up a picture of Mrs Bird looking to her mind ridiculous out here in the western deserts with her fancy clothing and her fancy ways. She shrugged. "Oh well. She's Mr Bird's wife and no responsibility of mine. But imagine wanting to get so dressed up out here. And that cloth her clothes are made of, the best in the whole store. Such a price!"

Marie Anne sat down. "That woollen cloth looks really warm but is so expensive. If only I had a few sheep, as we had back in Maskinongé, I could make woollens just as warm. I used to be a good spinner at one time. Wouldn't I love to knit some caps and toques and mittens? Hide mitts are better than nothing, of course, but knitted woollens are so much easier to work in and much cosier."

She stood up and reached for her goose wing in preparation for doing some housework, trying to get some of the dirt festooned around the upper parts of the hides that made a furry wall hanging,

"Well, wishing won't make it so," she thought as she brushed. "And there are no sheep around here for at least four months travelling that I know of, so there is scant chance any of them will wander into the stockade today. I might just as well forget my reveries. And much as I want to see Maskinongé again some day, it only upsets Jean when I mention it. He seems so like a young boy sometimes. But then that's one of the things I do love about him."

After some discussion of where they thought the best chance would be for the two of them to get all the skins they needed, Jean and Belgrade decided to work their way in a south-easterly direction. The grass should be more advanced than up where they had wintered and hence more succulent. Possibly the calves might be born a little earlier.

With minds made up in complete agreement, Jean Baptiste and Belgrade were anxious to be off at once, if not sooner. The women looked at each other and smiled in understanding. How like their impetuous men, they seemed to say to one another, and they turned at once to their packing chores. Marie Anne took time to run over to the infirmary and bid goodbye to Bouvier. She could see he would have dearly liked to come with them. That was impossible, of course, but he did pat her hand and wish her Godspeed.

In record time, the two hunters, wives, children, dogs, and horses set off with the morning sun on their left side to go south to hunt for calves – the spring hunt. As well as fresh meat, the calves provided the soft skins that were used for robes for the children and for storage sacks. Pemmican made later in the summer hunt was stored for winter use in the stomachs of the mature buffaloes.

As she jogged along on her horse, Marie Anne could understand why Jean loved to be off. Horse riding was a novelty to her, but she learned quickly. With Reine on a *panier* on one side and a three-day supply of meat on the other as a sort of balance, she started counting carefully on her fingers, one by one, hanging on to the reins as she did so. She was really sure, but she wanted to go over the days once more to figure when the little hunter she knew Jean was longing for would make his appearance.

"Sometime in the late fall," she said over and over to herself.

If she had made a mistake, she could not bear to give him such a disappointment, and anyway right now he and Belgrade were thinking only of the hunt ahead of them, a rather dangerous undertaking for only two men. The Indians liked to go out in a huge party so that they could surround the herd and separate a calf, itself herded into a tight circle with the cows and surrounded by the menacing great shaggy beasts facing outward, altogether a daunting prospect for only a pair of humans.

After riding south for four or five days, the two friends decided to make camp at what they considered a likely place for their headquarters. There was water nearby in a copse and a stand of caraganas to give shade when the summer became unbearably hot for the women and children. The women unrolled their hides, and the men cut saplings to use as supports for the hides to make a teepee. The shelters went up quickly, the horses were seen to, and the encampment was ready to be lived in. Amie and Marie Anne set off to the water hole to catch minnows in their buckets. There was corn to be planted with a small fish in each hill.

"Good for the corn, so a Blackfeet squaw told me," said Amie. "They always have good gardens, so I'm told, and I'm keen to try it."

The beans, squash, and pumpkin seeds went in next. Then the two women with Amie's toddlers and their papooses trotted off to the river to cut new shoots of willow. From the stripped willow poles, they wove themselves new baskets and backrests. It took them about a week to get their lodgings arranged to their liking and their gardens planted.

When finally they could look over their labours and feel satisfied, Marie Anne and Amie seated themselves on the ground between their teepees to enjoy a sunny respite from their work and to try out the backrests. They sat playing with the children and laughing together at the comical antics the children were getting up to, enjoying some leisure and both utterly relaxed.

Suddenly, Amie sat up alert and alarmed. "I hear hoof beats," she said. She stood up and shaded her eyes looking around in all directions. There was real alarm in her voice now. "Many hoof beats. Too many for our men! Too many for our horses!" She gasped in terror. "Look at the dust. Eeeeh!" she screamed and scooped up her baby, Marie Anne's toddler, and her own two young ones. With arms and legs sticking out at all angles from her clasped arms, she darted like a mother hen into the caragana thicket.

She bade the children all crouch down like baby plovers and, just like the baby birds, not move the tiniest bit until she told them they could. She grabbed a low-hanging branch and held it down and over, as though she were covering a nest, and crouched down herself almost on top of them. It all happened in seconds. If Marie Anne had not seen what happened, she would have thought they had vanished into the thinnest of thin air. Like magic, Amie had simply gone and taken the children with her.

When Marie Anne got hold of her senses, she saw a party of at least twenty braves – she could not tell which tribe – trotting up towards her and obviously intending to take a close look at these two lodges out all by themselves. Marie Anne thought at first they were Cree, but she couldn't be sure. Were they friends from the fort, or ... Marie Anne flew into the closer teepee.

She knelt down on the ground in the middle of the tent and got out her rosary with her hands trembling so much she had to hang on to it tightly lest she drop it. She prayed as she had never prayed before in her life. She repeated the rosary over and over with her whole heart. She prayed to every saint she could remember to spare her so she might bring up Reine. She prayed that Reine might be spared, and Amie and her babies. She kissed her medal and prayed every prayer she knew. With her hands clasped together, she implored every saint in heaven to show mercy to her and to Reine. Her head was bowed to her knees.

The flap of the tent was flung aside, and the sound of two heavy feet stamping inside made her cower even lower in terror. The noise ceased abruptly, and Marie Anne could almost feel a tomahawk coming down to crush her skull.

There was absolute silence in the tent. But nothing happened. The silence persisted. Terror and a little curiosity mixed themselves up in Marie Anne's mind, and without knowing what she was doing, she slowly, very slowly, raised her head and opened her eyes.

There were two brightly beaded moccasins, large ones, almost touching her knees. The reality of those two big feet six inches away from her suddenly made her lean back on her heels and stare up, all the way up, to the dark bronzed face of a very tall man, who in turn stared down at her, seemingly transfixed by the sight of a young white woman staring up at him. How long they both held this pose like two statues of stone, Marie Anne could never estimate afterwards. It seemed like eternity to her, but it couldn't have been more than a couple of seconds.

Abruptly, this imposing figure turned on his heel with his eagle headdress swinging around behind him, the feathers brushing hard against Marie Anne's knees and trailing in the dust of the ground. Marie Anne thought that her heart would surely stop then and there. She began to fall over sideways in a faint and instinctively covered her face with both hands, pushing out an elbow to break the fall.

A man's voice speaking in French brought her back to full consciousness. She thought she was imagining things. For a moment, she thought she would faint again. Taking a deep breath and making the sign of the cross to bolster her courage, she opened her eyes.

To say that she had been amazed when confronted by the Cree chief dressed in his full ceremonial regalia, and that he had left the teepee without touching her, would be understating the truth. But now to hear what appeared to be an Indian brave speak to her in perfect French completely unnerved her. Her shoulders shook. Her hands shook as she tried to wipe away the tears to look again at this apparition.

The brave spoke gently, realizing her distress. "My name is Batoche Letendre," he said. "I came out to the western countries as a voyageur, an *hivernant*, like your husband, I presume. I took a Cree wife, and now I am admitted to her band. So you see, I have become one of them."

Years of living out on the grasslands had tanned him, until now, except for his curly black hair, he looked no different from his fellow Crees.

"The chief was startled to find a woman by herself in a tent, and even more astounded to discover her white skin and blue eyes. You must realize, Madame, that he has never imagined in his dreams that such a human creature as you existed," he went on. "In fact, he wondered if you were human or some kind of spirit. So that is why he left the tent so abruptly and ordered me, his brave, a white skin, to question this strange creature.

"You must admit, Madame," Batoche smiled as he spoke, "with your hair plaited around your head like that like the colour of the grasses ripening, you do appear almost like a holy statue."

Batoche went on to tell her that he had been sent to see if perhaps she spoke the tongue of the Cree. He tried to reassure the pretty Madame Lajmoniere that the chief only wanted to assure himself that there were no enemies lurking in the lodges, and having found only herself, he had told Batoche to tell the white woman that he intended to do her no harm.

Now it was Batoche's turn to question Marie Anne. Trying hard to control the tremble in her voice, she said, "There are only two Canadians, and they are hunting down buffalo calves," she told him. "I am sure they will be back before darkness."

He bowed. It raced through Marie Anne's mind that to see an Indian brave in his facepaint bowing as though he were back east in some gracious salon was somehow all a part of this mad dream she was living through.

"I've lived with these Indians a long time now, and I am sure no harm will come to you, Madame. The chief has given his word that he intends you no injury. You must remember that you came as a great surprise to him. He had never seen a white woman in his life before, and he had never imagined that such a woman could exist."

Batoche smiled, bowed, and made his exit from the teepee.

Marie Anne still thought she might have imagined the whole episode. But no, she thought, suddenly remembering Amie's frenzied dash to the copse. The sounds of horses snuffling and whinnying and the noise of the men chatting over what to them was an extraordinary happening made her realize that it was no dream. She had encountered a tribe of Cree headed to the summer festivities in their best finery, and had somehow, by the grace of God, survived. Once more, the rosary came out of its pouch, and she gave her thanks. Too terrified to leave the lodge until she heard the braves depart, Marie Anne remained in her kneeling position motionless and listening in agony for any sound that might give away the presence of Reine and Amie.

Marie Anne patted her stomach. "Stay still, little one, I beg you. In God's mercy, do not move."

All day long, Amie and the children remained motionless and silent. When much of the heat had gone from the sun and its rays were lengthening, throwing long shadows on the grasses, Marie Anne peeped out of the lodge without moving her legs. It should be getting time for Jean and Belgrade to be back, she kept thinking. And what of them? Had they met a with a similar band, not so kindly disposed towards a couple of white men hunting in what they considered to be their territory?

At length, just as Marie Anne was on the point of breaking up and in her agony imagining that terrible things had happened, Jean Baptiste rode up and saluted the large company of visitors around his lodge. Belgrade rode up behind him. Both men then remained silent, staring about them intently for any small sign, any detail, to give them an inkling of the fate of their wives and children.

The visitors in their turn were lounging about on the grass, smoking and chatting and generally making a most pleasant picture with their horses tethered nearby cropping contentedly. The beauty of the group portrait at leisure was entirely lost on the two Canadians. More braves joined the group. They had been down at the river's bank. Horses from another direction whinnied and stamped and snuffled. The hair rose on the backs of their necks. There were a lot more men here than they had at first realized.

There was complete and dreadful silence from within the lodges and no trace whatsoever of their families.

The visitors stared at the newcomers and waited for them to speak. Batoche tried to make a signal to the other Canadians, but they did not recognize him as anybody other than a brave like the rest. He was so tanned he could have been Indian or Metis.

Jean Baptiste could not bear the tension, the not knowing, any longer. He bellowed out, "Marie Anne? Marie? Are you still alive?"

From inside the teepee came a tremulous little voice. "Yes, I'm alive. But I'm dying of fear."

Until she heard his voice, she did not know that Jean had returned. Now she was almost physically sick with fear, both for herself and for Jean confronting that entire band.

Jean approached the chief and bowed. He and Belgrade could both make themselves understood in at least one Cree dialect, the Tongue, which with small differences had become a sort of lingua franca amongst both Indians and whites. They assured their visitors that they had arrived at their lodges and that they wished to establish friendship with the assemblage. At a signal from the chief, Batoche spoke up in French, to the astonishment of Jean and Belgrade. They had heard of compatriots going "native," but as far as they knew it was a rarity. Batoche was the first Canadian-turned-Indian they had encountered. The conversation turned into a rather florid declaration on both sides.

Throughout the exchange, Belgrade wondered with dread what had happened to Amie and his children. He thought it most probable that at best, she had been taken hostage, perhaps even killed. He kept silent to see what the outcome of the extended greetings would be. It hardly crossed his mind that Amie could have escaped unharmed and was hiding.

From time to time, the two Canadians looked at one another trying to get a message across without words or gestures. *Where is Amie? Where are the children?* the looks said.

Jean was particularly wary, because although he had heard Marie Anne's voice so weak and fearful, there had been no sound from wee Reine. He was sick at heart wondering if Marie Anne had been tortured, and if Reine had been massacred along with Amie and her children.

In spite of his anxiety, Jean Baptiste used his famous charm on the chief. With the help of Batoche, he managed to convince the Cree that he and his companion were alone on the hunt and that they bore only the greatest good will to the chief and his band. The chief nodded and indicated that they would set up their encampment beside the Canadians for the night. He further stated that the Canadians were invited to partake of a feast with them and to join in afterwards with dances and general celebration around the fire. Both men bowed their profoundest thanks for the honour. Jean asked, however, if it would not offend the band if he might camp a little further away from them, as his wife was ill and needed rest without disturbance.

The chief considered the request. Then, after some pondering, he assured Jean Baptiste that since they were now friends, and he nodded around at each of his braves to indicate that none of them wished the slightest harm to come to their friend and the strange white-faced lady, he gave permission for Jean and Belgrade to break their camp and take Marie Anne farther away.

Amie, meanwhile, had raised her head just sufficiently to watch from her hiding place all that was going on. As soon as she thought she heard the chief give permission for Belgrade and Jean to break camp and move, she gave her tiny signal, uncovered her nestlings, and brought them all, still very frightened, into the camp to stand beside Belgrade.

His relief at the sight of Amie leading the little ones, carrying her papoose and Reine, all stepping with silence and with dignity inside the circle of braves to take her place beside her man, was so great he almost broke down and wept. It was the hardest thing he had ever done to maintain his self-control and stand stoically so as not to lose face with these people who had a completely different attitude towards their women, whom they regarded as useful in many ways of course but not to be compared in importance with men or a good horse.

As for Marie Anne, when Jean came into the lodge to fetch her, she all but fainted away again for the third time that day. Her relief and joy when she could at last hold Reine in her arms was so great she sobbed and laughed at the same time.

The four friends packed up their belongings with all the speed they could. Marie Anne's hands were still shaking, and neither of the men looked as cool as usual. There were no jokes passed and no gaiety, only a heartfelt relief that drained them all. To be off and away was everyone's first concern.

When they had everything packed up and had bade ceremonial goodbyes and wishes of never-ending friendship with the Cree, the four friends mounted their horses and rode off. After they had ridden four or five miles, they decided they had gone far enough. Quietly and silently, they made a new encampment, not as grand as the one they had left but good enough for their needs. Then the two men collapsed, congratulating each other that there had been no casualties, just a bad scare, no lasting harm done, but that it had been a close call. That was certainly true.

Marie Anne could not feel as sanguine as the men seemed to be. What would have happened if Batoche Letendre hadn't happened to be along? How many hunting parties were there all around them? Were these Cree on the warpath? Were their enemies next on the visiting list? Before crawling under their buffalo robe, Marie Anne and Jean knelt down reverently to give thanks as well as their usual prayers.

At last, Marie Anne's tears could flow naturally. She had held them back all day, and now the relief of being able to bed down in peace and physically unharmed with Jean and little Reine between them was too much. She sobbed for some time as Jean held her close and gently stroked her until she lay quietly. It was a pair of thankful parents who laid their daughter protectively within their embrace.

Marie Anne's last thoughts, as she drifted into a sleep of exhaustion, was that there must be a special providence, a company of angels, guarding her and her dear family. Her prayers had been answered, and they were safe for the night at any rate.

Next day, the men decided to break camp again and head back slowly to Fort of the Prairies, hoping for the best in the way of calf hunting along the route. They had planned to stay out in their encampment all summer, but that was now out of the question.

With the danger over, Amie was more upset at having to leave her neatly planted garden than by the terror she had undergone. Being part of a large group took on added importance to her. "It is not good for two women and their children to depend on just two men," she thought. She felt more conscious of her Cree upbringing than of being the pampered wife of one man, even if he did have white skin.

Marie Anne too was thoughtful riding back to Fort of the Prairies. The whole tribal way of existing seemed wrong to her and quite opposed to her religious feelings, but she could see as well how vulnerable two lone women out on the grasslands with only children and a horse or two could become.

"Without Jean, how could I manage?" she thought over and over. Not for the first time, Marie Anne ended her thinking by declaiming, "I'm not an Indian woman. I'm not Cree. I'm a white woman, and I married a Christian in a church blessed by a priest."

CHAPTER 13

Because their hunting had been cut short, the men had not been able to obtain as many calves as they had hoped for, yet the party still had to make a slow and laborious trek back to Fort of the Prairies. It took the best part of a week, and try as she might, Marie Anne found it difficult to keep up the pace she knew they all wanted. She was still nervous and very weary after her terrifying encounter with the Cree band. Jean helped her all he could, but he had the horse with the travois to lead. The Belgrades were similarly laden, so there was nothing for it but to keep on going, with each doing his or her part.

Both Amie and Marie Anne felt they had developed longer ears, the better to hear any sound which could signal the onslaught of a band of braves galloping up with ideas of fun at the expense of the weaker group on their minds.

"Please God, give me strength" was an almost constant prayer on Marie Anne's lips for the duration of the trip back to the fort.

Amie tried hard not to show her concerns and her worries, but Marie Anne could tell she was depressed. More than ever, she was realizing the value of safety in numbers and the sense of security in being part of a large group of plainsmen and their families in these dangerous summer hunts.

"I hate to see Amie so concerned," Marie Anne was thinking to herself, even as she was almost falling off her horse sound asleep. "It's almost like having one of my real sisters with me. This last two years has given us so much to share, and I feel very close to her. She is a true friend, and I know that she is missing her own people. What will become of us all?"

She dug her knees into the horse's flanks, trying to catch up with the others, and shook off her almost overpowering urge to slither off the horse and curl up wherever she was and sleep.

Belgrade had taken charge of the larger travois that was laden more lightly than they wished with the calf hides. The Belgrades' dogs ran alongside, their tongues hanging sideways out of their mouths. From time to time Amie's elder daughter was allowed to ride on top of the hides, bouncing along as the travois was dragged and appearing to enjoy it. How she managed to hang on was a mystery to Marie Anne, but the little girl, young as she was, appeared to be quite capable of taking care of herself. However, someone always had to ride along bringing up the rear behind the travois to make sure she was not suddenly caught unawares and flung off her perch onto the vast expanse of tall grass. It was now so high that she could not have been seen, even if she waved her arms over her head.

Occasionally they came across a prairie-dog townsite. The Belgrades' dogs flew off in a wild melee of chasing and barking. They all laughed heartily at the dogs' disappointment and their persistence in the chase when it was perfectly obvious that the prairie dogs would always outwit them.

No sooner had a prairie dog slipped tail-first down into his front entranceway and a Belgrade dog stood yapping over the hole than another one or two would appear from another hole, hurling a great deal of prairie-dog invective at the dogs in outraged squeaks. Then the onslaught began all over again and the little fellows, twitching their noses in defiance and rage, would slip down through a hole into the tunnels of their underground town, where they were perfectly safe until the most curious of them would raise a head and shoulders to peer around and see if the coast had cleared.

Watching the antics of both sets of dogs made a break in the routine and was welcomed as a rest stop by everyone. Marie Anne frequently dropped back to the end of the line. Looking out for Amie's daughter was her excuse, but it was now obvious that she was pregnant. It made the long hours of riding more wearying for her than she cared to admit to Jean or even to her confidante, Amie. From her vantage point at the rear, she could see all too well how puny and vulnerable the expedition would appear to marauders.

It was nearing midsummer when they returned to Fort of the Prairies. The two hunters planned to stay only for a short period until they had to ride out once again for the late summer hunt, the important one, indeed the crucial one that yielded them their store of meat for the winter. A bad year in the late summer hunt had more than once brought starvation to those who depended so utterly on pemmican.

The men were far from idle after their return, and on at least two occasions, rode out by themselves to the early summer lodge site to check on the women's plantings, although they did not admit to going out of their way to do so. Their main purpose was to hunt down a calf or two, even though it was getting late in the season for the prime skins. They also wanted to keep tabs on the major buffalo movements so that they would have a chance of bringing down a sufficient number of adults to feed their growing families. Another reason, of course, was to try to track the various band movements so hopefully another confrontation could be avoided.

In the meantime, the two women were kept busy stretching and boarding skins, working them into pliancy by pounding fat into the skin side. The calf hides being so much softer than the adult skins, they were used for the children's moccasins even though they did not wear as well. Calf hides were also made into sacks for storage of small skins and supplies, but not for pemmican, which customarily was stuffed into the buffalo stomachs.

When August was more than half spent, the little company set out once more for the open plains. Both women were fearful. They knew their men would be facing considerable danger, as all the hunters they knew went out in pursuit of the massive beasts in a large force. Belgrade and Jean Baptiste believed they could manage alone by wile and ingenuity rather than brute scaring tactics and preferred to do it their way.

Accordingly, they journeyed south and somewhat east again and arrived where their earlier camp had been pitched. Then they decided to pitch camp farther down the river. The old one still had memories best forgotten for them all, but both women wanted access to their crops and to harvest what they could find. The men felt that the Cree band, even if they were still in the vicinity, would be unlikely to pay another call unless to renew their plights of friendship, their curiosity having been satisfied.

To their delight, Marie Anne and Amie found that their plantation was doing well. The little stand of corn was tall with many a cob. The beans were well ripe, and squash had spread runners in every direction. They swooped down upon their garden gathering everything together, and with the help of the men transported the entire harvest back to the campsite, to be thoroughly dried in the sunshine. They knew that as soon as the buffaloes were dragged back to the camp, their work would be cut out for them butchering, slicing the meat for smoking, scraping hides, and rendering fat in their precious new iron pots. It was a task to make the eyes run with the smoke from the fires and their backs ache with lifting heavy chunks of meat and the hides, not to mention the iron pots. As it turned out, Jean and Belgrade obtained what they figured they needed without mishap, and the women were so fully occupied with their pemmican preparations they had no time to waste their thoughts on visiting warriors.

On the last night out before the return to Fort of the Prairies for the winter, the two hunters sat themselves down before the fire and leaned back on the willow backrests the women had made earlier in the summer. They were staying out of the way of the busy wives, who were seeing to the last of the preserving and keeping an eye on the children. Each man felt he had earned some relaxation after hard rides and tricky manoeuvres on horseback. They smoked their pipes in contentment and chatted. Both agreed that while the hunt had been successful, it was certainly not as easy to track down buffaloes as it seemed to be in their memories of three and four years gone by. And certainly it did not compare with the way the real old-timers told it.

They shook their heads. "Too many hunters," said Jean Baptiste, relighting his pipe and stretching his long legs.

"Too much killing," said Belgrade. "The Indians are all after that firewater too much. Have you noticed that there are a lot more fights breaking out nowadays?"

"Things are changing, all right," agreed Jean. "Have you heard them talking about killing a buffalo only for the tongue? I know it's their greatest treat, but to leave the rest of the animal dead and rotting … Well, I don't know. It's not the same anymore."

Belgrade nodded. "It's these drives that are so wasteful, forcing and scaring an entire herd into stampeding over a cliff, and then, as you say, cutting out the tongues and leaving the rest. Things can't go on this way."

Marie Anne, despite her busy hands, listened intently. Could it mean that there was a possibility that Jean would give up this kind of living, camping out, travelling from place to place, always on the move, leaving her so much alone all winter? But if he weren't hunting, what would he do? Hunting was his whole life. It was all he knew.

"It's going to be harder with the two babies," she thought, straightening her back and rubbing a sore place. "I must stop thinking of Reine as a baby. She's our little girl now."

Gathering up that little girl in her arms, she thought, "Reine will soon be too big to lift, and right now I need more rest." She turned and made her way into the teepee with the sleepy child on her hip.

At a reasonable hour the next morning, all four adults tumbled out of their sleeping robes and emerged from their lodges, stretching and yawning in the bright sunshine.

"We are getting to be lazy sleep-ins," grinned Belgrade.

After a wash and deciding to make the first meal where they were instead of later on their way, they had a hasty breakfast and then set to work packing up their belongings, the bulk of their larder for the winter, and the new hides.

Amie and Marie Anne mounted their horses. The men fixed the travois, making use of the tent poles. The packhorses were readied, and the men mounted their beasts. It was a cumbersome affair with the men riding and leading the pack animals. The strongest and sturdiest were chosen to bear the loads and pull the travois. Marie Anne had two saddlebags. Reine rode in one, and in the other was the meat they would need for the next three or four days' ride back to the fort. The little company of Canadian plainsmen set off at a slow and easy pace.

Suddenly, with no warning, Marie Anne's horse, trained to the buffalo hunt and lighter and swifter than the pack animals, snuffled the breeze. He was spooked. With ears laid back he started and reared, turned, and took off in a southerly direction, the scent of buffalo on the hoof bringing him to a full gallop. With whinnying screams, he seemed headed for the horizon and beyond, mane and tail flying as though all the winged horses of myth and legend were behind him trying to grab his tail.

When Marie Anne had caught her breath and realized what was happening, she dug her knees into the beast's flanks as hard as she could, ignoring the sudden knifelike pain in her groin. With one hand around Reine's neck to try to prevent her from being pitched right out of the saddlebag in this headlong rush, she grabbed as much mane as she could with the other, twisting it around her wrist and yanking and pulling with all her strength. She jerked on the reins. She thought she would pull the beast's mane right off its neck, but it only excited the hysterical horse and made him gallop faster. She had no stirrups, only her knees and one arm — that and grim determination to hang on at all costs.

She had no idea where she was going, just the thought ringing in her head: "Hold on! Hold on! Don't fall! Hang on for dear life!"

Marie Anne's horse was so frenzied that it was doubtful if it even felt her restraining attempts. She screamed, and he whinnied. Then she saw with horror that he was heading directly into a herd of buffalo. The air was already filled with the dust of their pounding hooves as they arranged themselves into their protecting circle. When she could see at all, Marie Anne could make out the heads lowered in the attack position and those menacing horns gleaming most eerily in the sunlight fractured by dust everywhere.

The instant the horse had reared and turned, Jean threw his leading reins to Belgrade and dug his heels into his horse, shouting to it as he did so. Horse and rider flew across the plains. He saw Marie Anne disappear between two of the enraged beasts. It struck him with horror that she was in the midst of the cows and heifers. The circle immediately broke and tried to reform to exclude the interloper.

Marie Anne's horse reared and plunged, reared and plunged, turned and reared again. Poor Marie's eyes were nearly falling out of her head with terror, and she could see very little except that she knew her mount was actually brushing against the enraged and terrified cows. The dust choked her, and the smell of the herd sickened her. With grim determination she had not realized herself capable of feeling, she hung on like death itself in a battle to the finish.

Jean Baptiste plunged straight into the milling herd between two buffalo ready to lock horns and crush this enemy, except that he was a second too swift for them. When he was able to pick out Marie Anne in the midst of the hysterical crowd of pushing, shoving, mooing animals, he made his way as best he could to her side. For Marie Anne, the smell of the huge bellowing beasts, the dust that hundreds of hooves had raised, the mooing of young heifers separated from their mothers, and the general din was a kind of nightmare she could not believe she was enduring.

In a curious flash, a scene like a picture of what Father Vinet had described to the children of his parish as the hell that awaited sinners in a life that was so different and was so many lifetimes ago now crossed through her mind. Somehow, Marie Anne clung to reins, mane, and Reine and stayed on top. The sound of the hooves terrified her more than anything.

The image of her falling off the horse, or of helpless little Reine being pitched out of her bag and horribly trampled in that inferno, helped her in her desperation. The horse reared, wheeled, reared, bucked, and reared again, but Marie Anne clung. Where her strength was coming from, she had no idea. She only knew that she must hang on forever if she had to.

After what seemed an eternity of this terrible frenzy, noise, and dreadful pounding, suddenly there was Jean at her side and his hand on her rein. With superb skill at steering his frightened beast and bringing it into a situation it was not keen to enter, Jean managed to get control of Marie Anne's horse as well, twisting now this way and that to avoid the lowered heads and horns.

No one was ever sure how he could have managed it, but Jean did guide both horses out of the muddle of the distraught herd and led them both to the safety of a copse of caraganas near a butte.

The herd, meanwhile, had charged off in the opposite direction and was soon out of sight except for the spiralling clouds of dust that told which way it had gone.

"Is Reine all right?" were Marie Anne's first words when her horse was finally brought up short.

"She is, my love. She is, and you are too!"

Jean wiped the sweat and the tears out of his eyes and lifted his adored helpmeet off her horse and into his arms. Carrying her over to the copse and settling down gently, he almost collapsed with relief after the scare of his life.

For Marie Anne, it was a different matter. Her water had broken sometime during her ordeal, and she was already beginning the throes of labour spasms.

"Jean!" Marie Anne heaved. "Oh Jean. The baby's on the way."

Amie rode up quickly to see to her friend. She leaped off her horse, threw the reins to Belgrade, and told him to fetch water.

Marie Anne was not in labour for hours this time. Her use of her thigh and leg muscles in her attempts to bring her horse under control had brought her pregnancy to an abrupt end somewhat ahead of schedule. Amie took charge and made her friend as comfortable as possible. With a tree to sit up against and Amie's two hands to grasp, her tattered nerves were steadied by Amie's words of encouragement. In short order, Amie was able to turn to Jean Baptiste and show him the small but very vocal son he had so longed for.

Jean took his tiny perfect little son in his arms and kissed the covering of small blond hair. "My son! My own little son," he kept repeating over and over.

Amie sent Belgrade and the toddlers off to search for moss and then began to figure out some sort of covering for the tiny mite. She couldn't help a little smile as she thought of all the preparations Marie Anne had made for Reine's appearance.

When Marie Anne was capable of saying anything at all, she smiled a wan and weak smile and asked Jean, "Please, make the sign of the cross over him and name him Jean Baptiste after you, of course, but as well I want him named Laprairie. That's where he came into the world."

Jean put the baby gently into her arms. "My baby," she said to the little one, "born out on the prairie, under the sky, who knows where exactly? My little Laprairie. And what an introduction! Right in the middle of a buffalo herd!"

The whole party rested for two days. Marie Anne tried her best, and it was a valiant best, to get rid of her terror and the recurring nightmares. She was still in shock and almost speechless with fright.

Her consolation was the tiny fair-haired blue-eyed boy she held in her arms and tried to nurse. Reine stayed very quietly by her mother's side. Her world seemed to have changed drastically ever since that bouncing, noisy ride.

After only the two days of rest, Marie Anne had to climb back on her horse – a different beast this time. She glowered at her runaway as she walked past him. Again she placed Reine in one saddlebag (fastened even more securely this time), provisions in the other, and now a precious bundle in a makeshift papoose on her back. She kept a tight fist on her reins with both hands, thinking as she did so that she doubted if she could muster that much strength again for a while. The party rode off quietly, slowly, and soberly to Fort of the Prairies. Jean had resolved to keep a much sterner watch on the doings of all his horses from now on.

"Could it be only two years ago that I was arriving in these western lands?" Marie Anne mused to herself. "Now everything seems so different. I am really in an entirely different world from back east. How I would love to see the village again. The roses here are beautiful, of course, and there are so many of them. But, oh! How I miss the ones in maman's garden, the ones that were brought all the way over the seas from the Old World. How sweetly they smelled. And I don't suppose I shall ever hear the sound of a church bell again. I remember how I felt about that before Reine was born, that the songs of the birds would have to be my beautiful substitute for the bells in St Sulpice. I loved the bird songs then and I do now, but I do feel the pangs of longing and my love for Canada. I wonder, shall I ever see Canada again? So green and so peaceful!"

Amie glanced from time to time at her friend so lost in thought. She felt a little concern for the wee boy. She had never seen a baby so small and with such a frightening blue cast to his skin, not at all as she remembered Reine. She wondered time and again if Marie Anne would be able to raise him, even though the tiny bundle in question had filled out a little in the past three days and had lost much of that bluish-white cast. His clear blue eyes fascinated Amie and her little daughters.

To the immense relief of them all, the rest of the journey back to the fort was made without any more surprises – no roving bands of hunters, no wandering herds of buffalo, just an antelope or two which was added to the pile of skins. Sometimes they stopped to watch families of ducks amusing themselves, quacking together happily in every slough and stream they came across. The children's eyes shone with excitement. Jean and Belgrade thought of duck for dinner. Marie Anne saw a mental picture of the duck pond back in Maskinongé. Amie admired the beautiful feathers, thinking what she could make with them.

When they reached the south shore of the Saskatchewan, they signalled for help crossing the river. A raft was dispatched, and Mr and Mrs Bird welcomed them on the wharf. The new member of the Lajimoniere family was subjected to a thorough scrutiny from both the factor and his wife.

Mr Bird was bowled over and delighted to welcome the tiny blonde baby. His admiration for Madame Lajimoniere was greater than ever for having given birth successfully to a baby prematurely under the open sky. Marie Anne shrugged. Since there was no time to set up a lodge after the buffalo encounter and Laprairie had made up his mind apparently that he would rather be where he could see what was going on than tucked safely away inside her, she told Mr Bird that she'd had no choice but to deliver, with Amie's help, her second infant out on the plains. With her customary smile, she pointed out to Mr Bird that even the weather was kind. They had not had rain for weeks.

"You must pass the winter in the fort again," Mr Bird told both parents. "Bouvier is now able to fend for himself, so there will be no need for you two ladies to nurse him any longer. There is no necessity for the Belgrades to remain inside the stockade if they would prefer to be with Madame Belgrade's friends and relatives." He paused and then added, "You are most welcome to take over the lean-to again. I think of it as the Lajimoniere residence now, and I would be very much relieved if you would both take advantage of it."

Belgrade considered Mr Bird's words. He knew that Amie was wishing to be back surrounded by the many tents of her people and her particular friends, the wives of Paquin and Chalifou. Belgrade too had missed some of the camaraderie of his two friends, and after the summer's experiences was more than anxious to establish a good working relationship with a larger group. He was quite happy to live with Amie's people in an Indian encampment, for this was precisely what he and Amie had been doing for well nigh six years. Feeling that he could be sure of a welcome in the group, he told Mr Bird that he would rather live outside the stockade for the coming winter.

"Life both inside and outside the fort in the various Indian encampments is becoming rougher and rowdier than in past years," he said. "As I am not an employee of the Hudson's Bay Company and value my independence, I am more than happy to move out and not feel myself beholden to the Bay or to you, Mr Bird, kind though you have been to both my wife and me." Belgrade bowed, and the men shook hands.

Chalifou and Paquin gave him a rousing welcome. Throughout the fall and winter, Jean Baptiste continued to go out with his friends on the trapping lines. They were friends, good friends, and would always remain so.

For her part, Marie Anne was completely engrossed in caring for the new baby and Reine. Now that Reine could toddle about, she found herself with her hands full constantly. Ensuring that neither the adventurous Reine nor the wee baby got into danger or mischief was all she could handle, along with her usual chores of drawing water from the river, cooking over an open fire, supplying the fire's constant need for brushwood, and trying to establish some sort of established order and cleanliness in the shed.

In addition to all her chores, Marie Anne occasionally met Amie and went with her to the woods outside the fort to set their snares when their husbands were away on their trapping expeditions.

"Rabbit makes a nice change," Marie Anne said to Amie one afternoon when the two were trudging back through the snow carrying a rabbit apiece between them on a stick.

Their papooses were on their backs, and their spare hands were guiding the little girls.

"You are a good person to go out with," said Amie, turning and smiling at her. "If no one could see the colour of your face, you could pass as Cree anywhere."

It was intended as a real compliment, and Marie Anne blushed with pleasure at her friend's words.

Unknown to Marie Anne, Mr Bird kept an eye on her comings and goings. He was particularly concerned lest anyone bother her and create a disturbance inside or outside the stockade. She was still an object of great curiosity to any newcomers to the fort, Indian or white. Mr Bird's reputation as a strict disciplinarian was high throughout the northwestern posts, and he wanted no scuffles or unpleasantness on account of the fair Madame Lajimoniere. With her two little ones to care for, Marie Anne was unfailingly grateful for his interest in the family and his many kindnesses. Mrs Bird remained a bit of a mystery to Marie Anne. Although she was friendly enough, she seemed to give herself enormous importance as the factor's wife.

Marie Anne had another troubling concern. Jean Baptiste missed the closeness of his three comrades when their four hide tents had been set up hard by each other. She knew he blamed her for wanting to continue to live in the lean-to. She knew he thought the lean-to was the next thing to a house, and she sensed his disappointment in her opting for what he termed an easy life. She wisely kept her thoughts to herself.

"Easy life," she sniffed and thought longingly of some of the amenities of that other life. "Some things are good, of course. But oh, how I would like to bring fresh loaves out of an oven."

She worried about bringing up Reine and Laprairie – Lap, they called him now – to be so very different from others around them. "Jean has Belgrade and the others, all good Canadians. The children will know only Indian friends. Is it fair to them? Jean just can't understand this. Or won't," she said to herself.

"If my children are to be brought up as good Canadians, there is some housecleaning to do around here. Enough of this pitying myself, or where will we end up?" She reached for a goose wing and started sweeping.

Winter passed quickly. The weather was good, not as cold as some old-timers could remember but yet with plenty of snow to make travel with the dogs and the travois easy for hunting parties. Every once in a while, Marie Anne wrapped up Lap and Reine and took them up to the store to have a chat with Bouvier. It was a pleasure for her and poor Bouvier, who still had problems with speech, to chat together in French. Bouvier made as good a recovery as could be hoped for, and true to his word, Mr Bird gave him many carpentry tasks. Bouvier was becoming an accomplished maker of furniture, primitive as it was, and his pride in his successes made him a favourite among the factor's staff.

CHAPTER 14

After a recovery from the New Year's revels, the inhabitants of the fort and the surrounding encampments settled down to the winter routine, which is to say, sporadic fights to settle old scores and celebratory drinking sprees after successful hunting forays. Marie Anne had to contend with little wet feet, for Reine loved to get out into the snow and play. Lap was still in his papoose, but he was an enthusiastic spectator of her games.

Marie Anne taught Reine to make angels in the snow as she and her sisters had done. Together, they would choose a clean patch of snow where no footsteps had marred the whiteness. The papoose had to be removed from Marie Anne's back and set upright so that Lap could watch.

"Lie down like this, your arms at your sides," instructed Marie Anne. "Now swing your arms out and up in the snow. Touch your fingertips together if you can over your head. Good! That's the way. Keep your arms in the snow. Now back to your sides. Now sit up and stand away from your marks without putting your feet in it. There we are. Angels in the snow!"

Reine laughed and clapped her hands with glee. Lap chortled at their pleasure. If Amie and her brood chanced by, they laughed too and admired the angels. But when Marie Anne tried to explain what an angel was, she was met with a blank stare. A flying person you cannot see who is not a person was not something Amie could grasp.

When they returned to the lean-to, Marie Anne had the problem of getting their clothes dry again. "You just can't make angels without getting wet," she told Reine. "I think it's worth it, even if the outer doeskins do reek of wood smoke. And how else are you going to be able to picture an angel with no holy pictures to guide you?"

She decided the only solution was to make new shifts and leggings for herself and Reine. "One to wear and one to dry," was how she put it.

Throughout Reine's second winter, it seemed to Marie Anne that she spent a good deal of time stitching new moccasins for the girl as well as for herself and Jean.

"Keeping up with wet footwear here is worse than keeping up with wet mittens back in Canada," she told her husband. "Reine's feet are growing so fast and the constant soaking and drying are so hard on moccasins, it's a real race to keep up with the need."

She sighed and wished, not for the first time since she came west, that she had knitting needles and wool to hand.

When Jean was far off on his traplines and gone overnight, Marie Anne and the children cuddled up by the fire. Then it was that Reine climbed into her mother's lap and asked for stories. Marie Anne described her life back in Canada, her home in Maskinongé, going to church, chickens in the yard, an oven in its own bakehouse that sat outside the vegetable garden, and the little house for baking bread. Marie Anne tried to describe what bread was like.

Reine sat wide-eyed, watching her mother and listening, trying her best to understand what her mother was talking about. Marie Anne would get so carried away, she fancied she could smell the loaves fresh from the oven. Then she wondered sadly if she would ever taste fresh-baked bread again.

To shed her sadness at such memories, she often sang to the children, both of whom loved to hear the old melodies. Reine's favourite was *"Therese s'assis dans sa chambre,"* and she asked for it again and again. Marie Anne often wondered what meaning the child could make out of the words describing a young girl, Therese, about to leave the pretty bedroom of her childhood with its bedstead, ruffled curtains, and dressing table to be married with a new bed and a new life.

Lap gurgled and smiled and nuzzled his mother and was, in truth, a contented little fellow. With the blue eyes of his mother that seemed to become a more intense colour with each passing week, he was a source of wonder and entertainment to all the Indian women around. Whenever he rode out of the stockade on his mother's back, he always gathered a following. Everyone wanted to touch him, to hold a tiny white hand or to have him grasp a brown finger. They all vied to get him to laugh his contagious little chuckle. None of his admirers had ever seen such a tiny human being and of such beautiful colours – white skin, rosy cheeks, bright blue eyes, and hair the colour of sunlight slanting on fresh fallen snow. He was growing day by day, and it was difficult to remember that the small but active and alert little fellow had been so pitifully weak and tiny on his arrival at the fort at the end of last summer.

Any time that Marie Anne set off with her lively pair – Lap on her back and Reine by her side – it was the rule rather than the exception for a crowd to gather. Cree, Assiniboine, Blackfeet, Blood, all crowded around to have a look at the enchanting baby. By the time the drifts of snow basking in the southern exposure were melting away, all the Indians remarked on how well Laprairie, the golden child, was filling out.

Lap, feeling quite secure from the vantage point of his papoose, played to the audience. When he gurgled, they imitated the sound. When he blew bubbles, they laughed at him. Some would break into a little dance for his entertainment. When he laughed, they howled with glee. Lap was the star attraction at the fort throughout his first winter. Marie Anne had only to take her water buckets and her children and head for the shore to have a contingent of laughing, pointing escorts. Reine held tight to Marie Anne's shift, a little intimidated by the size of the audience but so proud of her brother's antics that she bore no grudge at his popularity or the attention he got.

Now that Marie Anne felt at home inside the fort, she made her way more frequently to the factor's store. She and Amie were still called upon occasionally to work in the infirmary, although it was usual for Marie Anne to be put in sole charge this second winter. The two women did not see as much of one another as formerly. In the store, Marie Anne made a point of seeking out Bouvier and having a chat with him. He in turn looked forward to her visits and the chance to reminisce with her in French. He was grateful for her interest and gently stroked the children's heads while Marie Anne described for him in minute detail their appearance.

On one of her visits, she noticed a bolt of soft white cambric. She thought it might have been intended as bandaging material, but it gave her an idea. Instead of trudging out into the surroundings in all weather to dig out moss underneath a snow bank, she would save her pile of moss for emergencies and splurge on a few yards of cloth to make napkins for her baby.

Her Indian friends were curious but unimpressed. All that work, washing the soiled cloths in heated soapy water and then rinsing in more hot water – Jean Baptiste's wife certainly had some strange notions. The moss that got thrown out seemed to them a vastly better solution to the situation. It was indeed a chore for Marie Anne, but on the days when the snow was driven in blinding horizontal drifts around the log buildings and the winds shrieked, she found it a comfort not to have to go outside and face wet and cold feet for Reine and herself. In time, the clerks of the Hudson's Bay Company and their servants became accustomed to the sight of squares of white cloth fluttering on an improvised clothesline. It was a nostalgic reminder of their homes across the sea in the Orkneys or in the case of the Canadians, of their villages back east in Canada.

When the temperature dropped to bone-chilling degrees well below freezing, Marie Anne remembered how her mother had coped with her laundry. She had simply rolled each piece up sausage-shaped and then placed them all in a basket outside to freeze. After a short time, when all had frozen solid, she brought them into the warmth of the fireplace, and in no time they were ready for use. Marie Anne brought her frozen napkins in to be close to the fire in the lean-to with the same result. She recalled her mother's instructions only after a driving gale-force wind snapped her line and sent some of her precious napkins whirling off into the storm. Without clothes pegs, she had simply knotted the napkins together over and under the line. Marie Anne was proud of her improvisations and reasoned that while it was necessary to learn how her friends coped, there was no need for her to turn her back on all the ways of the white woman. She was learning to adapt, when to compromise, and when not to compromise.

One bright clear morning in the earliest days of what might be called spring, when yesterday's sunshine had melted the top of the snow but overnight freezing temperatures had left a slippery treacherous crust of ice, Marie Anne decided that slithering down the trail to the source of the water supply was too dangerous to try with buckets to balance, Reine to guide, and a papoose on her back. She could see herself with buckets full, water slopping out as she slipped, and having a bad fall, injuring Lap and maybe even Reine. She figured she could get hot water much more quickly if she slipped out by herself.

She admonished Reine to take good care of Lap and for both of them to stay as still as little ducklings until she returned. She was uneasy at leaving them, but she did not see how she could manage her buckets and her children too. It was almost more than anyone could do to move about on the icy surfaces with even one bucket. The riverbanks were steep, and while Marie Anne could see herself getting down swiftly, perhaps in a sitting position, getting back up without losing the water would be another story.

Sliding and slithering down the path, Marie Anne made good time. She drew the water and filled both her buckets and then, desperately trying to minimize the time the little ones were left by themselves with an open fire, she hung on to any protuberance that helped to steady her. At times she was on her knees, pushing the buckets ahead of her or digging her toes into any kind of foothold. She was fearful and uneasy, with a sixth sense of danger lurking that helped her make the trip back to the lean-to in record time. When she passed through the gate of the stockade, her relief at seeing no extra smoke coming out of the lean-to was so great she almost lost some of the buckets' contents.

As she hurried on the last lap of the trip, she noticed a Blackfoot woman running past her in a rather furtive way. The woman disappeared quickly; Marie Anne noticed that she was carrying a baby in a blanket but thought nothing of that. She had often seen the woman hanging around, and she was certainly one of Lap's admirers.

Marie Anne put her buckets down to get the hide doorway open. With a sudden great gust of fear, she thought that it was not closed properly as she had left it. At the same time, she heard little Reine sobbing bitterly.

Very much alarmed, Marie Anne rushed in to find Reine sitting exactly as she had been told, with her knuckles in her eyes and a heartbreaking howling.

"Where is the baby?" cried Marie Anne, chilled to the bone in fright. Reine could only sob and point with one fist to the opening.

Suddenly everything was too horrifyingly clear to her. She rushed outside and tore after the Blackfoot, sliding over the ice as though she were flying. She thought she could pick out the woman's tent among the Blackfeet lodges and charged ahead, now furious at the brazen effrontery of the woman in abducting Lap.

It was true. Although the woman had many children of her own, she had formed such an affection for the wonderful blue-eyed baby that she could not resist spiriting him away. At first she denied that she had the white baby at all, but when other women came up to see what the shouting was all about, several of them forced her to unwrap her blanket. There was Laprairie, unharmed and bewildered, staring around at the commotion with his eyes even wider than usual and the beginnings of a large tear about to run down his cheek.

At length, the woman admitted that she had been waiting many days for her chance to seize the pretty baby. When she noticed Marie Anne on her way to the river all by herself, she thought she saw her big opportunity. It was her intention to be a good mother to the white baby, she told Marie Anne. But when she realized the uproar she had caused, she changed her tune. She then claimed she had only meant it as a joke. She thought it would be great fun to pass off this extraordinary child as her own.

Marie Anne by this time had Lap safely in her arms, and she let the woman know in no uncertain terms that taking another woman's baby was no cause for joking. She thought momentarily of days long ago when, thanks to Belgrade and his idea of a joke, her glance of anger was supposed to be lethal.

"I just wish I had a bit of that power right now," she thought grimly. "Not to kill, of course, but just enough to teach them to leave my children alone."

Mr Bird, upon hearing the uproar and thinking he could distinguish Marie Anne's voice, came out to see what the matter was. He met her at the gate of the stockade. "Don't ever leave the children by themselves," he told her. "Not even for a moment!"

"Rather like locking up the stable after the horse is stolen," she thought. "That is advice I don't need now that I know that it happens so easily. I just wish I had been given it before this happened."

"You must understand, Madame," he went on, "that the Blackfeet especially, but indeed all the tribes we have living around here, do not think as we do about parenthood and our children. While taking a baby is a heinous crime to you, for them it is not such a wicked act. Always be wary of the Blackfeet. It's not for nothing that the others refer to them as raiders and traders."

Marie Anne made her way back to the lean-to in deep thought. "Just when I think I am beginning to know these people and to get along with them, I find I really do not understand something very important about them, except Amie. I do really think of her as a dear friend, and I trust her."

She smiled only a half smile and, feeling wan and worn out, remembered how she had no choice but to put her trust in Amie.

"I trust her all right. I had to when Reine was born and I had so much trouble, and then Laprairie. What would I have done without her then?"

Marie Anne shifted Lap to her other arm and pulled aside the opening flap of hide. She ushered Reine back into the safety of their home and, with an overpowering sense of thankfulness, shoved the flap closed tight, shutting out for the present all the difficulties and dangers that seemed to lurk outside. Kissing first the little girl and then her darling, rescued son, she continued to ponder.

"Amie would never do such a thing. I know she wouldn't. But of course, Amie and I have lived through so much together."

When next Marie Anne and Amie ran into each other, though, it became clear to her that Amie did not and could not quite see why she was so upset about the kidnapping. Every mother in Amie's band felt the same way. It was their custom for every mother in the band to mother any and every child in the band. Babies were frequently passed from the natural mother to another for suckling if the natural mother was not nursing well. Marie Anne was learning that these semi-nomads felt a deep and strong relationship with everyone else in the band. There was a close-knit tribal affiliation, but consequently the individual family bonds were weak compared to the white man's way of thinking.

Jean Baptiste and Jean Belgrade returned with a good catch of magnificent pelts, feeling every inch the triumphant hunters. After they had settled down into their family routines, they each noticed that a coolness had developed between the wives.

Jean tried to probe Marie Anne for the reason for the lack of warmth between them. "What happened when we were away? You two seemed to be the best of friends when we left. How did this come about?"

Jean lifted his wife's chin with one hand and slipped the other around her waist. He led her over to their sleeping hides. Gently moving the children over to one side, he kissed her with all the pent-up longing from his loneliness on the traplines.

A long time later, Marie Anne, still drowsy and contented, raised her head. "Jean," she whispered, "Jean."

The only reply was a sleepy "Um."

"Jean, we forgot our prayers."

Jean turned his head to her. "You are so right, p'tite. Tonight we say them lying down."

Marie Anne giggled. It didn't seem quite right, but on the other hand, no point in getting out of the covers and freezing.

Marie Anne had poured out an account of the terrible fate that had overtaken Lap as soon as Jean arrived home. Now she tried to tell him about the strange way that Amie had taken the whole episode. It was almost as though Amie had expected something of the sort to happen and was not at all concerned for the misery Marie Anne had shown.

Jean shook his head. He could understand her horror and disgust at the abductor, and indeed shared it. He had known the people of the western areas for long enough to know something of their attitude to family life and its subservience to the life of the band. But that did not lessen his grief when he considered what might have happened if the woman had abducted Lap and then immediately taken off with her band into the vastness of the prairies.

"Can't we go back east?" Marie Anne pleaded. "We are so far away from everyone who thinks as we do. We are so out of touch. Can't we go back and settle down? Lap was snatched away, and that woman pretended she didn't do it. Then she was going to pretend our baby was her son. Then she said it was all a joke. A joke! Amie doesn't see it my way at all. She thought I was making a fuss over nothing much. Making a fuss! Over my baby stolen?"

"Come now, come, my dear little wife." Jean Baptiste embraced her tenderly, and she wept piteously.

"Tell you what. This coming summer, we will go again to the prairies for our meat, but we will go by ourselves. No Belgrade. No Amie. No one else. Just us. Our own family, like old times, yes? Remember when we paddled up the Red River to Pembina by ourselves? It will be like that again."

Marie Anne snuffled a little into his chest and thought, "I must love this great crazy husband of mine an awful lot. It won't be easy, just the two of us. It won't be easy for him alone either. Of course there will be no baby born in the middle of nowhere under the sky like last summer, and I will have Reine to help me plant corn. I guess there is nothing more I can do about it. I've said my piece, and my good man has his mind made up. But he wants us to be all alone in the middle of who knows where and at the mercy of who knows what. So be it, and may all the holy angels in heaven guard us."

Accordingly, when the spring was far enough advanced for hunters to be on their way to the plains for the spring calf hunts, Marie Anne and Amie parted with a few tears on both sides. Chalifou, Paquin, and Belgrade, together with their wives, children, and a small contingent of Cree, set off together. Marie Anne watched their departure and waved until they were out of sight. The Cree and the Canadians did not look back.

"It's just not their way, dear one." Jean tried to reassure her that going out separately did not mean a complete break between them. "Here, come and lend me a hand with these things we have to pack."

Marie Anne walked slowly back into the stockade feeling bereft of friends, very lonely, and uneasy in a way she could not put into words.

No sooner had she settled into her daily routine – fetching water from the river, trying as best she could to sweep out the mess that seemed to come from nowhere in the lean-to, and thinking about her packing and helping Jean – than the flap swept open and a Blackfoot brave she did not recognize walked right inside her home. It had never been an Indian's habit to announce himself or to pause before entering another's home and Marie Anne's lean-to was no different from any other dwelling to this brave.

Marie Anne was stunned by the suddenness of this invasion and stared at the man in anger. The Blackfoot motioned her to come outside. She shook her head.

The man was insistent. Marie Anne gathered up both her children and held them tightly against her, one in her arms and one on her hip. It made a heavy load, and she glowered at the man, hoping to back down those staring black eyes and get him to leave before she would have to scream for Jean.

The Blackfoot walked over to her and, without more force than necessary, made it plain he wanted her to come outside. Forced out of her home, she was made to walk over to his horse. With elaborate gestures and his command of the Cree language, he made it plain to her that he wished to trade his horse for her white-skinned boy.

When Marie Anne realized that this man had the effrontery to want to barter her baby for a horse, she screamed hysterically and stamped her feet.

"No! No! No!" she yelled in absolute fury.

Her screams brought a crowd, including Jean and Mr Bird, on the double. The Blackfoot repeated his request, a perfectly natural one to him. Jean ordered him to get away from his wife and to take his horse with him. Mr Bird tried to placate everyone's feelings by explaining to the Blackfoot that the white woman would never trade her son for anything or anybody.

"All the horses on the prairie would not be enough. It is not the white people's custom," he said sternly. "Her boy is not for trade."

The Blackfoot shrugged. It was a fine horse he was offering, a very fine horse indeed. In his opinion, the white woman was a fool not to take advantage of his offer. From his point of view, he considered that if the white woman could make one white boy, she could probably make another, so what was the problem? It was his second-best horse he was offering. He turned and left the group with his head high. It was not pleasant to be so treated by a squaw, white or any other colour.

For that day at least, the matter of trading Laprairie was closed. But until she left the fort with Jean Baptiste for the hunting trip, she felt the curious stares of the Blackfeet as well as those of other tribes. There was no doubt about it. Lap was a prize, and more than one individual wanted to acquire him by fair means or foul. Marie Anne gritted her teeth. If she had known how to growl like a sow bear, she would have done so.

Trade children around indeed. What sort of people were these creatures? Would Jean never accept that now they were a family, a Christian family, and that they were quite different from the families of his friends? Marie Anne gritted her teeth.

A rift seemed to be growing between her and the whole world. Even Jean couldn't understand – or was it that he didn't have an alternative and so pretended that there was nothing to be concerned about?

"Those settlers Mr Bird talked about can't come soon enough for me," she said to herself, giving the old hide an extra whack as she went inside the lean-to.

CHAPTER 15

"Come, dear heart. It's time we were off and away. Help me with these packs, the lighter ones. This one is our quietest beast. Let's get the food pack on your mount. I'll hand you up Laprairie as soon as I get Reine safely stowed in your saddlebag."

Jean Baptiste was trying his best to turn Marie Anne's attention away from the unpleasantness of the morning and to put the greatest possible distance between the Blackfoot horse trader with the greatest possible haste.

"Oh Jean, I do so want to get away from here. Can't we ride east this summer and just keep going? I'm so afraid for Lap. That's two times now that he has been in such terrible danger. Why can't we give up and go home?"

Marie Anne mounted her horse and took the papoose from Jean to sling around her shoulders and her back. It took all her courage and inner strength to contemplate what she looked to as the loneliest time of her life, even with Jean beside her. She tried to smile, but it was a half-hearted attempt at best.

It was the first time since the abduction by the Cree that Marie Anne had even tried to smile. Jean took heart from it, hoping that it signalled the beginning of the return of her normally sunny nature. He knew that she wanted desperately to leave the prairies and return east to Canada. He tried to imagine how it would be for them back again in the east. He always ended up shaking his head in dismay.

"The smells, the sights, this splendid feeling of freedom, this wonderful expanse of grassland, picking up and moving wherever our wishes and a buffalo or two will take us, the hope of a great catch of furs, and a loving wife, my own Marie Anne – together we have the best life any man could want," he thought.

Marie Anne thought she understood his compulsion, and she had always agreed that this was the best possible life – challenging, but at the same time free and satisfying. That was before the two threats to Laprairie had altered her way of thinking.

"There must be more to life than this constant running, and now we are running away from the fort that had come to mean a sort of security to me." She was deeply troubled, and Jean's ray of hope that she was recovering from her shocks was dashed.

"Well," Marie Anne went on thinking as the lonely foursome and all their possessions started off on the calf hunt, "there is one thing I can think of right away that would be a great deal more to life than we know at present, and that is bread. Funny how once you have tasted it, you never stop wanting it. Here's little Reine, more than two years old, and she doesn't even know what it is. But I do, and one of these years I want to bake bread again. And I want to go to Mass again." She sighed a deep and heartfelt sigh.

"Ah well," she reflected as she dug her knees into her horse's flanks, "my daydreams won't come true this summer, that's for sure."

Mr Bird watched the pitifully small party setting off and hoped for the best for them. One woman, burdened with two children, one man leading a pair of horses and a travois – that was indeed a puny showing to battle those primitive enormous beasts and any number of roving bands. He turned away and went back to his ledgers. But the image of the little group setting off so pathetically remained with him. He had grown very fond of the children, and he had enormous respect for the gallant resourceful Madame Lajimoniere. He considered Jean Baptiste a brave and upright man, genuine praise from the laconic Orkney factor, and that was more he could say of so many of the free traders.

"I wonder what's to become of those two and their little ones?" he thought as he sat down in one of the new chairs that Bouvier had made for his office.

Marie Anne was by now an experienced hand in setting up the summer camp. They had ridden in a more or less northerly direction and farther west this summer. For some reason, Jean thought it might invite less interference from wandering bands. Marie Anne set to work at once to organize her garden, her little patches of carefully planted precious corn seed and her bean, pumpkin, and squash seeds. Her digging tool was any handy curved tree root she could find. If it broke, at least it could be added to the stock of firewood, and the only regret was that she had to find another tool.

She got her big iron kettle cleaned up and ready for rendering the fat from the first calf Jean would bring in. Together they set up their teepee, using the travois poles as supports. They had been a week finding this summer encampment, and they were both rather tired. Once it was arranged to Marie Anne's satisfaction, they sank down around their fire and rested.

"It seems very quiet all of a sudden, Jean." Marie Anne turned to her husband from the last of her chores. "Why does it seem so extra silent?"

Jean was about to remark about the peace and tranquillity of being together and by themselves at last after the constant racket they had grown accustomed to around the busy fort. Hammering and sawing, shouts, comings and goings – it was enough to drive anyone insane, or out onto the peaceful grasslands. He was resting his back against one of Marie Anne's handiworks, a willow backrest, contemplating the pretty domestic scene of his children being taught to say their prayers before being wrapped in their furry blankets for the night.

"It's peace at last," he said, "and it takes getting used to."

Marie Anne raised her head and listened intently.

"No, Jean. It is more than that. It's too quiet. You know, the sort of stillness just before a big storm, except that there isn't a cloud in the sky."

Jean changed his position to knock ashes out of his pipe, and as he did so glanced towards the spot where he had tethered the four horses.

"It's too quiet, all right. The horses have taken off!" Jean was up on his feet in a flash. "They've all gone! Look, Marie, I'll have to try to find them. You stay here with the children. There's nothing for it. I've got to get them back, and it's better that I go by myself. I can make better time." There was a desperation in his voice.

Marie Anne just stared, without a word or a tear. She was too numbed to answer. To be alone out here on the open prairies with two small children all night long was a devastating thought, but Jean was right. He raced over to the hobble posts. He couldn't tell whether in his haste to help Marie Anne with setting up the camp he had been careless and had not tied them properly, or – and it was a chilling thought – a raider had sneaked up on the little camp and stolen them.

Marie Anne opened her mouth to scream at him. How could he be so careless? She clamped her mouth shut just in time. No need to make him angry as well as frightened. What frightened her most of all was that he was frightened too.

"Dear God," she thought, "Will this boyish man never grow up? What kind of fool am I to love him so much, this man who can't tie up a horse securely? What kind of fool am I to be here in the first place?"

Loath as he was to leave Marie Anne and the babes alone, there was only one course of action open to him. He had to set out on foot to follow the hoof marks and somehow or other round up those beasts and get them back to camp. He could not allow himself to contemplate the alternative. If he did not bring back the only means of transport, the whole family would perish of starvation very slowly – unless by some miracle a band of friendly hunters happening to pass by would stop and investigate a camp with people but no beasts in evidence. Even so, it would have to be a friendly encounter indeed, or they could expect only a quick and merciful death from braves who had very little understanding of what he and Marie thought of as pity. It was a long chance, and he knew it starting off with a knot in his stomach.

Marie Anne watched him stride off with fear growing harder by the minute in her stomach as well. To be alone in this huge world all night! What would she do if coyotes came close? She clenched her fists.

"I'll think about that when I hear them," she told herself.

Jean Baptiste followed the tracks until it was too late to see properly what he was doing. Cursing that there was not even moonlight to guide himself by and fearful of losing their tracks and becoming lost himself, he took what shelter he could find near a slough and was up again at the first lightening of grey in the north-eastern sky.

Marie Anne hugged her little ones close to her and sang them to sleep. Their night prayers had new and significant meaning for her now, and she prayed once more to be protected from the perils of the night. She tried to get some sleep herself, but every sound, the tiny twitter of a bird's night call, even the movement of the grasses in a breeze awakened her. She stared into the darkness without making a sound, listening for any clue as to what had awakened her, with her heart hammering so loudly she was sure its beating would waken the babies.

Not even in the darkest, longest days of winter had any night seemed longer to Marie Anne, and here it was close to the shortest night in the year.

She sat up to listen more intently a dozen times or more, and each time cautiously and silently lowered herself back under the buffalo robe, terribly alone. Dawn came at last.

Marie Anne made her mark on her buffalo robe and prayed that tomorrow she would still be here to make the next one, and then scrambled to her feet thankful that she and the children at least were still in one piece. She fed the children, who of course wanted to know where Papa had gone. She managed to make up a perfectly straightforward story about Papa taking the horses away and promising, with her fingers crossed and a leaden feeling in her stomach, that he would soon be back. Then she set about her usual morning tasks, taking both children with her and keeping them close, going to her garden patch to pull up weeds.

Bent over her precious garden, Marie Anne was aware of movement behind her. Instinctively she reached for Reine and Lap happily playing farmers with a few seeds she had given them. She swivelled round to see what new menace she had to face. A herd of pronghorns came leaping straight for her and her garden. With a little one in each arm, Marie Anne stood up and did some leaping from side to side herself. Even a few of the graceful beasts prancing so lightly across her garden would have made a travesty of her carefully planned food supply.

At the last moment, it seemed, the leaders parted and the beasts leaped in their curious bouncing way on either side of the plantation. Marie Anne put the children down and wiped her face.

"What more can happen to us?" she cried out loud.

Reine's eyes were very big. "Those little horses almost jumped right on top us! When will Papa come home?"

Lap did not seem as disturbed and tried, in his toddling way, to imitate the antelope leap.

Marie Anne gathered them both close to her. "Nobody got hurt, my precious ones." She wiped her face again. "Papa will be coming soon, and then we shall have a story to tell him."

She tried to make her voice sound as convincing as she could. But how sure could she be that this would be the end of their trials? "Best to get back to work," she told herself, "and pretend that this is what we intended to do all the time. Oh Jean, where on this earth have you got to?" It took real discipline, but she picked a dead branch and started to weed once more.

About midmorning, she thought she heard hoof beats a long way off. Thinking only that it must be Jean returning with the runaways, she stood up and shaded her eyes with her hand, the better to peer into the far distance where the sounds were coming from.

At first she could make out only a cloud of dust, a large swirling cloud of dust. Thinking that Jean was certainly riding hard to return to them and feeling thankful that he was coming home in triumph, she straightened her shoulders and was preparing to welcome him.

The hoof beats got louder and louder. These horses were really coming straight for the camp at a full gallop. Suddenly, Marie Anne realized there were far too many hoof beats for Jean's four beasts. As they came closer and she could make out the shapes of riders and horses in the dust, she found herself staring at a band of the fiercest looking warriors she had ever seen.

Over the din of hoof beats, she could hear the yelling and blood-curdling shrieks of Indians on the warpath, waving their muskets and their knives. Marie Anne wanted to take her children and sink with them straight into the ground or fly up like angels into the sky – anything to get out of the way of what looked like an angry horde making straight for her. They were close enough now for her to see their headdresses, eagle-feathered and falling down to their saddles – not the floor length ones for ceremonial occasions. These were the headdresses worn into battle, with ermine tails, white- and black-tipped, waving and bouncing on their chests.

Marie Anne was horrified. These were Indians she had never seen before. Their faces were smeared with red dye – or could it be blood? Some wore headpieces, masks made of animal heads. How could they see where they were going? Their shifts were gaudily covered in what seemed to her to be hideous designs of great staring eyes and gaping horrible mouths, designed to frighten a foe into submission.

The band drew up and some dismounted within a few feet of her. Marie Anne had Laprairie in her arms and Reine by the hand pressed closely to her side. She held both of them as firmly and protectively as she could, realizing as she did so that she was at the complete mercy of these warriors waving their knives with the most menacing and bloodthirsty gestures, literally dressed to kill. It was the first time that she had encountered a band in full warpaint, and she was too frightened to faint. She just stood and waited for whatever fate was about to fall. One of her ghastly thoughts was that this strange group had somehow heard of the white boy and was about to take him from her. She clutched him ever more closely.

Thoughts raced one after another through her mind. She had been lucky so many times so far, by now surely her supply of luck must have run out, and these must be her last moments on earth. This time, surely, she would be massacred with her babies. Except for Lap, she thought in a kind of hysteria. Her boy they would surely take as a prize to barter with, and his father would never see him again.

After their initial surprise at the strange sight of a light-skinned woman and her light-skinned children with no man about, the braves surrounded her. Marie Anne found herself standing in the middle of a circle of threatening warriors with whom she could not even converse. Their language was one she had never heard, and they did not understand – or at any rate, professed not to understand – when spoken to in Cree. As Cree was more or less the official understanding, the lingua franca, over all the plains area that she knew, she was more and more perplexed to know who these people were and where they had come from.

The chief and his favoured warriors had not dismounted. They now rode into the circle, and the others moved back. Marie Anne found herself staring up into the nostrils of a dozen or more horses. She wanted to cringe and kneel, but something made her steel her backbone and stand straighter than ever. She was not going to let these savage-looking individuals know that she was terrified of them.

By means of signs, the chief made it understood that he wanted to know where the men were. Marie Anne did her best to pantomime that her husband was off seeking their horses, and he would come back shortly. She crossed her fingers as she tried to make that understood, and she devoutly hoped that it was the truth and that Jean would really be beside her in a moment.

The chief signalled his braves to look inside her lodge. They came out shaking their heads. Whatever it was they sought, they did not find it. The chief nodded. Doubtless he was trying to imagine why a man would leave a woman with small children alone like this and what kind of carelessness would allow him to lose his animals. Horses were the principal items of barter for all the plains Indians and the biggest prize from a raiding party. It was difficult indeed for him to understand why the horses and the man were not where they should have been.

The chief dismounted and threw the reins of his horse to one of his already dismounted braves. One of the braves rubbed the skin on Lap's face, perhaps to see if the pale colour would wear off. Neither Marie Anne nor Laprairie nor Reine moved a muscle. The little ones had been taught well to obey their parents and follow their example.

When it was obvious to the chief that these extraordinary humans were not able to do them any harm, he did not think it worth his while to have them tortured and killed. It seemed a better idea for the whole troop to be told to sit down and take their ease and amuse themselves until this strange creature's man showed up.

Marie Anne, still holding the children closely, looked around at these garish individuals loafing and making themselves completely at home around her lodge. The braves with the animal headdresses had taken them off, and she was at last able to see what a few of her visitors looked like without red and black stripes painted on their faces. She shuddered at the look of their painted faces. There was a sense of deliberate cruelty about these people that filled her with loathing.

After she had regained a little of her composure – after all, they could have killed her but had not yet done so – she signalled to the chief that she wished to attend to Lap, who was in need of a change of his moss. When the chief finally understood her, he nodded in agreement but without any emotion or softening in his face. She looked after Lap and then began very slowly and tentatively to take up her normal morning chores. The members of the band watched her in some curiosity but did not try to frighten or molest her or the children.

The chief indicated to Marie Anne that he and his followers would move on after he had spoken to her husband. At least that is what Marie Anne thought he was indicating, and she felt somewhat relieved. He told his men to tether the horses and that they were to stay where they were and wait. Marie Anne did her best not to betray her terror by her shaking hands, and she cautioned Reine to do the same in French. Little Reine, her brown eyes huge and staring, did exactly as her mother told her.

There was a store of fresh meat inside the lodge. Very slowly and deliberately, Marie Anne took her kettle and of course the children, and walked down to the bank of the stream to fill it. She walked slowly back as unconcernedly as she could force herself to do and set the kettle down by the fireplace. Then with equal slowness and deliberation, she dragged brush to the fireplace, Reine doing her little bit to help. She threw brush and some wood on the fireplace and got down on her hands and knees to fan the brush into flame. Then she walked with her back to the braves into the teepee to fetch the meat. Feeling savage black eyes on her back and every hair on the back of her neck standing straight out, she managed with all the appearance of a dignified self-composed chatelaine to get the meat, bring it out, and put it in the kettle. The kettle with its full load was heavy, but she managed with the same coolness to raise it and place it on the fire.

The band watched every movement with interest. She knew she had the fullest attention of each guest – every one of those hideously painted faces – and she forced herself to be calm. Reine took her cue from her mother and stayed by her side without uttering a sound. Lap was in his customary papoose and stared out at the strangers with no sound and no change in his facial expression.

While her pot was simmering, Marie Anne went back into the teepee. Jean Baptiste had a small quantity of tobacco hidden away. She got it out and, walking with her head held high, made the chief understand that she was offering him a present. Jean usually saved his tobacco for special occasions, and Marie Anne decided that this was a very special occasion right here and now. The chief accepted her gift with an equally dignified nod and proceeded to distribute tobacco to his men.

When she decided her cooking was ready for sampling, she pulled the kettle off the fire. By now every nose was twitching and every pair of black eyes swivelled about, yet with no change of expression on their faces. Marie Anne could never decide later whether it was because the paint made it impossible for them to smile or even look pleased, or whether they were not accustomed to showing any kind of response by means of facial expression whatsoever. Forcing herself still not to betray any kind of agitation, she cut the meat in pieces and served it out on the grass to each of the warriors. It was an amazing sight to watch those painted faces chewing and grunting, and the grunting and belching going on around her fireplace. She stood still and watched, realizing that she had at best only bargained for time with her attempt at hospitality.

The men hardly spoke, they just chewed and patted their stomachs. Perhaps it was a gesture to indicate they were pleased at being fed. Marie Anne hoped so.

Although the Indians covered their surprise as convincingly as Marie Anne covered her fright, they were enjoying her feast. This was a reception nobody had counted on. Every last morsel was scooped up and chewed with appreciation. The tobacco was smoked. The chief and his men were not just surprised, they were astonished and pleased. With many kinds of signs, they made her understand that they were now friends, and that they would not harm her. They intended, however, to wait until her husband returned.

If the preceding night was the longest night she had ever known, this day was the longest day of her whole life. Several times Marie Anne glanced up at the sun to mark its progress, and almost every time she could have sworn it had not moved. What would happen to her and the babies if Jean did not get back before nightfall was constantly on her mind. She prayed for Jean and his recovery of their horses. She prayed for her little ones, and she prayed for mercy for herself.

Eventually the shadows on the grasses did lengthen, and the sun seemed to be shining on them from a more westerly direction. Marie Anne thought it must surely be time to see what she could feed the children for an evening meal. They had both been such good little soldiers, no complaints, but she knew they must be getting hungry. As she thought about how she could feed the children with so many onlookers who might be getting a mite ready for another handout themselves, Marie Anne wondered how much longer she could keep up the pretence of the coolly collected white mother. She knew she was close to the breaking point. Still moving slowly with all the dignity she could muster, she began to walk towards the teepee to see what she had left after arranging the midday feast. Glancing past the braves, she thought she saw dust rising on the grasslands far to the southwest.

"Could it be Jean? Oh God, please make it be Jean," she prayed, and for the first time since the invasion, her hands began to shake uncontrollably.

She continued to stare into the distance, willing the dust to be caused by Jean and their horses. The possibility of more Indian visitors was almost enough to unnerve her completely. The horses galloped closer. She thought she could make out only four, and surely three were on leading reins.

"Maman," piped up Reine in a tiny whisper, "I see Papa."

Jean Baptiste rode up with all the missing beasts. They'd had a good long run and were lying down sweating when he came upon them well after noon. Catching them all and getting back had taken him hours. From the moment he had caught sight of the company around his lodge, he had feared the worst. Now his astonishment and relief at seeing Marie Anne apparently able to stand up unharmed and with both his children at her side was almost too much for that cool composure absolutely necessary for dealing with his uninvited guests.

Naturally, his first thought was for Marie Anne. She assured him that she was unharmed, that no one had touched her, and that somehow they all three had survived this long day. His tobacco was gone, she admitted with a wan smile, given as a present to the chief, and it had all been smoked away hours ago. She told him also about having fed their "guests."

Jean approved. "A very wise move, dearest. You bartered for time with that feast. There is nothing like the surprise of unexpected food to establish a friendly footing. Now I'll go and parley and try to find out who they are."

After many attempts at sign language, Jean established that they were a band of Sarcee, an affiliate of the Blood. With what Jean knew of the Blood speech, a conversation of sorts was started, which was slowly understandable to both parties. To Marie Anne's ears, the chief did not sound as friendly as he had before Jean arrived home. He now began to speak harshly and abruptly. Marie Anne watched in chilled, horrified silence. The chief's speeches were terse, and he had his warriors backing him up with fierce and unpleasant-sounding grunts. The precious medal inside the little doeskin bag she had made for it seemed the only part of her that had any warmth.

How many years had her medal comforted her? It must be three, she thought. The medal was her comfort, the medal and the son in her arms and the little girl pressed so trustingly against her leg.

She was too frightened to get out her rosary, thinking of the time when her prayers and her beads had so startled that other Indian band. This was different. She could smell the hostility.

She prayed silently, telling off the beads that hung around Reine's neck. Too frightened to move or kneel down, she just stood beside Jean in dumb horror, waiting for the outcome of this unpleasant conversation.

These Sarcee all dressed up in their warpaint, plumes, and finery had made her understand that she and her children were not in any danger. But that was this morning and then later after feeding them. What was going to happen now when the chief was speaking to Jean in such great heat and anger? Marie Anne felt all hope desert her.

After some exchanges, conciliatory on Jean's part, he turned to her to try to reassure her and let her know what was going on.

"It seems that our friends were hunting and crossed with these Sarcee. They had meant to be friendly, but the Sarcee took exception to their being on what they said was their territory. Since the Sarcee arrived in this area about the same time or a little after the Cree came from the east, I don't see how anybody can lay claim to all hunting rights around here anyway. The Sarcee came from farther west and north where there are mountains, snow all summer, so I've been told."

Marie Anne looked deeply into Jean's eyes. There was a sadness and a bitterness she had never seen before.

"There's more to tell, isn't there?" she whispered.

He nodded. "The Cree, I am sure, meant only to be peaceful. But somehow things got out of hand. The Sarcee butchered every last one of the Cree. They were looking for more Cree when they searched our lodge. They are really on the warpath."

Jean stopped a moment. Marie Anne could see that something else was coming. There was an expression of revulsion on his face.

"They are looking for the Canadians who apparently managed to escape. I imagine they are headed back to the fort as fast as they can."

Marie Anne swallowed hard, sucked in her breath, and was about to scream, sob, or faint. She hardly knew which.

"Careful, my precious one. Don't let these killers know you are upset by the news."

"But Amie?" whispered Marie Anne. "Who escaped? Was she tortured?"

"Try your best not to show that this news means anything to you, dearest, I implore you, or they may just get bloodthirsty enough again today to figure if you are so broken up about their victims, they are justified in killing us all. But I have terrible news. All the Cree were massacred. These Sarcee claim they spared no one. Took no women or children, which is unusual, only their horses. So you can see, it's a real tribal war and a fight to the finish. Four Canadians escaped, and they think there may be another too."

"Amie massacred? And her children? All of them? And Madame Chalifou? Madame Paquin?"

Jean Baptiste nodded gravely. Again by a slight raising of an eyebrow, he cautioned her to keep silent and not to betray any feelings. Marie swayed as though she were about to faint. Only Reine clutching her knees kept her upright. Controlling her sobs was the hardest of all, but it had to be done.

Jean Baptiste turned back to the Sarcee chief. "Now that you and your braves have had the feast of welcome and you know we are not giving shelter to those you seek, my wife and I will pack up and go camp elsewhere."

The chief held up his hand. The warriors grasped their knives. Marie Anne looked from Jean to the chief and back to Jean. She wondered what could be wrong now.

"No." There was no doubting what the chief meant. "You will stay here with us." He stood up, and although he only came to Jean's chin, he stared at Jean. The man had a commanding presence. "Five of our people have been sent by us to the fort. When they return to us unharmed, then you can go. If harm comes to them," the chief played with his knife and made a small circle in the air, "we know what we will do with you."

Marie Anne could make out the last of the chief's words only too well. Their knowledge that the four Canadians were heading for the fort as well and would doubtless let Mr Bird know what had happened to the Cree made both Marie and Jean realize there was scant chance of the five Sarcee arriving back to their band in good health. Their position seemed to be growing more precarious with each passing minute. She managed not to cry out or faint. In truth, she was too sick at heart for any new terror to register fully. She only swayed a little once towards Jean this time.

"Stand tall, p'tite."

It was a hissed command, and somehow the image of the little plaster saints in far off St Sulpice came to her mind and seemed to be helping her to stand as impassively as they balanced on their stands.

But yet, this swaying was the cue that Jean needed. He informed the chief that his wife was very sick and needed to be where she could have quiet and be alone. The chief looked at this pale woman with disgust.

Jean pointed out to the chief that a few miles off near the horizon was a clump of trees. He pointed to the copse of birch and said that he and his family would camp there overnight and return to the Sarcee camp in the morning. The chief stared hard at Jean for several moments. He had not great respect for any man, white or redskin, who would lose his horses. He stared at Marie Anne, who was now leaning piteously on her husband's arm. She looked ready to collapse in a heap. He considered the request of these two foreigners, these interlopers, at his leisure.

Finally, he nodded in agreement and waved them off with a shrug and a sneer.

Jean and Marie Anne lost not a moment in gathering up everything that belonged to them. They packed all their belongings with a speed they hadn't known possible and stowed it on the horses' backs. They packed the birch poles on one of the packhorses. Reine was bundled into her saddle bag. Lap was bundled into his papoose. Whatever could be found in the teepee that was edible was packed in the other saddle bag, and they were off, throwing themselves onto the riding horses' backs and getting them to a full gallop. The chief and his men did not even bother to watch them go.

When they reached the copse, they stopped on the other side just long enough to give themselves a small cold supper and jettison the teepee poles. There would be no travois on this trip. As soon as they had eaten, they remounted and were off again, hoping against all hope and reason that the

Sarcee would be too indifferent to their hostages and too occupied with their own doings to pay attention to them. If the chief were satisfied enough with the way he had handled these pesky white folks and considered that he had acted with a great deal of generosity in letting his prisoners camp off by themselves, the Lajimonieres hoped he would not bother to check that his captives were setting up their camp where they said they would.

As they galloped off, they each turned from time to time to make sure that the Sarcee had posted no lookout. As soon as they figured the Sarcee had made themselves comfortable for the night and were no longer interested in them, the Lajimonieres whipped their horses into as fast a pace as the beasts could gallop. They took the shortest way they knew for the fort and comparative safety.

With death at the hands of the savages right on the backs of their necks, the little family rode the rest of the night, guiding themselves by the stars and praying that no horse would stumble into a prairie dog warren. They rode all the next day, stopping only when it was absolutely necessary to water the horses and attend to their own needs.

Every once in a while, Marie Anne or Jean would try to glance backward over a shoulder to see if a cloud of dust were visible to indicate they were being pursued. Fear made a knot in everyone's chest. Even the horses recognized their anguish and did their heroic best. Laprairie was silent and big-eyed.

"It takes a lot to keep that child silent," thought Marie Anne. "He might not understand what is causing the tension, but he shares it."

It took five days of hard riding before they saw the shores of the North Saskatchewan River and the flag on the fort rising above it on the far side of the river.

Exhausted as they both were, Jean Baptiste and Marie Anne shouted as loudly as they had ever done in their lives for help in crossing the river. Their desperate situation gave them the last spurt of energy they needed.

Fortunately, their cries were heard. Clerks came running down to the shore in response to the urgency, the hoarseness, and the anguish in their voices. A raft was launched, poled, and paddled without delay across the river.

The horses were lashed on board. They were so spent they could just barely move on board and needed a hefty shove from behind. The Lajimonieres and their equipment were handed onto the raft, and everything was lashed together. The family looked so exhausted the clerks wondered if it would be a good idea to lash them on board as well. Another raft was needed and dispatched with as much haste as the clerks could possibly make. When everything was tied down securely and made fast, the little flotilla of exhausted horses and humans reached the other shore without further mishap.

As Marie Anne and her children, all three of them dead to the world with weariness, were carried ashore, the rest of the participants in the dramatic crossing – Jean and the rescue squad – heard the unmistakable pounding of many hoof beats.

The cloud of dust on the horizon they had so dreaded came into view, and even from such a great distance, there was a sound of angry men on the warpath, shouting and raging.

The Sarcee were in hot pursuit, no doubt about it, and furious at the way they had been tricked. The Lajimonieres had made it to the safety of the fort's stockade with less than a couple of hours to spare.

CHAPTER 16

Jean stumbled off the raft onto the wharf to be met and slapped on the back by Belgrade and Chalifou as well as Paquin, who had shown up after the others by himself. Each of them had tales to tell of a hair's-breadth escape and terrifying pursuit. Jean, although exhausted and too tired to speak, was relieved to have his friends' arms around him, supporting him up to the lean-to. Mr Bird and his clerks had already carried Marie Anne and the children home. Even Bouvier had made it down to the waterfront to ask anxiously about his friend, Madame Lajimoniere. When told that she was sleeping but seemed otherwise unharmed, he choked and sobbed in his throat in a most heart-rending way.

The three friends congratulated Jean again and again. After setting him down outside his lean-to, Chalifou produced a bottle of brandy and insisted that Jean take a few reviving sips. Then they had to hear first-hand how he had come across the Sarcee and what happened – and above all, since the Sarcee were so hell-bent on murder, how had Madame Lajimoniere survived?

"Tell us the whole story," they all insisted.

As he did, Belgrade interjected, "You mean your wife served up a banquet for those killers? She's a survivor, that one!"

Jean and Marie Anne slept the sleep of the dead for the rest of the day. Some hours later, Jean was able to tell his friends of Marie Anne's feast in some detail, the gift she made of his tobacco cache, and her steadfastness in the face of what seemed over and over again to be the prelude to a massacre.

"Five days of virtual nonstop race with death!" Jean was still shaken as he described their constant fear of telltale dust on the horizon.

Jean's three friends continued to slap him on the back and congratulate him on what seemed almost a miracle: that he had actually outdistanced the Sarcee and got back to the fort in the very nick of time. The three widowers were especially impressed by Jean's account of Marie Anne and her hospitality, preparing a real feast surrounded by the fiendish captors.

"Your Marie Anne's courage and her resourcefulness and her daring is going to make one of my best stories – if not the best – I hope to tell for years to come," Belgrade told Jean with a great deal of awe in his voice.

When finally, after some hours, Marie Anne was rested enough to waken and rouse herself to find Jean, she found the men still congratulating him with a heartiness she could not share. Her friends, their wives, had been butchered to death. How could it be that those men didn't do more mourning for their wives than she felt for her friends?

But even Jean Baptiste was surprised at her frequent bouts of tears.

"She was my friend, my dear true friend," Marie Anne told everyone with great sadness, still grieving. "Of course I miss her. I loved Amie as my closest friend, and I always shall."

Not for the first time in his life, Jean Baptiste went off by himself muttering that he would never understand women. Here she was safe in the fort, saved from massacre by her clever business of giving a feast, and all she could think of was Amie and the others.

"What if those Sarcee should happen to cross our paths again?" Marie Anne recalled only too vividly what Jean had told her long ago about an Indian's need for vengeance, back in Pembina when his first wife had tried to poison her. Marie Anne shuddered when she wondered what happened when the Sarcee chief found his captives had melted away into the prairies.

"Surely they would want to take out their humiliation on our whole family with unthinkable savagery. I don't want to meet them again, and that's final," she thought. She begged Jean to take them all back east.

"No, Marie Anne," he insisted. "I am not a farmer. I am a hunter and a trapper. Surely you must understand that by now. We stay and hunt."

Jean's eyes were black. She could see he was adamant.

It was the second time the two had ever had a serious falling out. Marie Anne watched in silent disgust how quickly Jean's three friends each availed themselves of the opportunity to acquire new wives. She watched with dismay how eager the young Indian women were to attach themselves to Canadians. It was obviously a mark of great prestige within the Cree to have caught a white husband.

"I suppose the day after I'm butchered, Jean will go gallivanting off with some Indian and forget all about me," she muttered out loud in great bitterness.

Jean overheard her. He strode over and tried to take her in his arms, but she turned her head away.

"No! No! My dearest one." He managed to get hold of a hand and raised it to his lips, kissing her fingertips. "You and I are different. We have a Christian family together. We were married in a church by a priest. Someday there will be priests out here and white friends for you. I know there will. I promise you there will. And never, never would I run away and leave you to fend for yourself amongst savages."

Marie Anne clasped her hands together and stood very straight like a small pillar of stone. "Jean, we are different, just as you say. Which is why I want to bring up my children as members of the church, not heathens. I am tired of wondering which precise day it will be our turn to be butchered."

Jean Baptiste fell silent. It was too sore a point to bring out into the open any further for one day. Husband and wife looked at each other in sorrow and in anger.

"Please remember one thing," Jean mumbled with a broken sob. "You are my dearest wife, my queen, and you always will be."

Jean reached for her hand once more, and in a moment they were in each other's arms. The argument was far from resolved, but each one realized again how utterly dependent they were upon one another.

"Whatever happens," Jean whispered into her ear, "we are man and wife. The priest said it was so. And I do love you, Marie Anne, my dear one."

Marie Anne snuffled. "I love you too, Jean, dear heart," she whispered. "I will try to be the wife you want me to be, but I cannot help dreaming of getting settled down somewhere some day with a real roof over our heads we can call our own. And not at the mercy of a stray band of savages."

Jean had no words. He could see that Marie Anne had a point, but what on God's green good earth was he supposed to do?

For the remainder of the summer, Marie Anne stayed close to the fort. Jean Baptiste went out on the buffalo hunt with his old friends, for as he tried to explain to Marie Anne, how else was he to provide the meat for his family in the coming winter? He made arrangements with the other Canadians to have their new wives, the young Cree, prepare meat for smoking and scrape hides for new sleeping robes. They were only too happy to oblige, as it increased their ability to do a bit of trading at the factor's store.

Jean shook his head sadly when he realized that these ladies were as anxious to trade for spirits as their male relatives. He disliked being the agent who gave them independent means to trade when all they wanted was firewater. His old friends were indifferent to what was happening to their new wives as long as the women worked cheerfully as wives had always done. Drunk or sober, they seemed to Marie Anne to be saying, what does it really matter?

The plains were changing all right, and not for the better in Jean's opinion.

Marie Anne did occasionally take to the plains, but only on short trips, never more than overnight. She planted new crops close by the fort. What if the Blackfeet did come and help themselves? Better that, she reasoned, than another run-in with the Sarcee. She made sure that she was always within an easy ride back to the safety of the fort.

Jean and his friends frequently talked the situation over together when they had ventured farther from the fort and were camping overnight. The encounter with the Sarcee was far from forgotten, and they all braced continually for a surprise raid.

"It seems as though there are more and more Indians coming around for fewer animals these past few years," said Belgrade one evening.

"That's how it has seemed to me too," answered Jean Baptiste. "Those Sarcee are coming from way farther north and west than they ever used to, and it's only because there is less game now where they were."

"Maybe our winters aren't quite as cold as their old stamping ground. I guess they find that attractive too," chimed in Chalifou. "No doubt about it. Times are changing." The men sucked on their pipes for some moments.

Jean Baptise mused, "I guess that Mr Bird may know something when he told me that when the game really starts to dry up, the company will want to bring homesteaders out here. Those company men back overseas will be wanting to make money out of some kind of activity in all these grasslands, that's for sure. And where you can grow grass, you can surely grow grains." Jean Baptiste threw more wood on the fire.

Settling himself down again, he continued, "In the meantime, so Mr Bird says, there is more demand every year for winter ermine and beaver pelts. He even told me that the number of ermine tails with black tips on a huge sort of shawl that an official is allowed to wear is governed by his position at court."

The men all laughed uproariously at that one. "Such a notion. So that's the real reason the price we are getting for winter ermine has increased a bit," observed Paquin, refilling his pipe.

Chalifou thwacked his thigh. "Well, I never. Mr Bird told me that the price they can get for beaver pelts has gone up a bit too in the last year, because the men of fashion back overseas are all wearing beaver hats! Beaver hats! That must be quite a sight. But the money we get is a bit better than it used to be, so here's to beaver hats, I say."

Paquain leaned back and stretched his legs. "There's getting to be some ill feeling about the way the Bay Company officers don't want their employees to take country wives. I think there'll be a mighty big load of trouble coming about because the factors are all keeping country wives anyway. Look at Mr Bird and his good lady."

"But when the company men go back to the old country and leave their women and children here with no support," said Belgrade, "that's when it seems a shameful thing to me. Especially when they promise to come back for them, but they never do. I've never heard of one Bay factor coming back for his family. The wives have a hard time waiting and waiting and trying to feed the children. No wonder the company is trying to stop it. Not that they ever will. It's a bad business all round."

"There's trouble brewing about that, and there's trouble brewing between the Company and the Nor'West," added Chalifou. "When the Hudson's Bay Company kept to the north and the North West Company centred around Fort William and as far west as the Red River, there was no real competition. Both companies kept pretty much to their own territories. But now that the Bay is moving south and the Nor'Westers are always moving farther west, those two are going to meet head on." Chalifou banged his fist into the palm of his other hand. "Then we'll have one almighty fight on our hands," he said with his pipe clenched between his teeth.

Belgrade shook his head. "With demand for furs getting bigger all the time and the pelts getting harder to come by, it's no wonder each company is expanding its forts. Have you noticed how when one company sets up a new fort, the other comes along and offers competition? The Indians are going crazy shooting anything that moves on four legs just to be able to trade for stuff they got along without before all this fur craze started. Everybody is going to be shooting anything that moves pretty soon. It's crazy. Why can't we all cool down?"

"If it weren't for this fur craze, as you put it, we wouldn't be here." Paquin stood up. "If there's to be a war between the companies, I intend to stay out of it and keep on selling my furs to the highest bidder. But right now I'm turning in. Goodnight."

"If there's a bidder left after the shooting," said Caplette, a voyageur drawn to their by fire the sound of French, and he stood up too. "I'm off to get some sleep."

Belgrade watched them go. "You know," he said, "things are shaping up to be ugly. Mr Bird told me that the Hudson's Bay Company is planning to set up more forts and trading depots right to the western sea as well as down to the southern limits of their territories."

Jean Baptiste leaned forward, staring into the fire as though he wished the flames could reveal the future. "We may be in for trouble from another quarter. Mr Bird told me that the entire area south of the Hudson's Bay holdings was sold to the Americans. He called it the Louisiana Purchase. The Americans want to establish white settlements throughout their west. When the Dakotas and the other tribes down there get wind of that, there will be trouble. It's beginning to sound like more than a three-cornered fight to me. Did you know it was the Emperor of France – Napoleon, he said – who sold all that land? It's a strange business."

Letendre, a newcomer, almost dropped his pipe. "The what of France? Emperor indeed. Well, I never. And this emperor is selling off land in the New World? Too bad we aren't around to buy it."

The others all laughed. "What with? Hey there, Letendre. When you get to be rich, why don't you buy New France back from the British?" Chalifou grinned at him and then looked thoughtful. "If we have to take sides, I'll be for the Nor'West. At least most of their factors are Canadians. How about you, Jean?"

Jean Baptiste studied the flames in the fire very carefully. At length he said, "How can I make a choice? I have a Canadian wife. I have to go wherever it's best for her and my children."

At the mention of children, Belgrade and Chalifou shrugged and looked at each other. "That's a problem we don't have any more. Children. Not this summer, anyway,"

Belgrade sighed with a great heaviness, and there was a deep sadness in his voice.

Jean thought that it was too bad Marie wasn't around to see that Amie's husband really was in mourning.

The men stretched, made up the fire, and turned in to their tents. Each one had sudden private thoughts about changes on the horizon and even the very real possibility of some kind of accident like poor old Bouvier. They turned to throw something extra on the flames.

As he made his way to his solitary tent, Marie Anne's loneliness and her fears, especially for Laprairie, and all the events of the past spring and summer weighed heavily upon Jean Baptiste. He wished with all his heart that she was waiting for him, snug and warm and welcoming. He ached to get back to her.

"How I miss her," he thought, rolling over to sleep.

Next morning, however, with the sun up early, hot and golden, and the needs for next winter's meat uppermost in their minds, the hunters set off about their business. Gloomy thoughts were only for the night, seemed to be the thinking of them all.

Jean set his jaw. "The faster we get the harvest we need, the faster I'm home," he said to himself.

All through the summer, Marie Anne was kept too busy to brood for long about her misfortunes and the loss of Amie and her other friends, but all the same, she missed them constantly. She had the buffalo hides to finish for their new bedding and fresh boughs to gather for their sleeping comfort, and always, she had to be on her guard to protect her children. But she had no close friends at the fort now except for Mr Bird, who was a busy man, and dear old Bouvier, who was always ready to set down his tools and have a chat.

The factor's wife was far too grand in her skirts and blouses of fine fabric and European cut to pay attention to the wife of a trapper, even if she were a paleface and her husband insisted that she live inside the stockade. There were plenty of country wives of the junior officers more suitable to be her companions than that paleface. The fact that occasionally the officers went home on leave promising to send for those country wives but never doing so made no difference to her. Sometimes those wives went back to their own tribal bands along with their children, and she saw no more of them. In her opinion, the bedraggled-looking white wife of that trapper should go and talk to other trappers' wives if she wanted company.

Marie Anne was left out of female society altogether. Despite her loneliness – for Jean Baptiste had to be away frequently on his expeditions winter and summer – she found solace in her two little ones. She recognized that Jean must be away. After all, his traplines and his musket represented their lifeline to the trade necessities at the company store.

She turned all her attention when he was away to teaching Reine and Laprairie what she could remember of the old ways and the old days: their catechism, their prayers, counting on their fingers. She tried to help little Reine understand that the few playmates the child had were neither beneath her nor above her, just different. It was hard for Reine to grasp when she could see other little girls playing together but she was not always allowed to join them. For the remainder of the summer and through the winter that she celebrated her third birthday, she stayed closer to her mother than before, when she and Amie's children had romped together. When she asked her mother if Amie's children had gone to heaven, Marie Anne was hard put to find an answer that would fulfil the tenets of her faith and at the same time recognize her deep feelings about Amie's goodness and her little ones. At times like this, Marie Anne wanted to break down and howl. She grieved more than she realized for her Cree friends.

When at last the crows returned, the crocuses seemed to spring through the snows which disappeared like magic, and the ducks and geese came quacking and honking home, Jean Baptiste approached her with a pleading that was new in their relationship.

"I do need you on the buffalo hunts, you know. What if we go far to the south this summer? I hear the hunting was better last year down there, and we will be far enough away to miss contact with the Sarcee. Besides, we will travel together in our own family group, so we can move faster if need be than in a large and cumbersome band."

Marie Anne looked thoughtful. "There are forts near where you want to go, are there? We won't be off somewhere where there is no hope of succour in case we do run into trouble, will we?"

It was a conundrum. Jean Baptiste assured her that from all he could gather from talking to many other hunters, the spoils were indeed better, and there was not the same bitter feuding among the different tribes.

"How will they feel about a newcomer?" Marie Anne's eyes were bright blue and cold.

"Cree is understood by everyone in the south areas, and we both speak Cree," was all he could say.

"What about forts, Jean? Are there forts or not?" Marie Anne asked him with a firmness in her voice that made him wince, especially as he had no firm answer to give.

Somehow, the argument seemed to be settled. Marie Anne didn't remember agreeing, but Jean went ahead and made all the plans of just where he was going that summer. Accordingly, as early in the spring as it was feasible, they set off once more together for the prairies and the calf hunt. Their plan was to travel so far to the south that the earliest possible start was a necessity.

When Marie Anne mounted her horse this time with Reine in a larger saddlebag that her father had fashioned for her and Lap in the smaller bag, she wondered how she would manage on the way back. Sometime in the summer of 1810, she knew that another Lajimoniere would be joining the family. It was already a trifle awkward for her on the horse as it was. She hoped against reason and hope that she would be near enough to a fort of some kind to get help. Mr Bird informed her that at least one factor he knew of had at one time practiced medicine, and though he would be more experienced in stitching scalps and setting bones than delivering a baby, at least he might be of help, but he didn't really know where any such factor was. He reminded her that at least a couple of the Bay factors had served as ship's surgeons in the Royal Navy at one time or another in their careers. Hoping to find a fort and hoping to find a factor who had had experience in midwifery was the longest of long shots, but as Marie Anne admitted to herself, what other hope did she have and what else could she do?

Once more Marie Anne had rolled up the hides for their bedding and hides for their lodge, and of course she had packed her big iron kettle for rendering buffalo fat. Tears came to her eyes as she thought of the day she and Amie had thought themselves so clever at acquiring their pots. She missed Amie's companionship deeply, even though they had not been as close for the last few months.

She straightened her shoulders and forced herself to think with extra attention only of packing the knives she needed for the scraping job ahead. She glanced over at Reine playing quietly with a cornhusk dolly she had concocted out of little scraps of antelope hide and a few beads for eyes and mouth. Smiling at the little girl so busily attending to her pretend baby, Marie Anne thought she would have to see about a new pair of moccasins for the child. It was amazing how fast the little feet were growing, and Lap needed a complete new outfitting from top to toe. Marie Anne rubbed her sore back. Yes, she thought, with another on the way and all the chores that had to be done, it was going to be a busy summer. She counted up on her fingers for the seventh or eighth time at least this morning. It could not be long now, she figured.

"Please God," she prayed, "let me get to wherever we are going and at least get the lodge set up before I have to go through another birth."

Jean and Marie Anne made their way almost due south, and eventually, after many days' ride, reached the Cypress Hills, within a day's ride of the southernmost reach of the Hudson's Bay territory. They decided not to go farther south. As they were leaving the fort, Mr Bird had taken Jean aside and warned him that the sale of land they had heard of, the land deal between the French and the Americans, had been in force for seven years now. It was more than rumour that the Americans wished to colonize their prairies with their own people from the eastern seaboard. Mr Bird warned Jean to stay well north in Bay territory, as he had heard of uprisings from Indians in the southern plains. Jean thanked him heartily and made a note to keep the advice well in mind.

"Another attack like last summer would really do it for Madame, my wife," he admitted.

The Cypress Hills beckoned them, and Marie Anne was grateful to be in a place where she could at least settle for the summer. The area was a favourite stopping place for many bands. Cree, Assiniboine, Gros Ventre, and Blackfeet all made it a meeting place, a good spot to rest and catch up on others' news as the various groups migrated north and south on the buffalo hunts.

For the past two or three days, Marie Anne had become increasingly uncomfortable on her horse. Her pregnancy was well advanced. The baby had dropped, and her back ached unceasingly. She saw the Cypress Hills as a sort of heavenly salvation. No more riding for at least a few days and the possibility of finding someone to help her, or at least kindly neighbours, buoyed her up and helped her to keep going. But as soon as they made their presence known and had selected a spot for their lodge, it became obvious to both of them that they were amongst stone-faced plainsmen and their families, and nobody wanted to enter into friendship with this white hunter and his brood. A white hunter married to an Indian woman was one thing, but an all white family in their midst? No.

While Marie Anne rested, Jean set up their teepee. This time he made sure the horses were well and truly tethered and that Reine and Lap stayed with him, even though they got in the way with their funny little attempts at helpfulness. Turning at last to Marie Anne, he realized that her time had come.

With no one else to help, Jean became her midwife.

He bade Reine take charge of Lap and not stir from just inside the opening flap of the teepee. Then he took charge of Marie Anne, doing as she asked, holding her hands, and helping her to sit up with his arm as her support. Fortunately, the third baby came into the world without mishap. The little girl was delivered successfully by her father. He followed all the instructions Marie Anne could give him in between her labours.

Jean held his wee daughter in his arms, an expression almost of disbelief on his face. "A miracle, a miracle," he kept saying over and over.

Weak as she was, Marie Anne smiled happily, thinking that for Jean it *was* a miracle. She remembered how she had felt when she first held Reine.

"After all, this is the first time he has been present at a birthing, and of course it must seem like a true miracle to him. And not only present," she thought, "but now he knows how to be a midwife!" In spite of herself, she giggled.

Jean Baptiste was a very pleased man and extremely proud of himself as he held up their third baby and kissed the wrinkled little red face and then his wife. He called the children over, and both kissed the new sister with awe and affection.

"Let's call her Cypress," said Marie Anne.

The children both nodded. They liked the sound of it.

"Why not, dear one, as she was born in the Cypress Hills."

So saying, he sprinkled a little water – not holy water certainly but water all the same – and christened her with the sign of the cross on her forehead then and there.

Jean made it his business to stay close to the encampment. Marie Anne was still weary after both the ride and her confinement.

"I'm still only twenty-eight years of age, but sometimes I feel a hundred and twenty-eight. I don't seem able to pick myself up and feel strong again as I used to do," she said to Jean one evening.

"It's not too surprising, dearest. We have all had a lot to disturb us these past years. But our life will get better. I know it will. You'll see." He grinned one of those wonderful smiles that lit up his whole face and still had the power to make her forget every bit of present discomfort.

When Cypress was less than a week old, they had an unexpected caller.

A small party of Assiniboine had arrived. Somehow the chief had heard reports about the remarkable little boy, the one with curly yellow hair, bright blue eyes – yes, blue, the colour of the sky – and a face that looked as if a wild rose had left its mark on each cheek. An altogether pretty sight indeed. The chief was intrigued and decided to have a look for himself at this unusual boy.

The Lajimonieres were puzzled by their visitor. He made it plain that he wished to speak only to Madame. Jean asked him courteously to enter the lodge, but the chief declined. He wanted to speak to the white squaw outside. Jean tried to remonstrate with him, declaring that Madame was not well and did not wish to rise. The chief became more insistent, and a crowd began to gather. Since no one in this group could by any stretch of the imagination be called a friend, Jean thought it better to ask Marie Anne to come out and see what it was he wanted.

Still feeling weak and tired, Marie Anne dragged herself out of her sleeping robe and stepped out on Jean's arm. The chief then took the reins of one of his best and most beautiful horses, a magnificent animal, and wrapped it around her wrist. Then he made motions that he wished to take the white boy in trade.

Marie Anne leaped back, throwing the reins at him as though they were red hot and nearly dropping wee Cypress at her breast. She reached for Laprairie and clasped him to her so fiercely that even Lap was stunned. She shook her head in fury.

"*No! No! No!*" she cried out in anguish.

The chief understood only that his offer was not enough. He selected another horse and wrapped both reins around her wrist.

Marie Anne flung off the hated reins as though they belonged to the devil himself and were burning a holes right through her arm.

"*No!*" she shrieked in desperation and started to cry. "Jean, you tell him that I will never sell my son. They will have to tear my heart out of my body before I will let go of my son."

With pride in her courage, Jean relayed the message, wondering as he did so how best to defend the family from this persistent fellow. He stood prepared to take on the whole tribe if need be and fight to the death.

The chief merely looked perplexed. The whole offer seemed a natural enough barter to him. He thought he had even been generous. Bargaining one child for another had been done so many times right here in these hills. He couldn't think what was making this woman upset. A very curious woman, he thought. He shook his head but decided to try again. If his two fine horses were not good enough, perhaps she would look favourably on his son as well as the two horses. He called his little boy to come and stand beside him. The little fellow was just about Lap's age.

"These two horses and my son for your son. That's a good trade for you." He stood back grinning. He was sure that she would not refuse so grand an offer.

Marie Anne wept more and more loudly. If she had not known how deep despair could be before, she thought she was plumbing the very depths of despair and anguish now. She covered Lap's hands and face with kisses and buried her head in his neck.

"*No, no, no, no, no, no,*" could be heard in sobs from the heartbroken mother.

The chief was nonplussed. So much grief over so ordinary a matter! At the new sounds of her racking sobs, he decided he had had enough from this queer woman. He shrugged his shoulders and spread his hands to show there would be no more bargaining, and he was not going to repeat his offer. With his head held high, he marched off giving his best impression to his warriors that he had changed his mind and the woman had been too greedy to make a trade. He had simply changed his mind about the child and had thought better of it. Perhaps the child was not in good health anyway, which accounted for that white skin. If the child were to grow up like its mother, getting so upset about trivial matters, he was better off not to have traded for him.

The Assiniboine mounted their horses and rode off while Marie Anne collapsed in a heap on the ground outside the teepee.

"Jean, I don't think I can live through one more of these encounters. That's the third time I have had to fight to keep Laprairie. I'll never understand their ways."

Jean held her close and patted her shoulder. "I can see we are going to have to think of the future, dear one. Maybe the time has come for us to settle down somewhere. But don't ask me to give up hunting. It's the only way I know to provide for us all. Besides you and the children, it's my whole life. Please don't ask me to go back to Canada. I couldn't go back a second time. By now, who knows? Our parents may be dead. I can't go back now and beg for land from my father, if he is alive, or from my brothers. I have too much pride to beg and anyway, I'm no farmer. We have nothing to go back to in the east."

"Oh Jean, dearest Jean, I think I know how you must feel. There's no land we could have from my family either. I only want to do what is best for us. It's just, well, that man made me so angry and so frightened and so sick at heart. Jean, what is to become of us?"

Jean tried his best to comfort her, but conversations with his friends and particularly with Mr Bird went through and through his mind. Things were changing, and quickly too.

He tried to shut the unpleasant realities out of his head and prepare himself for a solo affront on the buffalo.

Despite the inauspicious start, the rest of the summer passed uneventfully, if such a life of hunting enormous and powerful beasts could ever be termed uneventful. Cypress was a happy baby, as indeed all Marie Anne's babies seemed to be. She had the famous blue eyes of her mother and the brown curls of her father and was altogether a bonny little soul. Reine was overjoyed at having a new baby, a real one, and was learning to help in her care. Lap took the arrival of another sister in good stride. He already adored Reine and toddled after her everywhere.

At the end of the late summer hunt – a successful one according to Jean's modest standards – the family started back on the long route north and a little to the west to Fort of the Prairies.

Marie Anne was happy to be on the move again, despite the awkwardness of travelling with two small children and a baby. She fashioned a secure saddlebag large enough for Reine, who rode in state with her father. Laprairie graduated to Reine's bag, and Cypress rode in Lap's old papoose. Marie Anne sometimes wondered if there would be enough moss to go round and if she were destroying the entire growth of moss around the fort. She thought with thanks of the store of napkins stowed in the lean-to. They would be put to good use again this winter.

Husband and wife both rode and led the horses. It was a stately procession they made, and their daily prayers for deliverance from roving bands of unfriendly Indians as well as unwanted encounters with herds of buffalo seemed to them to be answered.

Fortunately, there was no need for speed this year. Marie Anne pondered whether their several guardian angels were all in agreement and on twenty-four-hour duty in guarding the Lajimonieres. Sometimes she wondered how long their luck could hold in trial after trial.

Many were the nights after the children had been settled down to sleep that Jean and Marie talked about the coming year, and the year after that and on and on. They discussed the increasing difficulty of one man trapping enough pelts to feed five mouths and one man alone in the dangerous business of bringing down sufficient hides to keep them warm and provide them with their dietary staple, pemmican.

"It takes a lot of work to dress the hides and make moccasins for the entire family, dear Jean. You wear yours out so fast and so do I, and Lap is forever getting into puddles and snow banks, and his get ruined faster than anybody else's. Besides, they are both growing like the grasses in springtime. There's a great deal of work in this roving life, much as I do love parts of it with all my heart. What a puzzle."

Marie Anne stared into the firelight. She tried to look into the future and work out how they were going to manage with yet another mouth to feed and goodness knows how many more to come. Not for the first time, she envied the women in the tribal bands with aunts, grandmothers, cousins, even less defined relatives, all ready to pitch in and help with everything needed – moss gathering, suckling, moccasin stitching.

"We are so alone, Jean," she said, taking his big hand in both of hers. "How are we going to manage?"

"We will have to make some sort of permanent headquarters for our young ones. I can see that now," said Jean regretfully. "But come, the children are sleeping, and it's time we were too."

Jean Baptiste built up the fire, took her by the hand, and led her into the old hide tent. Marie Anne took his hand in both of hers again. Some of the bitterness she had been carrying about with her since Jean first refused to consider going back to Canada when Amie was slain seemed to roll away from her and disappear. She felt lighter and happier at his words than she had been for months. At least settling down near a fort somewhere out here was better than all this travelling about like gypsies.

Next morning, as they packed and rolled up their belongings yet again, Marie Anne turned to Jean and asked, "Do we really have to go back to Fort of the Prairies, Jean? It seems such a great distance to the north. Isn't there a fort nearer where we could stay?"

"I think it best, my love, for this one last winter. I know Mr Bird well. We will be better off inside the stockade in our old lean-to than camping out or trying our luck at some fort where we aren't known. Trapping with a band of friends has a lot to recommend it, but living outside a fort as we once did is out for us from now on. I can see that now. I can see too what you mean about the difficulty of raising Reine in the middle of a band of Cree and Metis. And it looks as though Lap will always be a target for traders as well as raiders."

"And the children need friends of their own age, Jean. We can't go on isolating ourselves. Besides, they need to know more of our faith than we can give them. I tried to

265

tell Reine what a priest is, but it was so shocking to me – she just couldn't grasp it."

It was on the tip of Marie Anne's tongue to remind Jean Baptiste about the factor at Fort of Gibraltar and his friendly interest in them, but remembering the stories she had listened to of the difficulties between the fur companies, she decided to hold her peace. Jean did seem to be committed to the Hudson's Bay Company, if not by contract at least in his mind, and they had enjoyed the safety of Fort of the Prairies since Reine was a baby. Most of the Canadians seemed to be for the Nor'West, even though Jean's friends hung about Fort of the Prairies. She hung her head and thought with sadness that rifts seemed about to open between everyone – most of all between themselves and everybody they knew. It made it more important than ever for the two of them to stand together.

Her beloved Jean with his boyish love of hunting was her good man, and even a hint of willingness to settle down somewhere was a real change in him. Now when Marie Anne thought of Maskinongé, it was like a dream of years gone by. She could understand that Jean had too much pride to go home empty-handed of fortune, for they had saved no credit with the trading company. With three small mouths to feed as well, it was a conundrum indeed. She snuggled closer to him and passed into sleep unable to see what their future would be.

CHAPTER 17

The winter and spring of 1812 passed quietly. "What a relief that is to both of us as parents," thought Marie Anne. "No one trying to steal or trade Lap, so far at least."

It was true there were small upsets here and there, but nothing that Marie Anne could not handle by herself when Jean Baptiste happened to be off visiting his traplines with Belgrade and their Cree and Canadian friends.

Marie Anne frequently felt like a mother duck setting off for water with her two plump ducklings waddling along behind her and Cypress on her back. She still frequently went to visit Bouvier, who had made himself a valued member of the staff. He looked forward to her visits, sometimes carving little images for the children out of extra bits of wood left over from his carpentry duties. He made them all wooden crosses, crude but recognizable. Marie Anne was grateful, although she caught herself thinking the children could not grasp the significance of the crosses, and they did make a tiny bit more baggage to be carried about.

Belgrade and his new bride settled down together happily enough, and it looked to Marie Anne as though there would be a new Belgrade family starting up by late spring. She wished them both well.

Although she tried her best to extend friendship to the new wife, an easy relationship did not ensue. Part of the problem, which Marie Anne could understand well enough, was that she was must appear to be an old woman to a girl of probably no more than sixteen years. The discrepancy was not unusual, for a Canadian frequently chose a country wife or a squaw much younger than himself. Nevertheless, it came as a start to Marie Anne to realize the she must seem more like a grandmother than a contemporary in the eyes of the young bride. Marie Anne had noted with a mingling of dismay and amusement that when she passed her twenty-eighth birthday, according to local custom, she was now definitely classed as aged.

As well, she noted with some misgivings that Belgrade's new wife seemed as fond of spirits as her young contemporaries. Marie Anne turned her head in disgust. It seemed as though there were too many changes happening all around her, changes that were not, in her opinion, in the best interests of the little Metis, the children who after all were half Canadian and, in Marie's judgment, should be brought up in the knowledge and solace of the Catholic faith.

With no real companions left, Marie Anne felt very much out of things. This had been made obvious to her at Mr Bird's Christmas and New Year festivities.

"I'm neither fish nor fowl," she said to herself.

Now that the extreme and worrisome interest in Laprairie as a darling infant had passed and he was just accepted as another of the toddlers underfoot – albeit one with a remarkable complexion – she really missed the camaraderie of women friends.

Occasionally Belgrade came around to visit, and she particularly enjoyed his company. He and Jean smoked their pipes, swapped reminiscences, and ruminated on what they knew of the happenings of the world outside, gleanings from Mr Bird's slender store of information. The Emperor of France, she learned, was now at war with most of the Old World, and that included the English. Napoleon and the Americans were apparently allies, and what that would do to the border between the Americans and the Hudson's Bay Company was a subject they discoursed upon at length, coming to no satisfactory conclusion.

After their long talks together out on the grasslands the preceding summer, Marie Anne could sense a change in Jean's thinking. It was true that he was out as much or even more this winter on his trapping, but there had been no mention of a buffalo hunt next summer. Marie Anne waited in patient silence to see what Jean had in mind and what was in store for them all.

On a day in early spring when Belgrade and the others were preparing to go out onto the prairies for the first of the hunts, Jean Baptiste made his announcement.

"I have made up my mind," he told them all. "The factor told me that he had heard some startling news – news they had been expecting but rather a long time in the future, and as a statement of policy rather than a definite plan to be executed immediately. But Lord Selkirk, one of the most powerful men in the hierarchy of the Hudson's Bay Company, has purchased vast tracts of land from the Bay itself. He plans to bring out settlers, persons who in many cases were forced off the land they had farmed for generations. These settlers are to come from the old country – Scotland mainly, where the hardships are the most severe – and homestead on what are now his vast estates."

"Where is this place?" asked Belgrade.

"The land is near Fort Douglas in the Red River area," Jean went on. "Our factor wonders how that is going to sit with the Nor'Westers, since they thought the selfsame acreage was the hunting ground of their clients. He can see a few wrathful differences of opinion coming up over such a decision."

"Yes, I think I can too," smiled Belgrade, knocking his pipe on a convenient rock.

It became obvious to his friends that Jean Baptiste had listened carefully to Mr Bird. It had occurred to Jean that a man might benefit by such an arrangement. He took in all that Mr Bird was saying and wondered if it would be possible for a man to take possession of one of those large tracts of land for growing cereals and then continue to hunt and trap during the winter months.

Jean rubbed his chin and figured that if crops were not good, it might still be possible to ensure a supply of pemmican by going out onto the untracked prairies between the period of growth and harvesting. This might be just the way for him to get out of the dilemma – a fixed abode for Marie Anne and three children, but at the same time a place where he would be able to hunt and trap. He thought about it, and the more he thought, the more he liked the idea. It seemed like the answer to all their prayers.

Jean strode back to the lean-to. "Marie Anne," he said with an eagerness she had not heard lately. "Marie Anne, come with me. I want to talk over something important, and I want to talk about it outdoors. It's too big to think about cooped up over that fire. Come. I'll take Lap on my shoulders."

Marie Anne looked searchingly at him. Something must be afoot. She tied Cypress into the papoose, slung it on her back, and took Reine by the hand. Hardly daring to hope that Jean was deciding about their entire future and leaving the constant turmoil of the fort surroundings, she hurried after him. Once outside, Marie Anne harnessed one of Jean's dogs into the travois so that Reine could choose for herself whether to ride through the snow or tumble off and stumble around in the drifts. She picked up her rabbit snare with her usual care, just in case she saw some promising tracks.

Jean looked at the snare and laughed. "You won't surprise anything with this crowd, and I'm going to do some talking. This afternoon, we will not be playing stalking games." He swung Laprairie up and down to his son's giggles.

"Well," he said when they had gone a short walk from the fort. "Now that I have everyone's undivided attention, we are going east, back to the Red River."

He stopped to see what Marie Anne would have to say. Her eyes were wide open and shining. It seemed to be too good to believe.

"Please repeat what you just said," she said.

"I'll say it once more, but I think you heard me the first time." Jean Baptiste grinned at her. "This summer, we are all going on a long trip back to the East River."

Marie Anne grinned back at him. She had no comment; she was too happy to say a word.

"I thought that might just please you," he went on, still smiling.

Marie Anne could only nod her head up and down. Tears of happiness poured down her cheeks. Surely after all her pleadings and his absolute no, she was hearing things. She felt weak with the release of tension she had carried like a burden.

"We won't go to Fort Gibraltar this time. It will be Fort Douglas for us. We shall see how the land lies, and when they parcel out homesteads, I mean to be first in line."

Marie Anne's eyes shone with happiness through her tears. She stopped in her tracks, to the surprise of the dog behind her, and almost fell into his arms.

"Oh Jean," she whispered, hardly able to believe what she had heard. "Does this mean that we will be able to have our very own home, our first real house that's really ours? Something that we own, that belongs to us? With a real door and real windows?" Her voice was travelling higher and higher.

Jean laughed at her excitement. It fit right in with his mood, and he felt a lightness of heart for the first time in many months. He grinned down at her, and then, trying to bring her back to earth, he said, "Well now, just slow down a bit. First I have to fell trees, cut logs, fit them together, and hoist a roof onto the walls, so it can't be finished in a week or less. But yes, that is just what it means."

Marie Anne threw her arms around his neck and squealed with excitement. At the same time, there were tears running down her cheeks.

"It does mean so much to you, doesn't it, dear love?" he said tenderly.

Marie could only nod her head up and down. The lump in her throat and the tears pouring down her cheeks with the wide happy smile he loved so much were convincing proof, if proof were needed, that the courageous *hivernante* was about to get her dearest wish fulfilled. The only other wish was that there would be priests nearby this miraculous house, and a church.

"Perhaps all my dreams are coming true at once. Hold on," she thought, "one dream at a time." She wiped her cheeks with the sleeve of her shift.

"Now wait a bit, Marie Anne. Don't expect me to give up trapping altogether. For the first years, that will probably be the best cash crop we can rely on. But eventually you may just find yourself married to an elderly farmer."

She buried her nose in his chest and took a great deep breath. "Oh Jean. Oh Jean," was all she could say over and over.

The children both stared at their parents, wondering what the excitement could be about and deciding it must be something good, because both Maman and Papa looked so full of cheeriness. They pelted each other with snowballs. The dogs barked. Cypress woke up and yelled. In a short few seconds, the whole family had joined in a happy game of heaving snowballs at one another.

Finally, breathless from exertion and still laughing for no apparent reason to any passing Cree, the family gathered itself together. With the children still rolling about in the snow and a few more well-aimed snowballs, they headed back to the fort.

Marie Anne linked arms with Jean and tried to explain that it wasn't that she was dissatisfied with living inside a stockade in a lean-to patched with hides. It was just, well, with three small ones and the changes they could both see and foresee taking place on the plains, now that there was a possibility of the two of them settling down and living in their own house, a real house, she could understand now, very clearly, how much she had missed the comforts of a snug home in the last couple of years. Four walls, a roof, a well-fitted door, and windows to let in the light and keep out the blizzards was a blissful dream come true. The novelty of living as a free spirit, enchanting as it had been, was now wearing a little thin for pleasure.

Jean in turn patted her arm and admitted that to have the security of crops grown on their own land as well as joy from the freedom of hunting for meat was more and more appealing to him. "Especially so since Cypress's little papoose might just come in handy again." He grinned at her.

Marie Anne found waiting for spring more and more exciting with each passing day. She measured with her eyes how fast the snow banks were shrinking. The caws of the first crows brought her running out of the lean-to to welcome them back, with a light-heartedness she had not felt since Amie's death. She gathered bunches of the first crocuses and watched with glee when Jean brought out the old canoe that had not been used for three years. It had been stored out of sight behind the fort outbuildings and all but forgotten. Mr Bird watched him drag it out with approval and not a little nostalgia.

The canoe was repaired with care and a great deal of skill. Jean took Lap out with him to gather the spruce sap he needed to make the glue for patches. The little boy tried to be helpful, but like all two-and-half-year-olds, he succeeded in getting in his father's way most of the time. Jean was a good-natured and loving father who sat back on his heels to laugh at the mess his helpmate was making.

Watching them together, Marie Anne felt her heart singing to see them so contented with each other's company. "I hope this is the way they will always get along with each other," she said to herself.

While he was consistently good natured with the little fellow, Jean took great care that none of Lap's helpful mistakes would pass without his correction. The frail craft of birchbark had to be able to take on the current of the North Saskatchewan, a wide fast-running river. It had to be able to withstand whatever Lake Winnipeg could produce in mighty wave action. It was a long haul to Fort Douglas on the Red River below Lake Winnipeg, and Jean expected to be on the move the entire summer.

He knew there would be considerable danger from the river itself, although he and Marie Anne would be paddling with the current this time. On the other hand, it was many days' paddle between forts, which meant they would have to pause a number of times while he hunted to keep the family fed. They would be eating fish frequently, and duck's eggs, as well as any duck they could catch or shoot.

There was risk in the undertaking. Bouvier's experience was in both Marie Anne's and Jean's thoughts. To Jean, the risk was necessary rather than wait for the homesteaders to come out to Fort of the Prairies. This summer, there were three children. By next summer, all being well, Marie Anne would have another baby to tend. Jean had made up his mind to apply for a land grant, and he was going to make sure he was the earliest to get the best land.

"High time to be moving," he told himself.

Mr Bird, while approving of Jean's decision, prevailed upon him to wait for the supply boats. "You will have company at least as far as Lake Winnipeg," he said, trying to slow down the impetuous Lajimonieres so anxious to be off.

"I'm going to miss your little family," he told them. "I've become fond of all of you, and I'm thinking of your safe passage down the Saskatchewan. The Bay supply boats will have to leave you and turn north for York Factory at the mouth of the river, but I want to know for sure that you got that far at least."

The factor's words made sense, and to Marie Anne's relief, the actual departure date was put off until they could join the company flotilla. When Jean Baptiste told Marie Anne that Lord Selkirk was planning to send Europeans out to settle the Red River district and that she would have white neighbours for company, her excitement overflowed into whoops of joy.

"You sound like some of our present neighbours," Jean told her with a wide grin. "Your new friends will wonder where you have spent the last few years."

"Too bad for them." Marie Anne picked up Cypress and whirled her round while the baby grinned a merry toothless grin. "I'm just being happy the way everyone else shows it around here."

Jean laughed, Cypress cooed, and the older ones clung to the fringes on their mother's antelope shift and danced around with her in a circle.

When the supply boats arrived, the whole family was in a fever of preparation to be off. They could hardly contain their impatience while the Bay clerks tallied pelts and Mr Bird's ledgers were scrutinized.

Finally the morning of departure dawned bright and clear. The canoe was packed with great care. It was absolutely necessary that they travel as lightly as possible, with no unnecessary gear to be carried over the white-water portages. Reine was allowed her corn dolly, and Lap had a wooden horse carved by Bouvier, and both of course brought their crucifixes. The children were wedged into the midsection. There were last goodbyes to be said to Belgrade and the others. That was a hard parting. Marie Anne felt she was severing herself from a very special tie, and she could not help wondering if she would ever see Belgrade again.

For Jean too, the parting was sad. He and Belgrade had been through so much together, and Chalifou and Paquin as well. Mr Bird was on hand to wish them Godspeed and a safe journey. He patted each little head in turn and turned away quickly. The proud Orkney man was going to miss the gallant Madame Lajimoniere and the only white children he had seen for many a year. Bouvier came down and clasped hands with both Marie Anne and Jean, too moved to speak.

When the flotilla finally got under way, Marie Anne paddled bow with her papoose on her back, and the children waved a last farewell to their dogs and to Mr Bird. They were off on the long way back to the Red River.

Each day of paddling downriver was a day of excitement and anticipation. Marie Anne was glad to be using her paddling muscles once more. It was strenuous keeping up with the flotilla, but the boats were heavy with their cargo of pelts slowing them down a bit and she did her best. Mr Bird had made sure that food supplies in the flotilla were sufficient for the Lajimonieres as well as the Bay men. When they pulled into the night's camping spot, they were always given a warm welcome, and a place by the fire was made for them.

Each day they paddled east. Each day brought them closer to Canada. Marie Anne realized depth by depth how homesick she had been now that there might be a possibility of returning to Canada. Nothing had been said, of course, but the Red River was a long step in the right direction.

"Perhaps I shall see Canada and our own people again," she thought to herself. "At least this Red River settlement is on the way east."

She straightened her back and shoulders. The papoose was tucked in at her knees. No sitting up for Cypress, no gazing around and watching the scenery. The little one had to be content with a fine view of the great sky above her, strapped in as she was for safety, but she seemed well content with her position.

The entire trip down the river was without incident or surprise. Jean and a few of the Bay men occasionally took themselves off cautiously, for they were on foot, to replenish the store of fresh meat. Marie Anne rested, enjoying a small respite from the constant paddling.

She now knew for sure there would be another Lajimoniere to be fed in the New Year. Jean had suspected it, but when she told him, it seemed to him to be another reassurance he was doing the right thing for them all.

The company camped for two, sometimes three or even four nights at a time. The Bay men enjoyed the slow progress as much as the Lajimonieres were grateful for their company. At Fort Cumberland, they all stopped for several nights. The

Bay men had to pick up more pelts, and the Lajimonieres were glad to meet the factor again. He admitted that he had thought he would never again see Madame Lajimoniere in this world. That she was in good health and now had three youngsters with her was a source of amazement to him. He was almost speechless when told that not only did the white woman who could kill at a glance climb out of her canoe, but with new members of the family as well. This would surely be something to tell people back home in the old country when his leave came up. Getting his stay-at-home countrymen to appreciate what she had gone through and to believe him would be a real challenge to his storytelling abilities.

The factor had heard the account of Bouvier's fate from the Bay men and was anxious to hear from Madame herself how she had nursed the poor fellow. It came as a surprise to Marie Anne that she had earned herself a reputation as the *hivernante par excellence*.

As soon as the pelts had been accounted for and loaded on the company boats, they all set off again. The visit with the factor at Fort Cumberland had been a pleasant one for both the Lajimonieres. The white employees of the fort had all put down their quill pens at every opportunity to play with the small travellers; for many, it was a poignant reminder of home across the sea.

When the flotilla entered Lake Winnipeg, there was a leave-taking, with many a Bay man shaking his head at the bravery of that one canoe and its occupants taking on the treacherous waters of an inland sea. The Lajimonieres waved a sad goodbye when their escort turned north on its way to York Factory. Here the Bay Company ships were waiting for their cargoes of pelts destined for the courts and the fashionable world of Europe. Knowing that now they were truly heading in the direction of Fort Douglas far to the south raised the spirits of both Marie Anne and Jean Baptiste even higher

As he had done on the way up three years ago, Jean steered his craft close to shore. It meant a much longer journey paddling now east, now west, now north, now south, always skirting the jagged shoreline, but it was worth it to avoid the huge rollers that could have dumped them. When the breakers on shore made it impossible to take the canoe out, they simply stayed where they were for the time needed for the aftermath of a windstorm to subside. When finally they approached the bay at the southern tip of Lake Winnipeg, spirits were high indeed. Marie Anne sang as she paddled, and Jean chimed in with his deep ringing bass. Reine and Lap tried to sing along, and Pressie, packed into her papoose, wiggled a hand free and waved it in time to the music around her.

They were full of the keenest anticipation when they reached the fort. And so their disappointment was all the greater when the governor of Fort Douglas told Jean that the settlers were not expected that year at all. They both felt as though their dreams, their hopes, their world lay shattered at their feet.

The settlers had left Scotland too late in the year for the best sailing season. They had landed at York Factory as planned, but because the landing had been so delayed, it was thought that travel from York Factory all the long way south would be foolhardy. To encounter autumn storms and high winds on Lake Winnipeg would have jeopardized the whole enterprise. Facing bitter winter weather as soon as they arrived at Fort Douglas would have been an unnecessary hardship. There were many portages, and the canoes would have encountered ice for which they were no match. Either of the York or Nelson Rivers would have been an exhausting trip under the best of circumstances, but in freezing cold weather, it would have imperilled the whole Red River Settlement scheme, so Jean was told.

Jean could see the wisdom of their decision, but it did nothing to mitigate the disappointment they both felt. Marie Anne's hope for companionship and help – for it was obvious that another baby was imminent – were dashed in an instant. With the governor of the fort they held a hurried conference, the outcome of which was that the best policy for the Lajimonieres would be to press on to Pembina, where Marie Anne had passed her first winter, or most of it, and where Reine had made her entrance.

Jean was sure he would find some old comrades there, and with any sort of luck Marie Anne would be able to settle in before the baby arrived. Marie Anne wondered if she would encounter Jean's country wife, the potential poisoner, but she did not mention her concern to Jean, who had forgotten about the woman so completely that it did not cross his mind.

The family rested at Fort Douglas for a few days and then, sombre and subdued after the devastating news, took to the water once again. It took five days' paddle this time, and Marie Anne soon found herself too busy to be glum. The three small ones kept her continually on the hop.

At the fort in Pembina – a small fort to be sure – the Hudson's Bay factor made the family welcome and suggested they set up their lodge within the stockade. With gratitude they set to and erected their shelter, their winter home, and proceeded to make themselves as comfortable as possible. After her friendship with Mr Bird, Marie Anne found it much easier to communicate with the factor, a Scot, than was the case when she had first arrived at Pembina and elected to give birth to Reine in a teepee rather than enlist the aid of the Bay Company factor, the one who had helped deliver a child to one of his "boy" clerks. Jean soon found some old cronies – Cree he had hunted with in former years – and quickly made himself a part of their trapping expeditions. He was still remembered as an exceptionally skilled hunter and would have been welcomed anywhere in the area.

Once they had settled themselves in and taken time to look around them, both Jean and Marie Anne could see that the changes that had saddened them in Fort of the Prairies had been at work in Pembina too. Bands of Indians of various tribes hung around the fort, now reluctant to set up their encampments farther away than necessary from the factor's store of trade goods, and most particularly the factor's store of spirits. Cree seemed to be particularly vulnerable and were known at Pembina and throughout the northwest disparagingly as the "home guard."

Jean rode out with his Cree friends on the buffalo hunt in the late summer. He could see that the predictions of a decreasing yield of buffalo were coming true. He was also appalled at the method of buffalo hunting which had become popular around the Red River and Qu'Appelle, stampeding the beasts by means of a pair of fences coming together like an arrowhead at the top of a bluff. The animals were driven by many mounted riders shooting off rifles into the air to frighten the beasts into the trap. As they landed on top of each other at the bottom of the bluff, each would be killed outright by the fall or trampled to death. Not an animal could escape, and an entire herd would be wiped out in a day. Jean took only what meat he required and returned home earlier than his companions to Marie Anne.

Marie Anne's time came as she and Jean figured it would, just before the Feast of the Nativity. Again Jean was attendant midwife and deferred setting his traplines until after the baby was born and Marie Anne was strong enough to take over the running of the tentful. Perhaps it was because she had adapted herself so successfully to life on the open prairies, the semi-nomadic existence, and the lifestyle demanding considerable strength and agility that after the birth of her first baby, she had been able to produce the next ones almost as easily as did the Indian mothers. She was still never able to pick herself up and catch up with the band after a birth the way the Indian women could, however. She was thankful that she would not have to now.

Benjamin made his arrival without fuss or bother. He was dark-haired like his father and had the winning ways of all Marie Anne's children.

"Thanks be to God they are all healthy," Marie Anne said as she nursed her contented little son. "And with brown hair he may not be such a target for stealing or trading as Lap was, and for all I know, still is."

She shivered a little just thinking of those three times she had to fight like a sow bear to keep her firstborn son.

A couple of days of rest was something Marie Anne felt to be absolutely necessary after her confinement. She remembered with a faint sad smile how puzzled Amie had been about her friend needing to laze about after a delivery. Having her baby at Pembina was like coming home in a way, but yet with some big differences. This time Jean and Marie Anne had erected their teepee inside the stockade of the Hudson's Bay Company rather than outside the Nor'West fort. The forts were built close to one another, but the Bay fort was larger. Both the Lajimonieres sensed a feeling of trouble in the air, and Jean was no longer an independent trapper but now fully committed to trading only with the Hudson's Bay Company in the hope of securing his land grant.

As soon as the spring break-up arrived, the tent was dismantled, everything was packed once more into the canoe, and Jean and his family returned to Fort Douglas, all six Lajimonieres, to await the arrival of the colonists.

Spring turned into summer, and each day they went to the waterfront to peer downriver to the north, but no colonists appeared on the horizon. Husband and wife shared the horrible thought that Lord Selkirk, for whatever reason, had given up his scheme of bringing out homesteaders, and now the two of them were worse off than ever. The trapping had not improved at Pembina. In fact, far from it. It was plain to Jean that supporting a family of six in the old way around the Red River was not going to be possible.

Those were anxious days for the Lajimonieres. They turned to one another and always there was the unspoken comment, "Have we done the right thing?"

Late in the summer of 1812, Jean moved his family to Fort Charles, about twelve miles upriver from Fort Douglas. It was a small fort, and he reasoned that there might be less likelihood of the sorts of brawls that were becoming more and more prevalent in the larger forts. He still had to be away on the winter trapping trips. He set to work as quickly as he was able and built a log house, a very small one, their first real home. Somehow he got the sod roof on before the frost set in. In order to get it finished in the least possible time, he did not take time to saw out window holes or even floor it. It was shelter, a one-room shack, but little more could be said in its favour. As soon as he had satisfied himself that the six of them were established in their new home, Jean took off for the hunting grounds.

Marie Anne coped as best she could in the cramped space. She now had four lively children all under the age of five tumbling about on top of each other and getting into high-spirited squabbles under her feet. There were many times when she wondered if they had been so wise to leave Fort of the Prairies after all, but as she had learned to do all her life, she made a great effort to shed her melancholy and set to work to make the hut as presentable as possible and to teach the children their catechism or what she could remember of it. She was hard put to recall all that the priests had taught her and her mother's teachings as well. She wanted so much to pass on to Reine and Pressie, or Josephte a name to remind Marie of her sister, all that she had learned. Reine was already becoming quite a little helper to her mother when Marie Anne set a snare to catch an unwary rabbit that made so welcome a change from the everlasting pemmican.

Meanwhile, at the end of the summer at Fort Douglas, the first settlers did arrive. They were a bedraggled lot. Their route south from York Factory had been difficult, arduous, and exhausting. The previous winter, which they had been obliged to pass at York Factory on Hudson Bay, was more miserable and colder than anything they could have imagined. Many had died from the privations and hardships of a long sea voyage. Bad food, overcrowding at the Factory when they finally disembarked, and the inability of the Factory to cope with such an influx of wintering guests had sapped their strength, their spirits, and their endurance.

To her sadness, Marie Anne's loneliness was not alleviated by the presence of other white women in the settlement She saw virtually nothing of them because the distances between their shelters was far too great to make social calls feasible. The settlers spoke English with a broad Scots accent, and Marie Anne had difficulty in understanding anything they said when she happened to run into them at the fort. They in turn looked askance at this woman who looked white certainly but had taken to native ways and even dressed herself and her children in the heathen manner of the savage.

"So much for understanding and making companions of my white neighbours," Marie Anne said to herself.

In addition to the Scottish Highlanders, Lord Selkirk had arranged for two hundred Swiss nationals to come out and settle in the New World. It was a disaster from everyone's standpoint. The men for the most part were trained musicians, pastry chefs, and toolmakers. The women were skilled in lacemaking. It had not occurred to anyone, apparently, that these talents were not of immediate use in the rigours of Fort Douglas in the year of our Lord 1812. The Swiss missed their mountains. The general standards of cleanliness appalled them. They found the winters long, cold, and tedious. By the spring of 1813, family followed family as they all disappeared.

They were not prepared for the bare subsistence of frontier life and were even less inclined to weather the rough and primitive existence than were the Scots. Marie Anne and Jean Baptiste pitied them in their efforts to make such an enormous adjustment, but apart from knowing that they were in the fort, swelling the numbers of white people, the Lajimonieres had no contact, social or religious, with any of them.

That their general standard of domestic cleanliness appalled the newcomers brought Marie Anne up with a start. It made her realize how her notions of housekeeping had altered and how much she had adapted to necessity.

"Have I become a filthy savage as they said?" she asked herself. "Well, let them try to survive out on the plains as I have. Those ladies would have trouble keeping their hands clean enough to make their lace stuff."

She laughed at the very idea of lacemaking in a buffalo-hide tent with the fire making everything smell of wood smoke.

"And that's not all our tents and lean-to smell of," Marie Anne sniffed. "Good riddance," she thought, and then came the next thought: "I hope they send sturdier settlers out next time, if there is a next time."

She caught herself up short. "No more of that. Of course there's a next time. I hope, anyway."

With the arrival of settlers in their midst, matters between the rival fur companies became steadily worse. Most of the Canadians and the Metis gave their allegiance to the North West Company, with its headquarters in Montreal. It was mainly the Scottish settlers, the English, and the Orkney employees and their country wives with some Indians who sided with the Hudson's Bay Company.

That Jean had publicly declared his allegiance to the Bay had made him something of a stranger to the majority of the Canadians. Of course, he always stood out as an unusual fellow because he brought his wife out west with him. His hunting friends could appreciate that with his brood, a grant of land was very important to him, but still there was a growing coolness between Jean and the Canadian voyageurs.

"Hunters and farmers don't mix," he was told again and again. "Which are you anyway? You want fences for yourself, and you want open hunting ground as well."

Jean could well understand their questioning. At times, he felt torn in two.

Jean Baptiste did his best to provide for the family by trapping all winter. Marie Anne did her best to raise the children in a miserably overcrowded situation. As soon as spring made its most welcome appearance, Marie Anne went out to her garden, planting seeds of all kinds she had found and saved. She still felt she had to be extremely protective of all her children, particularly the little boys, even though their home was a few miles distant from the encampments and the fort.

There were many times in the winter of 1812 and the spring of 1813 when Marie Anne thought sadly that although she had dreamed for so long of being a homesteader, there were aspects of it in reality that made her look back on her days as a semi-nomad with some envy and not a little nostalgia.

CHAPTER 18

Throughout the long summer of 1812, Jean Baptiste had to be absent frequently for weeks at a time. There was no help for it. If they were to have food on the table in the coming winter, Jean had to secure their staple diet, pemmican, at the end of a gun. According to the calculations scratched on her robe, Marie Anne realized there would be another baby to join the four sometime late in the spring of the following year.

To her surprise, she found she missed life on the prairies – sleeping in the hide lodge and the feeling of freedom she loved in the vast open spaces. But with small people to manage, it was simply not practical anymore. Country wives and squaws managed because they were part of a large group. For one woman alone with so many children, following Jean onto the open grasslands was impossible. She turned to her garden with all the enthusiasm she could muster, and it was considerable. She also took the children on foraging expeditions to gather berries – anything edible growing wild – to enhance the pemmican. Her back ached and her shift felt tight, but harvesting had to be done. The year drew to its close with Marie Anne surveying a satisfactory store of dried meat and pemmican and Jean planning his traplines yet again. They were blissfully unaware of events going on far to the east of them.

The invasion of Canada by American troops; the several battles in both Lower and Upper Canada; warships on the Great Lakes; the struggles in Europe; Waterloo and Trafalgar; Napoleon's retreat from Moscow – nothing of these events reached their ears. They had no way of realizing how eventually the ripples from these far-off catastrophes would impeach on the western deserts.

They had too many difficulties of their own to spare much sympathy for the rest of the world, even if they had been aware of the turmoil. Just staying alive took all their energies. The winter of 1812–13 was exceptionally bitter. Again, Jean had to be away on his trapping for weeks at a time, desperately trying to accumulate enough furs to ensure his family's survival in trading credit at the fort, with enough left over to meet his needs for ammunition and a few other essentials.

In the spring of the year, Pauline, their third daughter, made her appearance. This birth was the first one for which Jean was not on hand, but Marie Anne was able to get help from the fort from the wife of a Scottish settler, a kindly soul.

The baby was born in a dwelling with a permanent roof, albeit a log shack. She was the first young Lajimoniere to have this luxury. Again, Marie Anne's incredible resilience and ability to rise above what were now exceedingly trying circumstances came to her rescue. Amazingly enough, all five children and Marie Anne survived the winter with a minimum of illness. Marie Anne had gathered maidenhair fern and prepared it as a syrup for anyone who coughed or sniffled. She made sure that this winter of all winters, living as they were in such crowded conditions, an adequate store of spruce gum was stored, which she used when boiled with water as a healthful drink to ward off colds and minor ailments.

The succeeding year passed in much the same pattern as the last, with one exception: Marie Anne did not produce a baby. Jean was absent a great deal of the time hunting, as he had to travel much farther afield than in the old days. Marie Anne's full attention was given to coping with her houseful. Lap began to show a great eagerness to assist his mother in her garden. He was a real help to her, and one day, as Marie Anne watched him taking care of her patch, she realized that he had a genuine love of and feeling for the land.

"I do believe that one will grow up to be a real farmer," she murmured with pride. "He takes after both his grandpapas, even though he has never seen them."

It did occur to her that a possible early memory of his experiences right before his birthing might be an influence to stay out of the path of buffalo for the rest of his life. She couldn't help smiling at her memories of that afternoon.

"It's a little bit funny now, but it wasn't funny then," she thought and straightened her back as she leaned on her improvised garden tool, a small branch.

In the spring of 1815, the already intense rivalry between the two trading companies took a turn for the vicious. Employees of the Hudson's Bay Company, thirsting for excitement and with the braggadocio that comes with knowing you have a larger force than your opponent, opened fire and overcame two forts of the Nor'West, one at Pembina and the other at Fort Gibraltar at the mouth of the Assiniboine River where it joined the Red. Both forts were thoroughly looted, and the spoils of open warfare were taken back in high glee to Fort Douglas. It was an irresponsible and foolish beginning to a tragedy. The conquerors, feeling flushed with their first victories, set out to take Fort Qu'Appelle about five hundred miles almost due west. It turned out to be no victory for the Bay hotheads. The Nor'Westers drove them off and gave chase. In the meantime, all employees of the first two Nor'West forts had been taken prisoner. Letters, documents, and instructions from Montreal were seized.

In retaliation, and after their success at Fort Qu'Appelle, the Nor'Westers stepped up their attacks and stopped messengers from Lord Selkirk, who had taken up temporary residence in Montreal, coming into Bay forts, and took them prisoner. Matters were becoming extremely grave, as all combatants would require the lifelines of food and supplies from Montreal or from York Factory to stay alive over the coming winter.

Marie Anne and Jean, a scant twelve miles away from Fort Douglas, both shook their heads aghast at the desperate plight these foolhardy clerks were putting the entire population in. It seemed as though a kind of madness had overtaken them all, in Jean's opinion.

All summer long, there were skirmishes and small incidents. They became accustomed to the sound of gunfire but never its implication. Marie Anne kept her children close by her, whether Jean was at home on one of his short and infrequent visits or not. She began to feel like a mother hen with her chicks hanging on to her ankles the entire day and night.

It was a state of war, declared or not.

Governor Semple at Fort Douglas became increasingly alarmed as the summer wore on. Supplies and communications were not coming through, and the situation would be beyond desperate if some action was not taken. At last, in the early fall, when he had decided that there could be no relief from Montreal without a special intervention, he spoke to Jean Baptiste.

He told Jean that he had been unable to get any reports through, and his concern was that he would be out of communication with headquarters in Montreal over the entire winter.

"Lajimoniere, will you take correspondence from me to Lord Selkirk in Montreal? You know the country as no one else does whom I can trust."

Jean was stunned by this request. It made him realize just how bad the situation was if Governor Semple had to turn to him for such an errand. He promised the governor he would think it over very carefully. The governor impressed upon him the need for secrecy and asked for his decision overnight.

Jean started totting things up in his mind. It would be a distance of over one thousand miles. He would have to go through dense bush. There would be nothing in the way of trails for most of the route. He would be at the mercy of any Nor'West clerks or traders lurking about, which meant he would have to give all Nor'West forts a wide berth. Even the Metis would look upon him as a war prize. Perhaps there would even be a price on his head if he were missed, and if it got around that he was travelling on behalf of the Bay.

It was a challenge to be sure. Jean Baptiste walked down to the wharf of the fort and strode up and down weighing the possibility of getting through against the fate of all of them if he did not reach Montreal or simply did not go.

He decided that the only way he could go would be alone and mushing every step of the way. It was far too late in the season to think of taking a canoe, and far too dangerous, as he would have to pass various Nor'West forts on the only route he knew. If he mushed with dogs, dogs required feeding. It would be a lonely trek through forest up and down difficult terrain, rocky outcroppings, and frozen waterfalls. The days were closing in on their shortest spans of daylight, and prowling wolves would be at their hungriest. He sighed, and his shoulders sagged. The nagging thought that kept cropping up in his mind was that someone had to do it, and as Governor Semple pointed out, no one knew the woods as he did.

He walked slowly up to the fort and entered the stockade. He found the governor walking heavily from his office to his residence.

"I may be crazy, but I'll go. No point in wasting a night's sleep trying to make a decision. I've made up my mind. But there is a condition. I want your word that you will look after my wife and my family and see that they are given every care and the protection of the Bay. May I have your word on that?"

The governor grasped Jean's hand and his arm. "You have my word, Jean Baptiste Lajimoniere. I will guarantee the well-being of Madame and your children to the best of my ability. You can depend on me."

Jean walked slowly home, wondering how best to break the news to Marie Anne.

"When I get to Montreal," he told her, "I will get to meet the great Lord Selkirk himself, dear one, and it shouldn't take too long. I will be back for the Feast of the Nativity or very soon after. I can ask him when he plans to parcel out the grants of land and let him know I want one, and a good one, too," he told her.

He laughed and showed more self-confidence than he felt. Worrying Marie Anne would not help anything, but he knew as well as anyone that he was undertaking a perilous commission, and he also knew that she understood just how perilous his mission would be.

The first part of Governor Semple's promise to Jean was fulfilled shortly when Madame Lajimoniere and her children were invited to move into a spacious residence, the most elegant dwelling she had entered since leaving Maskinongé and right inside the fort. The children soon made themselves at home in noisy excitement. They ran up and down the stairs – the first time they had encountered such a thing inside a building. Proper rooms with doors fascinated them all. Reine set about making herself a dolly bed for the old corn doll she had brought from far-off Fort of the Prairies. Josephte copied Reine, and together the sisters constructed what looked almost like a little bed with a cover made of a piece of cloth they had begged from Marie Anne. That they had a room all to themselves for sleeping and playing in was something so new and so exciting. The boys had their own room too.

"Now girls, this is not our real home," Marie Anne reminded them. "It's just until Papa gets home."

The children wanted to know where Papa was going and why, but Marie Anne told them it was something that wasn't to be talked about until Papa came home. Since their Papa was away so much of the time anyway, the little girls settled down and were not sure there was anything much different about this absence.

Although Jean had tried to prepare himself mentally for any untoward eventuality, he felt fairly sure that he could manage to slip through the forest successfully. That he had lived the life of an Indian over so many years he felt was going to help him go alone on roundabout routes and through uninhabited country. He hoped that from a distance, he would be taken for any trapper going on his rounds and not be recognized. Speed was essential. He felt sure that the Nor'Westers would not dream of anyone taking to the woods over such a long haul in wintertime. Until the bush information signal system was activated – trappers noticing tracks they could not identify and rumours of all kinds – caught up with him, he was confident that surprise was on his side. Still, and he had to bring himself down to earth, the way would be exceedingly hard, and he would be travelling through the Nor'West and therefore enemy territory.

Jean Baptiste said goodbye to Marie Anne, who staunchly held back her tears so that it would look as much as possible like just another of Jean's trap inspections, and promised that he would return by the Feast of the Nativity or a day or two later. They embraced and kissed each other farewell on All Saints Day, November 1. Jean hugged his daughters and slapped the two little boys on their shoulders.

"Take good care of your mother," he told them.

Marie Anne silently implored every saint in the calendar to watch over her Jean on this, a feast day. One last kiss between husband and wife, one long look deep into each other's eyes, and Jean harnessed his dogs, flicked his whip, and was gone.

The children soon settled down into a routine, with Marie Anne supervising their tasks. Although their home was now spacious and – even by the standards of the Red River – luxurious, there were many more chores to be done to keep it clean and in good order. The boys frequently made off by themselves to go to the store, lonely for masculine company.

All was not serene at Fort Douglas, however. Sometimes the clerks were short with the little Lajimonieres, and Marie Anne tried to get them to understand that there was a great deal of trouble a long way off and that the men were naturally upset. "Try to stay out of everyone's way," she told them with a weariness in her voice that betrayed her own misgivings.

Thankfully, Marie Anne ground up the scraps of her dried meat, her harvest, and put it away for the winter, for who knew what this coming winter would bring in the way of reprisals and dangers. "And thanks be to God that the boys will not have to be outside the stockade tending to our patch now. We will all have to go together to get wood. There's safety in numbers, I hope."

Many of the men at the Bay fort by now had second thoughts about their bravado in taking over the forts at Pembina and Fort Gibraltar. They did not have a garrison to defend themselves from a concerted attack from the Nor'West and their Metis. The action had generated bitterness among both Metis and Canadians, as well as the Indians who traded habitually with the Nor'West. In retrospect, it now seemed a foolish act. It also meant that their own forces were stretched too thinly for comfort in managing the trading that should be occurring at the forts they had taken.

By taking Fort Gibraltar in particular, the Bay men had ensured that the supply boats coming in the spring to Fort William would be unable to get through to the important base fort at Gibraltar Point for distribution of supplies to all the Nor'West posts sprinkled throughout the prairies. It was a desperate situation for the Nor'Westers and all who had come to depend so utterly on the arrival of the supply boats with ammunition and trade goods – their very means of survival. They realized they would be destitute by the following fall, and in all probability, many would starve during the following winter if the supply boats were prevented from servicing their posts.

The men guarding Fort Douglas naturally expected reprisals and that an attack would most probably come from the west by the Nor'Westers at Fort Qu'Appelle. They all realized now that it would be a vicious and bloody battle. The stakes were high, and neither side had the capacity to deal with prisoners. Each man kept a wary eye on the western horizon.

In the meantime, Marie Anne, her children, and all the members of the little community not actively engaged in preparing for an attack and the possibility of siege were going about their daily tasks trying not to think of the inevitable. Marie Anne remained her stalwart self and focused on caring for her household, although always at the back of her mind was the thought that her nursing skills might be called upon. Their living quarters had improved immeasurably, but the open fireplaces took both tending and a great deal of wood-gathering. Jean had left his family with a good-sized woodpile, but as she told the children as they went out to gather whatever could be used for kindling, "the more exercise you get in the fresh air, the more warmth and comfort you will enjoy inside the house."

Christmas, the Feast of the Nativity, came and went, and no Jean as he had promised. Then it was New Year's, and the company men, mostly Scots, tried their best to keep up an air of jollity. Then came the Feast of the Three Kings and Reine's seventh birthday, and still no Jean Baptiste. Reine asked her mother repeatedly if Papa would be with them for her name day, and Marie Anne – keeping her annoyance in check at the repetition of the question – answered her again and again, "We don't know, my little Reine. We don't know. It is in God's hands."

Each night at bedtime, all the Lajimonieres prayed especially for Papa, that wherever he was, he was safe and well.

The winter dragged on and on. Tension did not lessen within the fort. Spring came at last, and with it a slight lifting of the fear shared by all. Governor Semple sought out Marie Anne to enquire about her welfare. The unspoken question was, "What news? Have you heard anything at all?"

A tiny shake of the head on both parts made them part in worrisome sadness. Governor Semple would have given a great deal to know if Jean had got through to Montreal. Marie Anne just wanted to know how her Jean was faring and where he was. By the time the sun was high in the sky to give them as much sunlight as darkness, Marie Anne carried a heavy load in her heart. She made a great effort to be reassuring and strong, motherly, and above all patient with her brood.

"Jean assured me that he would be back by New Year's at the latest," she thought, "and that we would have a splendid reunion after he had earned the interest and favour of the influential Lord Selkirk himself. After all, wasn't this fort, Fort Douglas, named for him, for his family name?"

Marie Anne closed her eyes and tried her hardest not to think of what could have gone wrong.

Sometime in the middle of June in the year of our Lord 1816, on a hot and sultry afternoon, the sentries noticed a line of Metis horsemen in the distance. The alarms were sounded, and every able-bodied male sped out to defend the fort.

Here it was at last, what they had all been dreading, an attack. And how many Metis had gathered together, and how many mounted warriors did they have? Was it a full-scale attack with the backing of Fort Qu'Appelle? Each man charged his musket and nervously took up his position. A force of men was detailed to leave the fort and go to meet the Metis.

The Metis in their turn sent a messenger to ask what the detail wanted and why these men were interfering with them. As it turned out later, it was a small contingent of Metis without warlike intentions who were simply proceeding farther down the river, hoping to meet with trade canoes that they'd heard had, mistakenly of course, set off from Fort William.

Somehow in the exchange of shouts, which grew more and more lively and finally rude and insulting on both sides, a shot was fired.

Before any of the excited men, Bay or Metis, had time to think what they were doing, twenty-one bodies lay tangled up together outside the fort. Experience in buffalo-hunting on horseback with breech-loading rifles had transformed the Metis hunters into a superb cavalry force, reloading and firing at full gallop with as much ease as they had shown time and time again on the hunt. Their prowess was disastrous for the Hudson's Bay Company. Governor Semple was one of the twenty-seven casualties of what later came to be known as the Battle of Seven Oaks.

Only six Bay men remained alive. Inside the fort, there was consternation. The corpses were rescued and the country wives wept. As well as tending to the burials, they were fearful for their own lives. While the Metis had not entered the fort and put the entire population to slaughter as yet, there was a sick fear in every heart that this would happen, and soon. When the Indian reserves came up, this would be the usual course. No one expected the slightest mercy.

When the boys first heard the gunfire, they were excited, running from window to window to see what was happening. Marie Anne was beside herself with worry. The gunfire sounded too close for her pleasure. She bade all her children stay together and crouch down near the fireplace in the big kitchen room where they ate and lived together. Josephte, began to cry with fright. She was told to hold her tears and be quiet. Marie Anne was in no mood to be gentle. No Jean and now this! Would her trials never end? Some of the Bay men had dared to speak of Jean as though he were dead. She had stopped that sort of talk at once, but now this warfare was right on her doorstep.

"Where, oh where can he be?" she cried.

The children were quick to understand that their mother – who seemed able to handle anything – was concerned, and they huddled together drawing comfort from one another. The girls covered their ears at the sound of gunfire.

At last darkness fell. The silence was terrifying. Marie Anne had no idea what had happened until a timid tapping at the door brought her up short. She went to the door she had barred and piled up with furniture.

"Who is it and what do you want?" she whispered.

It was one of the Bay men.

"Madame," he whispered back. "It is terrible. I'm alive, just. You'll be needed at first daylight. The six of us left are in bad shape."

Marie Anne gasped.

"And the governor. Is he all right?"

"No, Madame. He is dead. There are many dead. It was terrible, terrible. And God help us if the Metis bring up reinforcements."

The little family gathered around one another as closely as possible, making a knot of silent children looking to their mother for her commands. They repeated the rosary solemnly together and prayed for deliverance. There was nothing else they could do. Marie Anne wondered wretchedly where deliverance could possibly come from this night in their awful and vulnerable position. She wondered again and again if this would be their last night on earth. With their protector dead, their position was truly terrifying. That the Metis might enter the crippled fort and put it to the torch was only one of their fears. Their house would go up like a tinderbox.

Suddenly, the silence was broken once again by a light knocking on the door. Even more terrified, if possible, Marie Anne – first telling the children to be still and not cry out whatever happened – went to the door and, leaning against it, whispered through the crack.

"Yes," her voice was a sigh. "Who is it?"

"It's me, Madame Lajimoniere. Your friend Pigouis. You remember me? When my wife had her baby and she was so sickly, you came and helped me. You helped me. You remember now? Yes? Now I come to help you. Look, the Metis will enter the fort tomorrow at first light at the latest. More Metis will be coming with horses. You come with me now. You and your children can stay in my lodge across the river. You will be safer there than here. Come quickly. You must hurry. We have no time to wait."

There was a desperate tone in the Metis's voice. If the Qu'Appelle Metis had poured into the fort at that moment, he would have been butchered along with everyone else they could find.

With hands trembling so much it took her some time to unpile the furniture and to undo the latch, she got the door open and bade Pigouis come in. She bundled up what she could of the most necessary possessions, bedding hides, and as much pemmican as she and the children could carry. Urging the children to slip out quietly and do whatever Pigouis told them, Marie Anne brought up the rear, stumbling with her load and leading two-year-old Pauline by the hand.

In her rush to keep up with Pigouis, she yet observed that the Nor'West prisoners had broken their way out of the lockup and fights were breaking out between the prisoners and the badly outnumbered Bay clerks who had escaped the afternoon massacre. Pigouis was absolutely right. They were anything but safe in Fort Douglas now. With Governor Semple dead, Marie Anne realized her peril only too clearly. Here she was, a white woman with five children – and where, oh where, was Jean? How could she protect her children?

The family made its way as silently as any Indian slipping through the forest. The stockade gate was open. There was no one to bar it now. They all ran to the river's edge and climbed into Pigouis's canoe, each one following Pigouis's instructions exactly. It was a heavily laden canoe, and Pigouis was not having any accidents. Madame Pigouis paddled bow, obviously very nervous at the risks she and her good man were taking.

Marie Anne came last. Completely unnerved by what she had been through in the afternoon and what she had just witnessed, utterly distraught at what the future might hold, she lost her footing on the slippery river bank. Trying to stand up under her heavy load, she lost her balance completely, and the foot that was poised to land in the middle of the canoe crashed down heavily on the gunwale. In a twinkling the canoe tipped, the whole family and all their cherished possessions falling headlong into the water. A few other Metis also trying to make their getaway came to help right the canoe, get the children out of the water, and rescue their possessions. Marie Anne they also rescued, dripping wet. She was so worn out and so distraught that at the moment her children were tipped into the water, she fainted. Pigouis's friends plopped her into the boat in the greatest haste and sped back to their own canoes. Marie Anne came to in the middle of the Red River surrounded by her soaking-wet household goods and, miraculously, her children, hushed and wide-eyed but otherwise apparently unharmed by their ducking.

CHAPTER 19

Though still groggy, Marie Anne was able to get herself out of the canoe and as far as the Pigouis lodge still clutching her loads. Madame Pigouis made the children sit close to the fire to dry themselves out. Now that they were safe, it seemed like a real adventure, and they chattered happily about it. Their mother was too unnerved to join in the general feeling of relief.

The news that Pigouis had gathered about the Metis coming back the next day was correct. Fortunately, no one else was killed, but every living soul in the fort was taken prisoner and transferred eventually by boat to York in Upper Canada.

It often occurred to Marie Anne in later years that although she had wanted so much to return to Canada, it was the Canada she loved, Lower Canada. To have been made a prisoner and taken to York on Lake Ontario in Upper Canada would have been three quarters of the way back, to be sure, but she had no taste for being taken anywhere as a prisoner. She shuddered too as she thought how out of touch she would have been with the last place Jean had left her and known of her whereabouts. There were many who pitied Madame Lajimoniere and thought of Jean Baptiste as one of the casualties of either the war or of hunting. She rebuked everyone who spoke of her Jean in the past tense, maintaining that he was alive and would return soon.

For the remainder of the summer, the Lajimonieres stayed with the Pigouis family. They were jammed into the lodge like rows of fish left drying in the sun. The Pigouis were kind and hospitable. Both husband and wife were Metis.

Marie Anne did whatever she could to be helpful. Hunting was far too hazardous with armed warriors ready to fight anybody with as much enthusiasm as they usually channelled into chasing after buffalo. The entire lodgeful found it the better part of valour to remain close to the lodge. The Lajimoniere and Pigouis families ate fish day in and day out. They all wished devoutly for a change of diet, but it was not possible, and indeed they were grateful that they had a food supply at all and close at hand. Fish seemed to agree with the children, but while she was grateful for anything to eat to survive, Marie Anne hoped she would never have to endure the fish diet again in her whole life. Even going far enough afield to gather berries was considered dangerous. The survivors at the fort kept a sharp eye on what was going on across the river and were constantly on the lookout for Bay troops and a skirmish.

Each night, Marie Anne settled her children for sleep, and each night they prayed for Jean Baptiste and that he would soon come back to them. She was frequently on the verge of tears, but she tried valiantly not to show it, and above all to show a brave face in front of the children.

"Papa is perfectly all right and was just delayed by his important business with Lord Selkirk," she told the children.

In her heart of hearts she knew, beyond any reasonable doubt, that Jean was alive. She refused to consider that she would never see him again. She knew how adroitly he could slip through the forest. At times, she had nightmares about him. She called them feverish imaginings and willed herself back to sleep. She prayed constantly that somehow the God she believed in implicitly was taking care of her beloved husband.

Gradually, the nights lengthened. The geese flew south high overhead, honking and generally disputing whatever it is that geese so enjoy arguing about. Marie Anne and the five little Lajimonieres turned out to watch the great wavering Vs in awe. But the geese exodus signalled the end of summer, the end even of Indian summer. All around them on the east side of the Red River, there was a sense of peace, a sense of respect it seemed for the beautiful world around them – blue sky, the grass a golden bronze, trees turning into golden beacons.

"Where, oh where, is Jean?" was Marie Anne's first thought each morning when she opened her eyes and looked around at the closely packed bodies in the Pigouis lodge.

"It's overcrowded now," thought Marie Anne. "What on earth will it be like when the children can't run in and out of the lodge like puppies tumbling about and playing? Our hosts have been kinder to us all than we can possibly deserve or ever imagine paying back. I've got to stop thinking every day that Jean will be back tomorrow. That tomorrow may not come."

Appalled at what she had allowed herself to think, if only for a moment, she nearly broke down. "No, I mustn't think such a thing. Of course he will come back. And when he does, we will have to get him in here in this lodge with block and tackle, it's so crowded."

Their hosts urged her not to think of moving out. For one thing, where would she go? They had room. Somehow, everybody could manage. A well-filled lodge meant everyone stayed warmer. They brought up many arguments, and all were truly meant to be generous and convincing. Marie Anne thanked them but still felt she should try to find some kind of shelter within the area of Fort Douglas.

"This side, not the side the Nor'West has taken over," she pointed out with an attempt at light-heartedness.

Her hosts shook their heads. Their offer was indeed genuine. The Lajimonieres had not worn out their welcome.

At times, Marie Anne stole away by herself, venturing out on short tours of exploration in which she gathered wood or a few berries. One day she came across a decrepit and abandoned log hut. The Pigouis told her that a Canadian, an *hivernant*, Bellehumeur by name, had walked away and left it years ago.

"That's an auspicious name," Marie Anne said to herself with her old decisiveness. "Though it's in a mess right now, I believe with the help of the older ones, we could chink it and make it liveable. A good name and a good omen."

No sooner said and decided upon than done. Marie Anne proceeded to move her family and whatever they still possessed into the hut, and to the best of her ability make it waterproof, more or less. "Thank goodness I have no need of moss for a baby," she thought.

She and the children gathered what moss they could find and used it to chink the log walls. The roof leaked.

They tried pieces of sod, but it still leaked here and there, and there was little they could do about it.

"Not as impressive as the governor's house we borrowed across the river," they all agreed, "but it's home, and let's make the best of it."

All fall, the family lived quietly, storing up what they could catch of anything edible for what seemed a hopeless task: to stay alive all winter long. Day after day, the family fished and smoked the results until they were thoroughly fed up with the smell of the smoking fires and the fish drying. They had the smell in their noses, in their sleeping skins, in the hut itself, and certainly in their hair.

"Will we ever get rid of this stench?" Marie Anne asked. "What a dreadful smell. The only good thing about it is that it's food."

Nearly all the colonists had disappeared to the east where, reports had it, it was easier to get a start and the winters were not as severe. No one really knew if the Nor'West would send troops to wipe out sympathizers of the Bay who had managed to cling to their allotments. Whether the entire area would revert to hunting ground again or whether the homesteaders would get a toehold on their grants and start putting up fences, no one knew for sure. It grieved Marie Anne to see the would-be homemakers' hopes dashed and to watch them leaving. She had not made any particular friends among them, but still it had been a comfort to know a handful of white families lived in the neighbourhood.

"It's no wonder those poor souls want to get away to Canada and go farther south," she thought. "Who can put hearts and backs into the land when it may all be wrenched away from you? Yet I was looking forward so much to a settled farming life. The only people with whom I have any understanding are the Metis. The Red River settlers just passed us off as backward savages when we were only too willing to help them. Ah well, at least the one Scots lady helped me when I had Pauline."

Fear made a bitter taste in everyone's mouth, for the colony, dwindling month by month, was anything but independent of the supply boats. And who would be coming to relieve them next spring? Prospects were grim for survival.

As the darkest days of the winter approached, the Lajimonieres tried their utmost to mark the Feast of the Nativity with some sort of joyousness. Marie Anne had never lost the habit of putting a mark on her sleeping robe so that she would know when the various feast days came. The children tried to show anticipation for their mother's sake. Marie Anne tried for the sake of the children. It was a hollow sort of preparation, but each one put a valiant effort into it.

On one of darkest afternoons of late December, the family gathered around the few planks that made a table in their hut. They were trying to fashion a little crèche out of dried and inedible berries, duck feathers for angel wings, sprigs of evergreens – anything to mark the birthday of the Prince of Peace. It was taxing their ingenuity. As they worked, Marie Anne taught them a carol she remembered from the long days ago at the presbytery, *"D'ou viens tu, berger?"*

A loud thudding at the door brought the carol to silence. Their hearts pounding, the children instinctively rose to their feet, clutching the table with fright and preparing to bolt for the Pigouis's lodge if they could get through the only door.

Marie Anne tiptoed to the door and, with as much courage as she could bring to it, demanded to know who was there. Again someone banged on the door. Marie Anne pulled the wooden latch and opened the door a crack.

"Who is it and what do you want?" she asked, managing to keep her voice steady though she shook with fright. All she could make out in the late afternoon gloom was a weary looking *coureur de bois* standing patiently in the doorway.

"Well," said the stranger, bowing in a most courtly manner, "will you not bid your husband enter your home, Madame?"

Marie Anne nearly fainted on the spot. "Jean," she whispered. "Is it you? Really and truly you?"

Jean caught her just as she was about to fall. The children ran to the doorway and pulled him inside. They leaped up and down in his arms. They all cried and laughed and tried to speak at once. Jean, of course, laughed the loudest of all. Worn out as he was, his delight in the pandemonium he had caused inspired the children to greater and greater heights of joy. Delight, relief, tears, and laughter all tumbled out on top of one another until the rafters rang and everyone was exhausted.

Laprairie had to be measured to see how much he had grown in the past year. Reine had to sing the carol they had just learned.

"Where are you coming from, shepherd? Where are you coming from? *Papa* is more like it," she said.

Everyone roared with laughter. Everyone had a chance to show Papa something that Maman had taught. Laprairie seemed to grow even taller with pride when his mother told Jean how much help he had been, the little man of the family. And Benjamin, too, she said quickly, when she noticed the beginning of a tear of envy at the praise heaped on his older brother.

"We have all prayed for you every single night, Jean," Marie Anne told him. "And each morning, too. Our prayers are answered, as we knew all along they would be. Let us give thanks."

"Indeed," Jean replied. "You know the old saying, speak of the wolf and you see his ears," and he roared with laughter once more, overjoyed to be with his own dear ones at long last.

Finally they all settled down, packed closely together in the small hut and begging Jean to recount his adventures for the whole year. *More* than a whole year, corrected one of the children, who got his head ruffled in a kindly way for his pains.

"From the beginning," came a chorus of happy young voices.

Jean told them that he has started off well, and all had gone as planned. He had a few minor adventures, nothing serious, no injuries, no bad illnesses, no bears stirring out of hibernation, no packs of wolves after him, not even any strangers marking his route and following him. There were moonlit nights, and he followed the stars as a guide. He arrived in Montreal just when he thought he would after thirty-six days of travel, on December 6, just two days before the Feast of the Immaculate Conception.

"Where is Montreal? What is it? Is it bigger than Fort Douglas?" Benjamin and Lap wanted to know.

Jean paused to fill his pipe and – puffing contentedly with Pauline on his lap, the two boys seated at his feet, and Reine and Josephte hanging on every word – began to tell them about a place with so many people living in it, you couldn't count them all.

"Some people go about in carriages. They sit behind in a sort of wagon with two, sometimes four wheels and a man to sit out in front and drive the horses. It's quite a sight, I can tell you. The ladies wear little bonnets decorated with feathers, and the men wear tall shiny hats made out of those beaver pelts I catch. Now what do you think of that? And buildings. So big! Do you know, Lord Selkirk was staying in one of the largest of all, made of stone with a stone fence around it topped with iron railings and a path wide enough for his carriage to take him right up to his big front door."

Reine and Josephte wanted to know what was inside the house. "Coverings on the floors made of wool patterned in every colour to think of, and wooden panels on the walls. It was very grand."

"Did you get to meet Lord Selkirk?" asked Marie Anne, bending forward at his account of a place that was so much grander than her memories of his parents' home.

"Indeed I did, my dear. At first the servant who opened the door to me didn't think much of what he was looking at, and he told me to leave any messages I had for his lordship. I told him that I had come direct from Governor Semple, and that my business was with Lord Selkirk and no other. Well, he let me come into the house at that. Told me to wait in the hall. The next thing I knew, a handsome man walked up to me and shook my hand. 'You must be tired from your journey. Come into my study, and I will send for refreshment for you,' he said to me."

Jean shifted a bit. "It was Lord Selkirk himself. He had his man bring me wine and a good meal and lots of it. While I ate for the first time in more than a day, Lord Selkirk read Governor Semple's reports. Then he questioned me, and I told him everything I knew about the conditions at the fort, the troubles the settlers were having getting used to our weather, and how they found it hard to learn our ways. Although I told him I had convinced some of the men that the only way to survive was to take buffalo at least for sleeping robes and hanging on the walls of their cabins, some wouldn't listen to me. Truth to tell, I think he was surprised to find I knew a few manners and I didn't wear a war bonnet and paint my face."

Jean paused for breath, and his audience laughed delightedly.

"At first, you know," Jean went on, "Lord Selkirk could not believe that any single human being could possibly have come this long way from the west and through enemy territory and have survived. But I told him I survived all right and more so after my good dinner. He found the news I brought him exceedingly grave. His house was much grander than my father's home, sweetheart, and it was only one of many in Montreal. And the churches, dear, you should see them."

"Jean," Marie Anne interrupted him. "The news that you brought him is out of date now. You have heard that Governor Semple was killed, haven't you?

"Pigouis and Madame Pigouis were so kind to us," she went on, "the whole family was so kind. We would have been rounded up the very next morning and all of us sent as prisoners to York. That's in Upper Canada, isn't it? The Pigouis rescued us and saved our lives and saved us from being sent away. We lived with them all summer, but it was so crowded. At first I didn't know what to do. Then one day I came across this cabin almost hidden in undergrowth and weeds. It's been a godsend. It's not much as homesteads go, but it's home, and it's much more than home now that we are all together again, dear Jean."

Jean nodded that he had heard that Governor Semple died in battle. "You can't believe how I felt when I heard that, because my every waking thought was about what happened to you, to all of you," he said, glancing around in pride and thankfulness at five pairs of bright young eyes staring back at him, some blue, some brown.

"Then what happened, Papa?" Lap was hanging on his father's every word.

The others all nodded.

"What has taken you, dear Papa, so long to get home?"

Jean settled back once more and continued. "Lord Selkirk gave me to understand that as I wished to settle down in the Red River Settlement, he would see that I got a handsome tract, one of the best."

Marie Anne's eyes shone.

"I hope he remembers his promise," he said, rubbing his chin. "So much has happened since. We discussed the possibility of bringing out more homesteaders again in the future, and I ventured the opinion that for a settlement to prosper, there must be religious as well as farmers. Otherwise, there is no stability. I told him I thought that was one of the biggest drawbacks in getting a settlement started. I told him that many of the Canadians were concerned that their children, Metis, were denied any knowledge of the Catholic faith. This situation has gone on for so long that a great many Metis are old enough to marry, and those children by right should be raised in the faith. I pointed out to him that the other stumbling block was the antagonism of the two fur-trading companies. It was against all their interests to be warring with each other."

"Oh Jean! Did he listen to you? About bringing out priests, I mean?"

"My darling, have you forgotten that your husband can talk his way into and out of, well, almost anything?" Jean bent over and kissed her in sight of the children. It made them all happy to see their parents so loving with each other.

"The great Lord Selkirk has promised to petition the Bishop of Lower Canada to send us out priests. Now what do you think of that?"

Marie Anne could hardly believe her ears. "Priests? Out here? When, Jean, when?"

"As soon as the bishop responds to his request, which I hope will be soon."

Marie Anne sighed with satisfaction. Her dearest wish was about to come true, and it was her Jean who had accomplished it.

"But now, my brave young family, do you not want to hear the rest of my story and hear how I spent the next whole year?"

"Yes, yes. Please go on, Papa," chorused his listeners.

Jean told them that he had been invited by Lord Selkirk to stay with him in his house and rest for the arduous and equally dangerous trip back. But he declined, tired as he was, because he was so longing to be back with his great news as an offering to Marie Anne for the Feast of the Nativity. He decided to start out at once, and feeling well pleased with himself and his reception at the hands of the most powerful man in the Hudson's Bay hierarchy, he obtained new snowshoes and a dog team and waved goodbye to the bustling metropolis of Montreal with no regrets. He made good time as far as the region near Fort William, gliding along and thinking about the reception he would be receiving soon from his beloved and beautiful wife. The promise of priests would make her so happy, he kept thinking.

His reveries were broken off when suddenly he was ambushed from behind. He knew he should have been on guard. It was his own fault he had been daydreaming and not fully alert. To his anger and humiliation, he was seized and taken prisoner, a fine captive of the North West Company and his fellow Canadians who knew of his preference for the Bay. He was taken to Fort William and made a prisoner of war of the Nor'Westers, spending the next entire year languishing in their foul-smelling jail, unable to get any kind of word to Marie Anne.

"How did you escape? Did you kill your guards?" It was young Benjamin.

"No! I did not, you bloodthirsty young fighter, Benjamin," and his father laughed and tousled his hair. "No, nothing like that at all. In the meantime, Lord Selkirk raised a regiment of soldiers at his own expense, the Meuron regiment, mostly veterans of the war that was fought with the Americans in 1812, and fine fighting men they are. Well, when the Meurons arrived at Fort William and attacked, the

Nor'Westers were beaten. The Meurons took possession, and I took the opportunity to bid my captors farewell."

Jean grinned. "I came straight to Fort Douglas, as I wanted to bring the news that the Meuron regiment is on its way to take the fort back for the Bay, and I have no doubt they will manage it easily. First thing I did was to ask around about you and stay out of sight of any Nor'Westers, you can be sure of that. I was directed across the river to Pigouis, who told me you had all survived the battle and were safe in Bellehumeur's old cabin."

"You mean there is still a war going in? We are going to be in the middle of another battle?" asked Marie Anne, her voice breaking and anxiety making creases in her forehead.

"This time it won't be so bad. We are going to be on the winning team. When it is all over, we will have our grant from Lord Selkirk registered to us." Jean hugged his daughters and kissed them.

"You seem so sure, Jean. I do so hope you are right. This fighting and killing is worse than anything I have lived through since we came to the Red River. Won't the Nor'Westers send out their men to take it back again? We are on a dreadful seesaw."

Jean leaned forward and took Marie Anne's hands in his own. "I don't think there is too much to worry about now. Both companies have lost so much revenue over this foolishness that I hear their backers, their shareholders, are upset on that score. I can see the day coming when they merge and shake hands, and it will be coming soon. Anything else would be arrant stupidity. They may be a mite greedy, considering the fortunes they are making out of our furs, but they are not complete fools."

"What will that do to us, Jean?"

"Nothing really, dear one. It will mean that we all bury our hatchets. If there is only one fur-trading company, we won't have this insane warfare. And we will all have to pull together, because I hear rumours that there is an American company, it's called the American Fur Company, run by a man named Jacob Astor, all set to give our people some competition. I would say that border they talked about so much that came with the Louisiana Purchase will become a reality as far as the Canadians, the English, and the Americans are concerned. What the Indians will make of it remains to be seen. But I have heard that the American company gives better prices on furs. That will entice the hunters from this side of the border to trade with the Americans. I also hear that the American company sells its spirits cheaper. If there is to be more trouble, this is where it will come from, I'm thinking."

Marie Anne got out the wooden bowls that Laprairie, with the dubious help of Benjamin, had carved. Her joy at reunion and the news of the priests was tempered slightly when she considered the likelihood of another battle and the disturbing news of the new fur company offering cheaper spirits. Jean remarked on the bowls and congratulated the boys. Marie Anne put together a special meal, the best the larder afforded, in honour of Jean's return. The usual dried fish was augmented by the last serving of pemmican she had been saving in hope for just this occasion.

A great sense of tranquillity permeated the entire little home. The fire crackled, and there were little jokes and giggles around the table.

"Bellehumeur," murmured Marie Anne, "what an entirely suitable name for this place. But it will be wonderful to get back to our own home again. I wonder what happened to it in all the troubles. I hope it's still there."

After their meal, the table was pushed aside. Jean and his family recited the rosary together in a circle around the fire. When Jean got up off his knees, he made up the fire, and soon everyone was tucked in under the buffalo robes.

For the first time in over a year, Jean and Marie lay together side by side in an embrace that threatened to stifle her. She wriggled a little to get her breath, and Jean clasped her more tightly. His deep contented breathing delighted her.

"He needs a good sleep," she thought, "and so do I. What a miraculous Christmas Eve this is." She fell asleep herself in the midst of praising all the saints she could remember. Snow fell all night, making a silence so deep it seemed no humans and their wars could disturb it.

Jean was the first awake. For a long time, he just watched his beloved wife smiling in her sleep. Then, so quietly as to not to disturb his brood, he moved over on top of her, hungering for her after thirteen months of enforced celibacy.

CHAPTER 20

After the immediate excitement of Jean's return wore off, life soon returned to something like normal. He went off to trap – not far, it is true, and he always returned each night. The demand for beaver pelts was higher than ever, and he wanted to make life a bit easier for the family as soon as Fort Douglas was Bay-dominated again and open for business.

Each day the survivors of the skirmishes and battles looked anxiously up and down the river, not daring to hope that the Meuron regiment that Lajimoniere had spoken of was on its way. The few Nor'Westers posted sentinels to keep a sharp lookout. The remaining Scottish settlers and all who were Bay supporters kept their watch, wondering how a regiment of men would possibly get through in the winter weather.

The fearful watchers had no way of knowing that Jean's tale of an approaching regiment was correct. They devoutly hoped it was true, but they were increasingly anxious as the weeks wore on. They were not to know that Lord Selkirk's men had taken a more southerly route than the voyageurs paddled when the waters were open. They were coming on snowshoes, mushing their way from Lake Superior and past both the Upper and Lower Red Lakes, continuing west from the Red River and then north through forest to the Assiniboine River well west of Fort Douglas. It was a roundabout way to approach the fort from the west, to be sure. Their strategy depended on surprise, since the Nor'Westers would certainly not be expecting them from the direction of Fort Qu'Appelle and even more especially in the worst time of the year, in freezing cold temperatures and blinding snowstorms.

After a gruelling march, the men needed rest for a short time, but they were not idle. Far enough west and away from the fort so that they could work undetected, the men felled trees and constructed long ladders, which they planned to carry with them for a scaling operation at the stockade. What was remarkable was that the men should be in any condition to fight a hand-to-hand battle after so lengthy a trek through the inhospitable and frozen wilderness.

The men of the Meuron remained hidden and settled down to wait for a good opportunity to exploit their most important weapon, surprise.

They were not kept waiting long. Appalling weather – a blizzard of blinding snow, driven horizontally across the open space between them and the fort, with howling winds shrieking and drowning out their sounds as well as making them invisible – ensured the secrecy of their movements. With the wind at their backs egging them on, they carried the ladders up to the base of the stockade. Grey ghosts in the storm, they placed the ladders against the stockade walls and climbed up the ladders like squirrels being chased.

Before one Nor'West sentinel recovered his senses and could believe what he was glimpsing, and with no time to alert his fellows, all were overcome and taken prisoner. The fort fell within an hour and without a casualty on one of the snowiest days anyone could remember in February of 1817.

Within a week, the new Bay factor completed the change in command. The Lajimonieres took up residence in the house Governor Semple had originally allotted to Marie Anne, and the children were ecstatic to be back in the grand home. Marie Anne set to work with a scrubbing brush from the store and many pails of water to get the place back into the sort of shape it had been in before they left so precipitously. Soldiers of the Nor'Westers, some with country wives, had taken it over, and the general housekeeping was far from Marie Anne's standards for so gracious a home. Reine and Josephte were both eager to help, and Marie Anne found pleasure in training her daughters in the domestic arts she had learned as a girl.

For the remainder of the winter, the family happily tidied up the messes and mended broken spindles and chair legs. Marie Anne knew a sense of security she had not enjoyed for years as the Meuron took over the fort's defences. She and the children became accustomed to hearing the men drilling and the shouted commands. Throughout the night, regular watches and the stamping feet and cries of the watch gave her a sense of stability and comfort, a luxurious novelty.

By spring, the larder was running dangerously low, and Jean Baptiste was keen to get off into the hinterland for the calf-hunting. Since all the Indians made it a practice to take their wives with them to dress and scrape skins and perform most of the butchering, Jean pleaded with Marie Anne to come along. This hunt, he assured her, would be far pleasanter for her, as well as safer. This time he was going with a large party, and in addition to plenty of horses, they were taking out the Red River carts, the homemade vehicles that took a pair of horses to draw. Surely, he begged, she would be willing to ride in a cart out to the prairies once more.

Marie Anne shook her head. She felt she simply could not face another summer of a makeshift garden and five children, three of them anxious to play with other children of their own age. That and the overpowering smell of rendering fat, not to mention the all-pervasive smell of meat drying and smoking – no thank you, she had made up her mind.

One other concern haunted her. With less supervision, what might Laprairie get up to, and was he still the object of strangers' acquisitiveness?

"I'm staying with the children here," was her only comment.

Reluctantly, Jean Baptiste took off without her. He had missed his beloved greatly over the year of imprisonment. He had missed her greatly when he had to be away tending his traplines in the wintertime. He had been hoping that she would consent to go out with him one more time for the summer hunts. But there it was. She had said no, and a steely blue in her eyes told him that there was no going back on her decision.

As well as being loath to be parted from her more than was necessary, he had misgivings about Marie Anne and the five youngsters alone without masculine protection in what was becoming a fairly rough military outpost.

"It's no place for a lady," he thought to himself several times a day. "But what else can I do but leave her if she won't go with me? We all have to eat."

As the days brightened and lengthened, the men of the regiment were put to work improving the amenities of the fort, erecting new structures and generally making their presence felt. There still seemed to be plenty of time, however, for those off duty to congregate around the parade square, gambling, regaling each other with tall tales of their lurid pasts, fighting at times, and generally roughhousing. Lap, now an impressionable nine-year-old, and Benjamin, a curious little six-year-old, were both attracted to all this new activity. Marie Anne saw that they were certainly learning, but she did not know what they were learning, and she did not like it. She grew increasingly concerned that as the summer unfolded, the boys would be hard to manage without their father's influence.

"In the meantime, heaven only knows what bad habits they could find worthy of copying from those troops lounging about on the square," she worried.

Marie Anne decided to approach the new governor, Mr McDonald, and seek permission from him to set up a large tent – big enough for the whole family – and spend the summer camping outside the fort. She felt she could direct the activities of the boys on a plantation, and she could better protect Reine, who was rapidly becoming a very attractive wee mademoiselle.

After listening to her anxieties, Mr McDonald agreed with her. The fort was not a suitable place for the five children of Monsieur Lajimoniere in his absence. He directed that the materials for a large canvas tent be made available and that a detail of men should erect it for her. After having had the responsibility in the past for erecting her own tent, with Jean's direction and help as the Indian custom was, Marie Anne was delighted to stand back and watch as this service was performed for her.

The summer of 1817 passed uneventfully. Although Jean Baptiste was absent for nearly all of it, at least Marie Anne had the satisfaction of being able to picture in her mind what he was likely to be doing. It was certainly a better feeling than the awful summer and fall when she had no word from him and did not know whether he was dead or alive.

The children were pleased to be out camping again, especially the boys. It was grand fun, they decided, to be out in the open in the summer. The boys had acquired seed potatoes from the mess at the fort, and these along with wild turnip seeds they had gathered and saved from the past year as well as wild onions added greatly to the scope of their expected harvest.

As Jean Baptiste had predicted, the two rival fur companies mended their differences and declared a truce – a merger, in fact. Lord Selkirk busied himself in settling restitutions that each company claimed from the other. Fort Gibraltar was restored to the North West Company and once again took its place as an important centre of trading, completely rebuilt, to the delight of the Metis and the Canadians who had remained loyal Nor'West traders. Plans were made at once to enlarge Fort Douglas so that it would remain one of the principal trading posts of the Hudson's Bay Company for the prairies and an important supply base for the western forts.

During a brief return to his family in midsummer between the calf and the buffalo hunts, Jean Baptiste overheard a couple of the Meuron soldiers talking about Lord Selkirk's arrival at Fort Douglas. He lost no time in striding over to the factor's store.

"Is it true?" he asked the clerks.

They indicated that indeed Lord Selkirk had come out to the Red River to see for himself what the settlement looked like and was even now preparing to give over tracts of land to bona fide homesteaders. Again with a quick decisive stride, Jean went over to the governor's house and bounded up the steps, pushing past a sentry and rushing headlong into the main reception room.

Clerks and Lord Selkirk's staff were taken aback to see this tall man roughly dressed in buckskins but obviously of European descent come through the doorway heading straight for Lord Selkirk himself.

By the time they recovered from the shock of it and at least one of the staff had tried to stop him, Lord Selkirk and the interloper were greeting each other, hands thumping shoulders, with all the warmth of old friends. It was a joyful reunion for each of them. After their initial heartiness had subsided somewhat, Lord Selkirk drew Jean over to his plans and showed him what he proposed to do with the real estate he had bought himself from the Bay. Every so often, Lord Selkirk turned to Jean to ask him again about the journey and his return. It was certainly obvious that he had not forgotten the bravery of the intrepid voyageur, who had undertaken so perilous a mission of eighteen hundred miles in midwinter, alone, and had made it to Montreal in just thirty-six days.

"A remarkable achievement," he said again and again. "Now that I have a much better perception of the distance you travelled and the terrain you covered, I am more impressed by your dauntless courage than ever."

When Jean explained that it was Lord Selkirk's own regiment, the Meuron, that had overtaken Fort William and enabled him to slip out of prison and make his way back home a year and a month after he had set out, Lord Selkirk was pleased and clapped him on the back.

"What a year you must have spent," he said.

Jean merely shrugged as if to say it was over now and best forgotten.

Lord Selkirk drew a line enclosing a vast portion of land directly opposite Fort Douglas, with excellent frontage on the Red River.

"This tract is for you," he said. "You have earned it. And with it goes my thanks for your loyalty and your courage."

Turning to his clerks, he bade them measure out the indicated portion and record it as the homestead of his friend Jean Baptiste Lajimoniere. It was to be expected that the Lajimoniere tract would be one of the largest and most favourably situated, but even Jean was astounded at the size of the grant.

Lord Selkirk showed a firm grasp of the issues and situations in the settlement. He had listened carefully to Jean Baptiste back in Montreal and had studied all reports with care. He could now see for himself how greatly the Canadians missed the comfort of their faith. Rough and swashbuckling though many of the *hivernants* appeared to be at first meeting, when they felt their lives at stake in the bush or on open grasslands, they fell to their knees and repeated their prayers, their Pater Nosters and Ave Marias. Vows made in imploring deliverance from peril to whichever saint each felt had his individual protection at heart were later scrupulously fulfilled. They were particularly keen to have their acknowledged children brought up in their own faith and to be able to have instruction for their country wives.

Jean was pleased to hear from the lord himself that his plea of three years back – when he was asked what favour he wanted for his bravery and answered "Priests. Priests is what we need most" – had been taken seriously. Lord Selkirk had had many an interview with the Bishop of Montreal urging him to send out priests without delay. The bishop seemed reluctant at first. There were many with an interest in the North West Company who saw homesteading and a religious community as being in opposition to their pelt profits. At length, the bishop agreed to dispatch two missionaries to Fort William, but they returned at the end of the summer to Montreal.

"Just as well my wife hasn't heard how nearly her fondest dream almost came to pass," Jean remarked to Lord Selkirk. "So near and yet so out of reach. It would break her heart to know of it. Better that she not know how close her heart's desire was last summer."

Lord Selkirk took Jean's arm. "This is not the end of the matter, I can assure you. I see the need, and I will approach the bishop again."

Before he left Fort Douglas, Lord Selkirk made a solemn promise to Jean and to all the Canadians assembled on the parade ground that he would himself plead again with the bishop to send out two resident priests to Fort Douglas and to Pembina as well. He would continue to pursue the matter with the bishop until their spiritual needs were given his blessing. He suspected that the influence of the managers of the North West Company on the bishop was to blame for the bishop's seeming unwillingness to send priests. The Nor'Westers were actively dissuading settlement to encourage the lucrative fur trade, and somehow the bishop seemed more sensitive to their demands than to the plight of the French hunters in the field.

As Lord Selkirk was leaving, he held up their petition with over three hundred signatures, saying, "This will be delivered into the bishop's own hands, I can assure you."

The men assembled raised a cheer. Privately he had decided to call on the Jesuits, to enlist their aid in convincing the bishop of the need for proselytizing in the western deserts.

As well as dispensing the lands he had himself bought from the Bay, Lord Selkirk made treaties with the representatives of the various tribes trading with the Bay out of Fort Douglas. There would remain plenty of free hunting territory, he promised them. Traders, hunters, and homesteaders were united in praise of the successful outcome of Lord Selkirk's visit.

Lord Selkirk's next project was to conclude a similar series of treaties with Indians trading out of Pembina. As a trusted friend and adviser, one who knew the area well and the minds and speech of the persons he would be dealing with, Jean was invited to accompany Lord Selkirk as a guide and interpreter to the fort at Pembina. Jean was pleased and flattered to be asked to join the company of Selkirk's aides and staff.

Marie Anne was almost overcome when she was told of the extent of their holding. She was concerned that Jean would be away again at Pembina, but as he explained to her, he had received such favour from this powerful leader he felt he had no choice but to join the mission.

Negotiations at Pembina dragged on and on, and it was late October before all business was concluded. Lord Selkirk and Jean parted company with many protestations of thanks on both sides – the lord to journey through the Red Lakes to Minneapolis, Montreal, and finally London, and Jean back up the Red River to his family at Fort Douglas.

With the satisfying feeling of having helped to forge an attitude of tolerance and mutual esteem between old enemies, Jean Baptiste lost no time in hastening back to the tent outside Fort Douglas. The first frosts were already whitening the land each morning, and the nip in the air, although exhilarating, was more than enough to remind him that a dwelling of some sort had to be erected for this family in jig time.

Thinking about the house he was planning to build upon his own land put a broad grin on his face. As he paddled up the Red River, he sang with the greatest joy in his heart. It almost seemed as if he made the woods on either side of the river echo with his ringing voice. As the canoe rounded a slight curve in the river, a startled deer turned and bounded off, its white tuft of tail bobbing up and down. Laughing with sheer happiness at the way his attempt at music had been received by his frightened audience, he realized with a start that he had not thought to reach for his rifle.

"I'm getting to be an old farmer, and that was a fine buck in velvet," he thought, and then contentedly broke into a new song.

Upon his return, he and Marie moved their tent and their belongings across the river to their handsome new property. Together they walked about surveying the lie of the land this way and that, trying to decide where to locate their home, their very own home. Marie Anne had definite ideas about the placing of windows. Just planning it gave them so much pleasure and satisfaction. The children found the idea of permanence hard to grasp. They had all moved about so much since birth that one house for all seasons of the year was a novel concept.

Jean had definite ideas about the position of the fireplace so that the house would turn its back to the wintry blasts and keep them snug.

Marie Anne requested a south-facing windowsill where she could grow a plant or two, her eyes sparkling. They walked about their property with their arms around each other and visions of a real family homestead about to become a reality.

The two boys were interested in the planting of crops. Their mother had so often spoken of wheat and what it was to eat bread that they were determined to get hold of some kernels and see for themselves what they could do to bring this remarkable stuff to the table. In her imagination, Marie Anne saw huge fields of wheat, their very own, waving golden brown in the sunshine and ready for the harvest. She sighed in happiness and anticipation of the tantalizing smells that would be coming out of her kitchen in just a year's time.

The first tentative swirls of snow brought them all back to reality with a depressing thud.

"It's going to be an early winter this year, or I'm much mistaken, dear heart – or should I be calling you queen now that you have an expansive realm of your own?"

Jean and Marie were approaching the tent. Marie Anne laughed and squeezed his hand. "One queen in the family is sufficient, and our own little Reine is growing into quite the queen, name and all." She laughed.

"What I'm thinking," Jean went on, "is that the winter is upon us, and I don't see how I can get trees felled and the walls of even a small hut up before the snow flies. I'm afraid it's a make-do dwelling we will have to be content with this winter." He put an arm around her shoulder.

"What can we do, Jean? I think I'm getting too old in the bones to live through another winter in a hide tent. Isn't it possible to go back to the house we had in the fort for just this one last winter?"

"Afraid not, love. It's been commandeered for other purposes. And I'll still have to hunt for furs. You would have to contend with troops in the fort. No, we will be wintering on our grant all right. What I have in mind is a sod house, dear. It won't be elegant. In fact, it won't be much of anything except a mite warmer than out of doors. We should be here on our land and quite apart from other considerations, I want to watch the way the snowdrifts and which way the runoffs go. That's the only way we have of figuring out which way to push a plough. You see? I have remembered a thing or two about farming."

"A sod house?" Marie Anne's voice rose in a wail of disbelief and frustration. "Jean, I've seen them. They are dark and damp and really bad for getting colds and feeling sick. So far we have such a splendid record of health in the children. You can't mean it. I hate to think of living even one winter in such a sordid cave."

"Of course you do, darling wife. But let's face it. It is much too late in the year to get anything up off the ground with a roof on it. I'm going to be hard put to dig out enough space for us all to lie down and stand up together. We'll have to take a leaf out of the prairie dogs' way of coping and tunnel underground as fast as we can. I know. I know. If I hadn't gone with Lord Selkirk to Pembina, I could have got it started, but even then I doubt if I could have had time to get any kind of liveable house built. I do think it was important that I went with him as a guide and interpreter when he particularly asked for me, and he has been so good to us."

Marie Anne swallowed her disappointment. It was hard to do, but Jean was right. There simply was no alternative. Their grant was certainly the best of all, and she was proud of Jean for the way he managed everything.

"Still, it seems a backward step," she said. "It will be the very worst kind of shelter we have had since we came out to the west together. Let's hope and pray it really is the last of the makeshifts we have been calling home for twelve years now. I never thought after all these years, I should be living like a bear in a cave of mud."

Marie Anne's disappointment was not the least bit lessened when she saw what she would be contending with all winter long. There was no time to make what might pass as a window. There was not even a glassed section on the door. The expansion at Fort Douglas had meant that every last piece of window glass was spoken for, and there would be none until the supply boats arrived in spring.

When the snow fell and winter arrived with a vengeance, the family was squeezed in together in darkness all day and all night except for the light of a fire and a candle. Shivering with cold, they learned to live as much as possible outdoors in the six or seven hours of daylight. When snow fell heavily, as it seemed to do during the long nights, it took the combined strength of all of them to force the door open a crack so that they could make a start at clearing a path through the drifts to the creek, which supplied their water needs only after the boys had broken the ice with an axe.

With Jean absent so much of the time – for hunting and trapping were still the mainstays of their existence – Marie Anne found the winter of 1817–1818 the hardest one she had been called upon to bear. The boys were kept busy splitting wood and keeping up the fire, their only source of heat. Five children and their mother frequently went out to set snares, hoping to catch a rabbit for a treat of fresh meat. She had heard many a tale of illnesses arising from the unsanitary conditions that were well nigh impossible to avoid in living quarters that were nothing more than half tunnel, half dugout. She thought wistfully of Bellehumeur's cabin, but it was not on their property.

The one bright star on Marie Anne's horizon was the memory of the petition that Jean had signed for Lord Selkirk. There were more names on it by the time it had been presented at Pembina and Lord Selkirk had borne it off. Although he had told them he was going back to London, he had promised that as he passed through Montreal on his way, he would make sure the bishop received the petition without fail.

Reluctant though he seemed to be to disturb the activities of the North West Company, the bishop could not ignore the pleas of more than three hundred Catholics and the prospect of gathering hundreds more, the Canadians told each other. They all lived in hope that by next summer, they would have a priest of their own who would stay with them over the winter. They had heard about the missionaries at Fort William who had left before the freeze-up. As the Canadians pointed out to each other, they and the Metis were out on the prairies during the summer, and a priest was needed year-round.

"Lord Selkirk is a Protestant, but he's a good man," Jean remarked to Marie Anne. "He understands our needs. He told me he is going to send out a Protestant minister as well, and a teacher, too. He knows it's the only way to get a stable community established in this settlement he has set his heart on."

Jean paused for a moment. "And put his money into as well."

CHAPTER 21

Long before winter lost its grip, Jean Baptiste arrived home from his pelt hunting. Somehow every body squeezed in a bit to make room for the largest member of the family. It meant yet another sleeping robe hung up on the mud walls every morning to dry out a bit and air, more or less. Each morning, he went out with his axe accompanied by the two boys to chop down trees for their new home.

By the time geese came winging in from their winter vacation, honking furiously to let the *hivernants* know that spring was really on its way, huge pile of logs were stacked for the work to come. The ringing of Jean's axe and the crash that followed seemed almost like an answer to the birds' insistent calls. The day the girls explored a small lake on the property and spotted the first pair of pelicans looking for reeds in a marsh, they came running back home.

"We saw pelicans! Down by the pond!" they called out delightedly. "Now spring is really here."

It was as if the entire world were telling Jean to make haste and get the house up. As soon as the weather broke and a patch of ground appeared in a sunny spot showing through the snow, the family moved with the greatest sense of release into their old hide tent. Marie Anne closed the door on the sod house with a bang.

"I vow I shall never sleep in that bear cave again. Better to sleep in the open under the stars before anyone lures me back inside that hole."

Jean Baptiste laughed at her determined foot-stamping and mentally resolved to use the door somehow, perhaps in an outbuilding. It was the only part of the winter's shelter that had any usefulness whatsoever in a proper house.

Everyone helped. The boys worked hard under the direction of their father, and the three girls were pressed into a work gang gathering rocks and stones as heavy as they could carry for the chimney piece. Marie Anne did double duty as chief helper to Jean as well as cook and homemaker, feeding and caring for seven people.

To receive the priests in their own home was the secret dream that had sustained Marie Anne throughout the interminable darkness of the gloomy sod house. To have the new home up and habitable by the time the priests arrived was her goal. Day by day, she watched the walls growing higher. Her spirits rose with each log secured in its place. A doorway was cut and dressed, and then windows. Busy as she was, Marie Anne was as happy and as full of song as the birds in the trees. As soon as it was possible to get small areas cleared of stumps and stacks, the boys became agile full-time farmers. Rocks too heavy for the girls to lift dug from their first tiny fields became hearth and chimney, hauled by stone boat. Others became the start of a stone fence around their first field.

The boys organized work parties for their farming projects when they were spared from their father's operations.

Even Pauline, now five years old, was put to work collecting one-eyed chunks of potatoes cut by Josephte and dropping them one by one into holes dug by Benjamin. Marie Anne went about the many other tasks she had to do to feed the family and keep them clothed and more or less clean. She kept her eye on the three smallest, were absorbed and happy in the importance of their work.

"To have Reine helping me is like having another pair of hands," she thought, which made her break into song, the old folk songs from the life that now seemed part of another lifetime altogether. Everyone within hearing range joined in.

"It makes my job go faster to hear my angel choir," Jean called out when they paused for breath or to start a new tune.

Wonderful news started drifting in with the arrival of the first of the trade canoes.

"The bishop of Montreal is sending two priests," one clerk in the company store was heard to remark. "Imagine, two of them!" The Fort Douglas folk exchanged the news, hardly daring to believe it. "One for here, and one for Pembina. That's what I heard." The rumour ran all over the fort. "More settlers on their way too, and Scottish folk as I hear."

The news was on everyone's mind. "They say he is sending a Protestant minister with them and a teacher too. Can you believe it? We are going to need some sort of constabulary right through the whole western lands too."

The talk buzzed around the fort and across the river. It was all anyone wanted to hear about. Some of the Metis were by now full-grown men and women. Marriages were planned. There were a few Canadian fathers who felt it was more than high time a priest blessed and regularized their own arrangements as well as celebrating their offsprings' weddings. Indians and Metis were intensely curious about these souls coming such a long way to save theirs.

They peppered Marie Anne with questions. What did priests do? What happened in the ceremonies? What did they look like? What sort of clothing would they wear? Would they look different from the other Canadians? How? How should one speak to them? Was it necessary to wait until they spoke first?

Marie Anne laughed and told all her interrogators to wait and see. "They are good people and will be kind to us all," she said.

With those scraps of information, everyone had to be patient.

Jean Baptiste worked on his house as hard and as fast as he knew how. Help was hard to come by, but Laprairie — now known as Jean Baptiste after his father, and P'tit Jean for short — helped his father in every way he could. The priests would need some sort of accommodation, and it was arranged that Jean Baptiste would be one of the *hivernants* on the building team. Anxious as she was to see her own home roofed, Marie Anne was proud and pleased that Jean would have a part in the actual building of the chapel to be erected on the east side, their side, of the Red River.

The first day that the priests could reasonably be expected would be sometime around the end of the first week in July. The Canadians were at fever pitch by the end of June. Lookouts were posted, and many others came to watch as well just so they could say they were among the first to sight the canoes.

"I can't stop singing," Marie Anne thought with sheer happiness. "And here I am scampering about like the children. I must try to remember I am a dignified matron, the mother of five," she thought to herself and giggled. Jean and the children were highly entertained. Her happiness was contagious, and every neighbour and inhabitant of the fort and its surroundings shared her anticipation.

Finally, on a sunny morning, the twelfth day of July in the year of our Lord 1818, the big trade canoes were sighted, their flags streaming out behind them. The *mangeurs de porc* had decorated themselves and their canoes more than usual in honour of the occasion.

Feathers, ribbons, painted symbols on the canoes – everything they could think of had been done to make the entrance of the priests a colourful and momentous occasion.

The factor of the fort, Mr McDonald, himself a Catholic, spared no expense of his own or the company's to make the reception on this day, a Thursday, the most joyful the fort had ever known. The Lajimonieres paddled furiously across the river to be present at the moment when the priests' feet first touched the ground.

Father Provencher and his junior, Father Dumoulin, the priest assigned to Pembina, could not possibly have had a more moving reception. At first it was planned that it would be solemn and marked with dignity. But when the boats were actually sighted and the entire population ran down to the shore, such an outpouring of joyous sound burst from every throat that formality was forgotten, and the two imposing friendly figures found themselves surrounded by a joyous dancing mob.

Everyone present and, most of all, the Metis and Indians were struck by the dignity and bearing of the priests. Both wore their cassocks, and after the initial noisy outpouring of welcome, a reverent hush fell on the entire crowd. Mr McDonald proudly escorted the handsome strangers slowly up the hill to the fort, with the crowd falling back in awe at the procession. The priests shook hands and blessed the devout as they passed.

Marie Anne and Jean Baptiste made sure they were among the first to be given a blessing.

"Kneel beside me and clasp your hands so," she whispered to Reine and Josephte, and then with one arm around Pauline, she knelt herself.

With a young son on each side of him, Jean bade the boys, "Down on both knees beside me and put your hands together."

Others followed, and the whole entourage sank to its knees. Marie Anne wept with joy as she watched the priest's hands actually blessing the heads of each member of her little family in turn.

Many of the Indians remarked afterwards that they never imagined such a sight and that they felt these two men were indeed sent from God. After inviting the women and children to come closer and sit at his feet, Father Provencher began to explain his mission. Marie Anne's tears continued to flow. She felt an enormous weight lift from her shoulders and a sense of profound release.

"Staying put in the far western countries was the right thing to do after all, in spite of my doubts and all the times I felt my last moments on earth were upon me," she thought.

"What trials I have lived through, but today my fondest wish comes true."

For the rest of her life – and she lived to her ninety-sixth year, the mother of eight children altogether and the grandmother of Louis Riel, the patriot – Marie Anne treasured the memory of the gentle voice and friendly manner of the priest and his fatherly address on the hill outside the fort. Trials there would be in the future – the Red River in flood, locusts harvesting their crops for them, summers with no rain – but she and Jean Baptiste remained steadfast in their faith and in their belief that the bounteous open prairies would always somehow take care of them and their loved ones.

Even though they had done their best and worked until their backs ached, the men had not been able to make the chapel and a cabin for the priest ready in time. Now that Father Provencher had arrived, the men were spurred to even greater speed. Mr McDonald prepared a large hall in one of the fort's buildings so that religious observances and ceremonies could begin without delay.

The fourteenth of July was announced as the day that all mothers were to bring their children under the age of six to be baptized.

As soon as she returned home, Marie Anne began fashioning as best she could something suitable for Pauline to wear at her christening. The other Lajimonieres, all over the age of six, had to wait until they had received formal instruction in their catechism before they could also be baptised by the priest. The family returned to the fort, all in their best attire such as it was, on Saturday morning for the baptismal Mass. Pauline was suitably decked out in a little shift frock of white cambric fabric cut and stitched simply in the Indian style.

"Let's gather the prettiest flowers we can find and make a little crown for her," Reine suggested to Josephte.

The girls rushed out early in the morning when the dew was still fresh to gather wild roses to plait them into a wreath for their sister' hair. Pauline's four older brothers and sisters walked to the fort alongside her, making an honour guard. Marie Anne and Jean Baptiste walked behind the little procession with their hearts almost bursting with pride and love.

Now that her dream of settling down in a real community with a priest and soon a church was actually true, quite unexpectedly a memory came upon her, so vivid it surprised her and momentarily blotted out everything else. She saw herself as a young girl of thirteen, the age of Reine, trudging slowly along that dusty road in Maskinongé on her way to the priest's house beside St Sulpice. How condemned she had felt, how rebellious and angry and miserable. That splash from the handsome young son of the richest family in the district hadn't helped. Nothing lay ahead for her but housekeeping and drudgery year after year for the rest of her life cooped up in a prison. Marie Anne suddenly smiled.

"How wrong I was," she said to herself.

The vision vanished. The contrast between that day and this one made her grin as she used to do in her early girlhood. Jean Baptiste looked sidewise at that familiar ear-to-ear smile of hers and pressed her arm a little closer.

Surely, she thought, she had been favoured more than she or anyone could deserve. How proudly the four escorted wee Pauline, such a dignified little girl.

Marie Anne pressed Jean's arm more tightly. They gazed at one another without words. No words were needed. The terrors and anxieties of that whole year of his captivity were worth it for this, he thought. She gave thanks in her heart for Lord Selkirk's friendship with Jean and his promise to her dear good man now so well fulfilled.

If there was a small cloud that day to dull her happiness, it was that dear Amie and Madame Paquin and Madame Chalifou were not there to share her joy.

"I could have been godmother to all our friends' children," she said to Jean.

With his free hand, he took her hand in his and held it tenderly. "God must have had other plans for you, dear heart. Today you are standing up as godmother to three hundred children. Godmother to three hundred! That's quite a responsibility."

"Of course you are right," she said softly. "My, how grateful I am to see such changes. And more to come, I'm sure."

Together the Lajimoniere family led the procession of traders, voyageurs, clerks, settlers, Metis, Indians, Protestant settlers, and a great assembly of children up the hill to the first Christian service in the western country. No one in the fort was going to miss this grand celebration.

FOOTNOTE

The Hivernante

The story is based on a true-life account of Marie Anne Lajimoniere, née Gaboury, born 6 November 1782 in Maskinongé, Lower Canada, a village on the Mastigouche River near Trois Rivières. She died in St Boniface in 1878 at the age of ninety-six, mother of eight children. Jean Baptiste Lajimoniere went out on the buffalo hunt every year until his death in the mid 1880s. None of the four boys hunted. They all farmed, and the girls each married a farmer. Marie Anne became the grandmother of the patriot, Louis Riel. She spent her last years with her eldest son, also Jean Baptiste, who wrote an obituary for his remarkable mother. This was augmented by M. l'Abbe G. Dugast who gathered anecdotes by word of mouth from the oldest inhabitants of the Red River and published The First White Mother of the West in Montreal in 1883. A century later Lise Perrault of Val Marie, Saskatchewan, translated the work into English, and it is this account which has been the basis of my researches and the spelling of the Lajimoniere name.

ACKNOWLEDGEMENTS

To so many friends go my deepest thanks for help and encouragement, particularly John Parry, Marili Moore, Marianne Beaudry and David Block and with a special thank you to Lise Perrault without whose help, The Hivernante would never have been written.

CPSIA information can be obtained at www.ICGtesting.com
Printed in the USA
LVOW11s0757130515

438244LV00001B/45/P

9 781491 752586